For —
   Beautiful, Sweet
Mickey — Such a
Pleasure seeing
and being with
you —
      Bobby

On Stage at the Ballet

My Life as Dancer and Artistic Director

Robert Barnett *with*
Cynthia Crain

McFarland & Company, Inc., Publishers
Jefferson, North Carolina

Photographs are from the author's collection unless otherwise noted.

LIBRARY OF CONGRESS CATALOGUING-IN-PUBLICATION DATA

Names: Barnett, Robert, 1925– author. | Crain, Cynthia, 1951– author.
Title: On stage at the ballet : my life as dancer and artistic director /
  Robert Barnett with Cynthia Crain.
Description: Jefferson, North Carolina : McFarland & Company, Inc.,
  Publishers, 2019 | Includes bibliographical references and index.
Identifiers: LCCN 2019026990 | ISBN 9781476679105 (paperback) |
  ISBN 9781476637327 (ebook) ∞
Subjects: LCSH: Barnett, Robert, 1925– | Ballet dancers—Biography. |
  New York City Ballet—History. | Atlanta Ballet—History.
Classification: LCC GV1785.B3474 A3 2019 | DDC 792.8092 [B]—dc23
LC record available at https://lccn.loc.gov/2019026990

BRITISH LIBRARY CATALOGUING DATA ARE AVAILABLE

ISBN (print) 978-1-4766-7910-5
ISBN (ebook) 978-1-4766-3732-7

Front cover: *left* the author and his wife, Virginia, with George Balanchine
after an Atlanta Ballet performance at the Alliance Theatre in Atlanta
(author's collection); *right* the author in a photograph for Balanchine's *Western Symphony*, third movement (by William McCracken, author's collection)

Printed in the United States of America

McFarland & Company, Inc., Publishers
  Box 611, Jefferson, North Carolina 28640
    www.mcfarlandpub.com

To my Family, Dorothy, Merrilee, and
the Dancers who have been in my life for all these years,
with my love and sincere thank you for their faith
and help in making my journey possible.

Acknowledgments

It is my pleasure to recognize the former students, professional dancers, colleagues, friends and family who contributed to my autobiography *On Stage at the Ballet: My Life as Dancer and Artistic Director*. As my friend Barbara Milberg Fisher said in the Acknowledgments in her book *In Balanchine's Company*, "A memoir, it turns out, is all about other people." I now understand what she means.

My autobiography was launched at an Atlanta Ballet event in September 2017 when two close friends, Lynn Cochran and Sharon Story, said: "Bobby, you have to write your autobiography. Now!" I told them that I needed to find someone to assist me. At the same dinner that night was the dance historian and writer Cynthia Crain. By early October the two of us were at my home in Asheville, North Carolina, talking and writing. Thank you, Lynn and Sharon and Cynthia.

There are numerous contributors to my autobiography to thank who were interviewed, which assisted me in recalling many wonderful memories of those early days as first-generation New York City Ballet dancers and staff. Barbara Horgan, Balanchine's personal assistant for so many years, and a co-founder of the Balanchine Trust; Nancy Reynolds, Director of Research for the George Balanchine Foundation; and former New York City Ballet dancers Janice Cohen, Jacques d'Amboise, and Barbara Walczak. Barbara and her co-author, Una Kai, who was a New York City Ballet dancer and a ballet mistress, published the book *Balanchine: The Teacher*. It is an excellent resource that was invaluable in the writing of my book. Also very helpful was the interview with Barbara Milberg Fisher. Her book, *In Balanchine's Company*, provided lots of details on those international tours that we first-generation New York City Ballet dancers and staff took together in the 1950s, as well as the annual Labor Day party she regularly attended that my wife Ginger and I used to host. I thank you all for not only helping me to recall some of the great times we shared, but also in recalling the facts accurately.

There are many, many former students and professional dancers (and some became colleagues) that I taught, coached, and mentored throughout their illustrious careers, who lovingly gave their time for interviews or contributed letters, playbills, correspondence, and all sorts of documents, to assist in the writing of my book. These contributors are Anne Burton Avery and her husband Eddie Avery, Lynn Petters Cochran, Carolyn Luesing, Gwyneth Dixon, Dawn Mullins, Lynda Bradbury Courts, Lane Bradbury, Caroline Cavallo, Julianne Spratlin, Joey Carman, Maniya Barredo, Maiqui Manosa, Wei Dongsheng, Naomi-Jane Dixon Clark, Christian Clark, Pamela Taylor Tongg and Kathy McBeth Hutcheson. Additional colleagues and Atlanta Ballet friends who contributed are Sharon Story, Carole Goldberg, Andrea Pell, and Jane Dean. I thank David Robinson for the hours he spent proofing and editing. Natalie Foreman receives high praise and much applause for guiding Cynthia and me through the production process. There are Ellen Sorrin and Nicole Cornell at the George Balanchine Trust; Kina Poon, New York City Ballet archivist; and Christopher Pennington, Robbins Rights Trust, all who were very helpful with questions and requests. At the Atlanta Ballet there is Tricia Ekholm who helped with photographs and who provided direction to beneficial resources.

I thank dance writer Joel Lobenthal for his assistance on this project. Joel interviewed me in 2011 for an article in *Ballet Review*, and his transcribed notes were beneficial in writing my autobiography. I thank Royal Phillips for her encouragement. Virginia's sister, Sally Darling, read chapters and her editorial comments were very helpful and appreciated. There is my family to thank for their contributions and support—my sons Robert and David, their wives Elizabeth and Jackie, and my grandsons Aaron, Ryan and Austin.

I am so very grateful to all of you who helped to make this autobiography possible.

Table of Contents

Preface: Not While I'm Around

I was going to be a fashion designer when I grew up. Dancing professionally was certainly not something I thought about at the age of eighteen when I graduated from high school. Balanchine, Nijinska, Youskevitch, Robbins, and Ashton—these were only a few of the legends in the history of classical ballet who were unknown to me. But that was about to change. A person's life is a series of unexpected happenings. Mine was no exception.

Thanks to my mother, I was tap dancing at the age of eight and was really good—good enough to show off my talent and boyish charms performing at lots of ladies' social club events in the small town where I was raised—Conconully, Washington. In 1943 I enlisted in the Navy, and I strutted and danced in a few officer's clubs. It was while I was in Japan that Michio Ito, a friend of Martha Graham's, picked me to perform in a GI musical he was directing. He encouraged me to take classical ballet classes. Upon my return to civilian life, I moved to California and began my classical ballet training from Bronislava Nijinska, Vaslav Nijinsky's younger sister. Learning the proper classical ballet foundation from a world-renowned teacher prepared me for my first professional gig, which was with Colonel de Basil's Original Ballet Russe, for his ten-month tour of Spain, Portugal and North Africa. In December 1949, I auditioned for George Balanchine, Jerome Robbins, and Lincoln Kirstein at New York City Ballet. Out of about two hundred of us who auditioned, I was the only male accepted. Two hours later I was in a studio rehearsing a new ballet with Jerome Robbins. New York City Ballet was founded in 1948, and we first-generation dancers were as close as twenty-something sisters and brothers can be. We took classes and rehearsed together. In what little leisure time there was we went to the movies, visited record shops, and ate many meals together at one another's tiny apartments. We toured together, to places that at that stage in my young years seemed like adventure-thrilling countries, including Europe, Asia and Australia. In

1

1958, I received an offer that was a new direction in my professional ballet career when Dorothy Alexander asked me to take on the roles of associate artistic director and principal dancer in her Atlanta Civic Ballet. Along with my wife, Virginia Rich Barnett, the New York City Ballet dancer and former student of Miss Dorothy's, we moved to Georgia. Dorothy retired in 1961. Merrilee Smith assumed the directorship for the 1961–1962 season, and I became the third artistic director of Atlanta Civic Ballet starting in the 1962–1963 season. Atlanta Ballet is the oldest continuously operating ballet company in the United States. The company's 90th anniversary is in 2019. Sixty-plus years since my first day on the job, I am still a member of the Atlanta Ballet family. In fall 2017, I set excerpts from Balanchine's *The Nutcracker*—"Candy Cane," "Sugar Plum Fairy," and "Spanish"—on some Atlanta Ballet 2 dancers. In summer 2018 I was back in the studio, setting Balanchine's *Tschaikovsky Pas de Deux*.

In a career that has covered eight decades, I now have a new role to add to what has been an extraordinary journey. I put my fingers on the keyboard to write this book. It is a formal thank you to the many individuals who have helped me on this path I chose to take. First, there are my parents, Jim and Vera, who in 1909 drove a stake into the ground in Conconully, Washington, to take advantage of the Homestead law. Our house lacked electricity, indoor plumbing and telephone. But there were the kerosene lamps for light; the outhouse for a toilet; and horses to ride, so that Dad could tend to the daily tasks of running the ranch. Because of my parents' hard work, frugal spending habits, and dedication to saving their earnings, my two older sisters and I never lacked the resources and the money for the education and training needed to achieve the careers that we wanted.

Second, there are the many individuals to thank who helped me in realizing my aim, my never-wavering passion, to pursue a professional career in ballet. Besides Michio Ito there is the Russian-born Bronislava Nijinska, a former choreographer with Sergei Diaghilev's Ballet Russes, whose reputation as a great teacher had preceded her immigration to California. I was twenty-one years old, and had just mustered out of the Navy, when I found Nijinska's school in a neighborhood near Hollywood. Another important teacher and role model is David Lichine, who picked me to move to Europe and join Colonel de Basil's Original Ballet Russe tour. Then there is Mr. Balanchine. It is because of studiously watching Mr. B that I learned how to direct a ballet company. Later, when I was the artistic director of the Atlanta Ballet, he was exceedingly generous, allowing me to have his *The Nutcracker* and *Serenade* ballets, as well as lots of his other ballets, without charging a royalty for any of them. Most important, because Mr. B hired me to dance in his New York

City Ballet, I met the dancer Virginia Rich. We married in 1957, in Atlanta. Mr. B was at our wedding. Last, but not least, there is the genteel Southern lady, Dorothy Alexander, to thank. Miss Dorothy, as she was called by her devoted students and company dancers, met Virginia and me at the airport the day we arrived in Georgia, immediately embracing us into the loving arms of the Atlanta Civic Ballet family. These are only a few of the important influencers and mentors acknowledged in this book who led (and sometimes pushed) me along the memorable path in my long professional ballet career.

A second purpose for this book is to pass along to future generations my knowledge and experiences. My methods for sharing, for passing it along, have involved traveling to dance studios and theaters in cities throughout the world teaching and coaching. I have lectured at colleges and universities, and at international dance competitions and regional dance associations, where I have talked with students, professional dancers, instructors, choreographers, balletomanes, and anyone wanting to learn more about ballet. I have been privileged to set some of George Balanchine's ballets, such as *Serenade*, on pre-professionals and professional dancers at schools and companies throughout the world. Setting a ballet is my way of showing Balanchine's style of technique and his choreographic ways and means that made the American ballet evolve and progress to the international prominence that it is today.

Balanchine once said to me, "Bobby, my choreography will disappear, or be watered down, once I am gone." "Not while I'm around," I promised. This book is my gift to future generations on the importance of ballet as an art form, and it passes along the lessons and tips of the trade I learned, as well as expresses my gratitude to those individuals, both the living and the departed, who were significant in assisting me to live such a beautiful, meaningful dance of life.

Chapter One

The Early Years

Okanogan, Washington. That's where I, Robert James Barnett, was born on Wednesday, May 6, 1925. My birth was at home, and I arrived a little too early, at seven months. I weighed 2.5 pounds. Still, I was the lucky one. My fraternal twin was aborted at around five months. An aunt was there to help with my birth. She put me in my new crib—a shoebox lined with cotton soaked in olive oil—which was placed on the dropped-down lid of a wood stove to keep me warm. For the first few months two aunts helped Mom take care of me, twenty-four hours a day. Throughout the day and night one would squirt a few drops of milk inside my tiny mouth, using an eyedropper, so that my underdeveloped stomach would not be overly strained.

Okanogan is the county seat of Okanogan County and is 200 miles east of Seattle. In the 1920s it had a population of around 15,000 independent-minded, hard-working migrants who were dedicated to taming and cultivating the western coast of America. There was no television, probably no radio yet, and no telephone in my house. At least we had indoor plumbing and electricity, though, much to the relief of my fifteen-year-old sister, Winnie, and eight-year-old sister, Lois, who were born twenty miles up north close to the rural town (if you can call a community of 200 people a town) of Conconully, Washington.

Actually, the Barnett homeplace where my sisters were born was not in the town. It was between Conconully and Okanogan, in a gorge, now called the Barnett Gorge by the State of Washington. The views were gorgeous, but it was a harsh place to live, especially in the sleet-stinging, snow-blinding winters. The only toilet was outside, in the outhouse. Nor was there a well on the property for drinking and cooking. Mom and Dad had built their modest house two miles away from the best source of water required for the family's daily needs. It was a spring that supplied water for Mom's garden, which was important to the family's livelihood since there were no grocery stores nearby, and which provided the water essential for drinking, cooking, cleaning, and bathing. To get the water for our household and personal needs required that Mom and baby Winnie ride on horseback the two miles to the spring every morning and every afternoon, seven days a week. Mom sold cream, which she carried in a cream can to sell to a local creamery in Okanogan to earn extra money, and on either side of the horse's back hung a large, metal cream can, about three feet tall. At the spring, she filled the two cream cans with water, which were securely strapped across the horse's back to keep the precious water from spilling on the return ride home. Mom was incredibly strong. For Winnie's baths, and then Lois's after she was born, for instance, she poured water in a tub, about the size used at a child's birthday party to bob for apples. She then would lift the heavy water-filled tub from floor to stove. After the water was hot she lowered the tub to the floor and waited for it to cool before bathing Winnie and Lois. It would be years before I heard these stories of my sisters' rough upbringing in Conconully. As the younger sibling, with two much older sisters to see to my every need, for the first five years of my life I was pampered and spoiled rotten.

My sisters Lois (left) and Winnie were ages eight and fifteen in this photograph taken in either Conconully or Okanogan, Washington.

Because of my dramatic entrance into the world, even my uncomplaining mom must have been thanking the stars that she lived in Okanogan at the time of my birth, instead of the somewhat store-less Conconully. She was thirty-two and healthy. But when one is bed-ridden, with a premature infant, conveniences like store-bought goods and family members close by to help out are a plus. While it may not have had the hustle and bustle of New York City or Chicago, Okanogan did have a few stores selling the basic necessities: sugar; flour; and bolts of cloth for making dresses, dish towels, and diapers. There were also some of what we simple, rustic people thought of as luxury items, like the mouth-puckering sour pickles swimming in brine, the huge, heavy wooden barrels on the floor. And there were those often taken-for-granted comforts to be grateful for in Okanogan, like electricity and an indoor toilet. Most important, given my premature appearance on the scene, having my aunts nearby in my dramatic first few months had to have been a real relief for both Mom and Dad.

Dad was overjoyed with my arrival, although it is not clear that he was as enamored with living in Okanogan as were his girls. He and Mom had started their married life fifteen years earlier in Conconully. They had been ranchers but had sold their 640 acres and livestock when they moved to Okanogan. Dad was thirty-eight years old when I was born, and while most jobs in the town supported the local fruit orchard industry, he was selling Dodge automobiles.

Here I am as a baby, feeling safe and happy in my sister Winnie's motherly arms, Okanogan, Washington.

At nine months I was a healthy fat and sassy baby. Then I got pneumonia. Mom did not believe in taking prescriptions or over-the-counter pharmaceuticals, including penicillin (which wasn't around yet anyway) or aspirin. She believed that drugs should come naturally, from the earth. Thus, instead of taking me to the local doctor Mom placed mustard plasters on my chest. She put eucalyptus leaves in a tea kettle filled with boiling water. She made a tent over a bed. Throughout the day and night she stayed next to me, both of us inhaling the soothing eucalyptus steam until I could breathe normally again. Growing up I suffered the occasional cold and for the first early years of my childhood I was a "croup baby." Mom's natural concoction to cure ailments such as the croup was to gather ashes from the wood stove and mix it with a few drops of kerosene.

In her home-remedy medicinal arsenal was a black pill she bought from a doctor that she mashed up and mixed with water; she added a little sugar, too. Then she spooned it into my mouth. The taste was terrible. But it worked. It usually didn't take long, maybe a day or two, before I was cured. I suffered the inevitable scratches, sores and rashes. Poison ivy I could swim through without suffering the mildest itch, but I was highly allergic to poison oak. And then there were the mosquitoes. Part of being raised on a ranch required nights out camping with Mom and Dad. There were no tents or comfortable sleeping bags. Instead, Mom gathered pine boughs from trees. She'd layer the thin branches, about a foot thick. A blanket was placed on top of each pine-bough bed. In certain seasons of the year the mosquitoes were thick and fierce. One night while I was sleeping on my pine-bough bed there were so many bites to my face that when I woke up the following morning my eyes were swollen shut. Mom had to dip a rag in ice-cold water from a nearby creek and lay it on my eyes to reduce the swelling. Because of my fair skin sunburns occasionally happened, and Mom applied vinegar mixed with water to reduce the pain. There were the common stomach complaints, and the usual childhood diseases Mom nursed me through, such as chickenpox, mumps and red measles. I did not get any vaccinations, though, until I was an adult, when I enlisted in the Navy. Nevertheless, I survived and thrived in those early years. Mom was still mentally sharp and physically mobile when she died at age ninety-nine. At age ninety-three I follow Mom's lead of choosing natural methods and supplements, rather than prescription (unless absolutely necessary) or over-the-counter pharmaceuticals, to keep me from getting sick in the first place or to cure the occasional bug. I get an annual physical examination, but also see a homeopathic specialist as needed.

I am about age three and dressed to the nines in this photograph taken in Okanogan, Washington. Mom made my suit.

I'm not sure why my parents gave up ranching in Conconully before my birth and moved to the more domesticated town of Okanogan—maybe for financial reasons. And there were those basic conveniences associated with living in a town the size of Okanogan. A big plus was the railroad station—a real advantage for towns and cities in the mid–1900s when the interstate highway system was in its infancy. There were no, or very few, eighteen-wheel trucks hauling goods from big cities to rural farm towns throughout the U.S. So, the railroad system made the transporting of goods, such as flour, corn, seeds and whiskey (important for adults) and candy (important for us kids), more efficient. A railroad station caused more people to move to the town, which caused more banks and retail stores to be built, which made shopping and life in general for the inhabitants more comfortable.

Even so, my parents decided that city life was not to their liking. After several years of living in the big city of Okanogan I guess Dad found life too routine, too dull—a salesman standing on a car lot all day hoping to sell a Dodge car compared to a rancher riding across his 640 acres of homestead land, branding bulls and breaking ornery horses. The call of the wild must have been too much for my adventurous forty-three-year-old dad and my thirty-seven-year-old mom to ignore. I was five years old when they moved back to the Conconully area in 1930.

It was in Conconully that my dad, James "Jim" Garfield Barnett, had married my mom, Vera Idella Berry, in 1909. He was twenty-two. She was sixteen. Most likely my parents had met in school or at the small bakery-restaurant owned by my maternal grandmother. Mom was born in Lake Charles, Louisiana, in 1892. Her father died soon after her birth, and she and her mother moved to Conconully to join my

My dad, James "Jim" Garfield Barnett, and mother, Vera Idella Berry, married in 1909 in Conconully, Washington. Dad was twenty-two. Mom was sixteen.

My mother's mother, Grandmother Agens, is in the center of this photograph wearing a very stylish hat for the early 1900s. From left to right in the back row are my step-grandfather Mr. Agens, my dad and my mother. From left to right on the front row, on either side of my grandmother, are my aunt Blanche and my uncle Roy.

grandmother's brother. He had studied finance and had a job at a local bank. Because my grandmother needed a job she opened a bakery-restaurant and became a successful businesswoman. Dad was born February 7, 1888, in Missouri. He and his family had moved to Conconully from Missouri when the State of Washington was just beginning to attract an increasing number of adventuresome individuals wanting to settle in the raw West. He said that his family moved to Washington because it was hailed as a "land of opportunity"; not because of gold mining (Conconully was a copper-mining town), but because a man could "plant a stick into the ground and get quite a bit of property." At that time, it was not unusual for men and women, such as my parents, to have no more than a fourth-grade education, although both my parents ended their formal education in the eighth grade. Women were not expected to go on to high school; marriage and raising kids were their tra-

ditional roles. Dad did not consider going on to high school either, because it was not common for farm boys or cowboys to go to high school, and also because he would have had to ride his horse two hundred miles or more every day to Spokane or Seattle. Before Dad and Mom married he had had a job in a livery stable, taking care of horses being boarded by town residents on a long-term basis or visitors on a short-term basis. Feeding, grooming the horses' coats of hair, keeping their hooves cleaned of pebbles and dirt, shucking and shoveling manure and keeping fresh-smelling hay on the floor of each horse's stall were some of his responsibilities. Mom had worked, too, at her mother's bakery-restaurant, before and after school, and on weekends.

The "opportunity" my dad was referring to was the 1862

James "Jim" Garfield Barnett and his siblings, circa 1894, when Dad was age six or seven. From left to right on the back row are my uncle Charlie and uncle Elmer. From left to right on the front row are my dad, my aunt Lola and uncle Orville.

The woman in the photograph at left is my mother, Vera Idella Berry Barnett, when she was about thirteen or fourteen years old in 1905. The photograph on the right is of my mother with an unknown friend.

Homestead Act, a law enacted by the federal government to persuade men and women to move to America's less populated states, such as Washington. Immediately after saying "I do" Dad and Mom became homesteaders, meaning that they obtained their ranch land in Conconully by pounding a stake in the ground and paying a small fee, about $15.00. Originally, the law restricted the number of federal land a person could claim to less than 200 acres, but it was eventually increased to 640. A homesteader had to build a house that was at least twelve by fourteen feet, improve the land (such as by growing crops or raising cattle on the property), and maintain permanent residency for five years. After five years a homesteader could file for a deed of title. Filing a claim at the county courthouse made the contract with the government binding and prevented someone else from claiming the same property. It was a cheap way to start a ranch or farm; however, the money, time, resources, and especially the physical labor required to make the farm or ranch a success made many homesteaders give up and walk away from

My dad when he was a teenager, circa 1903.

their claims before the five-year period was up. It was a rough existence, and there were some tough times. But Mom and Dad were not quitters. Little by little Dad acquired a lot of cattle and a good string of horses, and he needed hundreds and hundreds of acres to raise them on. Some of my parent's mountainous land was rocky and covered in timber—firs, pines and cottonwoods—land not conducive to feeding the horses and cattle. Rangeland, therefore, was required to feed the animals in the summer months and to grow

enough hay to feed them in the bitter winter. Dad grew the hay needed to feed the horses and cattle on the land he owned. But he had to lease range land from the government, where he grazed the livestock to fatten them up in the summer months. In the fall he sold the cattle and some of the horses. There were no cattle drives, as portrayed in the Hollywood movies. The buyers came to Dad, driving their trucks, and wheeled their live purchases away.

Purchasing cattle to raise and then sell was uncomplicated. But finding horses to own was a big deal. According to the stories I was told, soon after moving to Conconully Dad had started riding with some friends of his, Northwest Indians, up into the mountains where herds of

Dad wore chaps to keep his thighs from being rubbed raw from breaking broncos and riding horses for hours of the day, Conconully, Washington.

Dad riding one of his many horses he owned in Conconully, Washington.

free-range, human-wary horses could be found grazing in unclaimed government-owned pasture land. Together, the men would drive a herd of wild horses into a canyon draw—one entrance and exit—barricade it and choose which horses each person would own. They next began the dangerous process of lassoing and breaking. There wasn't enough time to tame each horse completely, so they were green-broke: able to be ridden by a cowboy but too wild yet to be ridden by a greenhorn. After camping for days in the draw, Dad would take his horses home and brand them. He must have suffered the inevitable saddle sores and muscle aches, but, to my knowledge, he never broke any bones from being thrown by a bucking bronco. Nor did Mom ever show any sign of worry that Dad might be seriously hurt. In those days horses were as necessary as automobiles are today. Not only did they safely transport us over miles and miles of steep, rocky trails and unpaved roads, but they were used to plow fields, to carry Mom's water, and to herd the cattle Dad bought and sold every year.

My homesteading parents had lived on their ranch in Conconully for about one year when my sister Winifred Deon "Winnie" Barnett was born in 1910. For seven years she was an only child until sister Lois Madeline arrived in 1917. Although I was not born when Mom and Dad were homesteaders, and only heard the stories later, I did have most of the same experiences as my parents and sisters because ranching duties, whether or not

Dad and some of his Northwest Indian friends in Conconully, Washington, circa 1908. From left to right are an unknown Indian, my dad, an unknown woman (maybe Felix's common-law wife), Dad's close friend, Felix, two unknown Indians, and my dad's brother, my uncle Orville.

Dad took great pride in competing in local rodeos. Here is a shot of him riding a bucking bronco at a rodeo in Okanogan, Washington.

one is a homesteader, are the same. I remember Dad being away from the house for many hours every day, and some nights, occasionally for a week or more, overseeing and caring for the hundreds of horses and cows he owned. Ranching is hard work with unpredictable hours. When a horse colics, for instance, a rancher doesn't wait to finish eating his dinner, or to get a good night's sleep, because the horse's stomach could rupture. Ranch chores are never ending and, often, time sensitive, such as timing when to mow the hay-fields to have enough food on hand in the ground-freezing, snow-storm winters to feed the livestock and keep them from starving. Maintaining a ranch is a family enterprise and ours was no exception. While Dad specialized in raising the cattle and horses, Mom specialized in managing the household responsibilities, like cooking and cleaning; caring for the barnyard animals; seeding and cultivating the herbs and vegetable gardens; keeping up with the financial accounts; paying the bills and the taxes; and keeping us children healthy, clothed, and educated. Mom's garden was huge and bountiful. While there were apricot and peach trees on our land, there were no apple orchards, even though we lived in apple orchard land. But these she could buy or barter. At the end of the growing season she would boil and then can vegetables and fruits (tomatoes, onions, cucumbers and peaches, for example). We didn't have an icebox, much less a refrigerator, so Mom stowed the cans and jars in the cold root cellar. Those vegetables that didn't require canning, such as cabbage, parsnips, potatoes and carrots, were stored outside in an earth mound in the garden, and to dig the vegetables out of the ground in those long winter months required a pickax. To keep meat on the table she gutted and butchered deer that my dad had killed. She butchered hogs and cured the meat in our smokehouse. She wrung chickens' necks, and we often had roasted chicken on the table to eat. There were some beautiful lakes and streams close by and we ate lots of fresh fish—trout and perch. Mom would gut them and cook them for breakfast. She baked the bread we ate every day, and her fruit pies could have won first place at any county fair. It seems ridiculous now but breakfast consisted of fruit pies; fresh fruit from the garden, such as melons; sourdough pancakes; biscuits and gravy. Also, there was ham, cured in our smokehouse, or deer meat, thanks to my dad's excellent marksmanship. Wild deer meat is not generally liked by most people. But Mom knew exactly what oils and vinegar and spices to combine for marinating the meat, which got rid of the unpleasant, foul wild-game taste. It was a lot of food to eat just for breakfast. And while such a rich diet would be considered unhealthy today, Dad and I stayed active enough to deserve the calories. We were both skinny. Mom's domestic chores were endless. She painted the bathroom and kitchen cabinets. It was not unusual to find her standing on a tall ladder painting anything that required a new coat of paint, both inside and outside the house. Because of her inexhaustible energy our house was always spick-and-span clean.

Just because we lived in a rural part of Washington did not mean that Mom was not appreciative of the latest fashion fads. In rural areas, the mail-order catalog for shopping was a necessity, and she regularly read the *Sears and Roebuck Catalog* to stay in the know and to order items. Part of her routine Saturday trip to the nearest town was to buy staples, such as flour and sugar, but the list of purchases also included those goods to keep us properly clothed. Dress patterns she could design and make herself, but materials for making our clothes required that she buy the cloth, thread, and buttons or snaps she wanted. Mom had a Singer sewing machine and her feet made the pedals sing every time she used it to make and to mend our clothes. How she did it all I will never know. Many years later when I was married, and my widowed mother retired, my wife exclaimed that she could not imagine a life like my mother's. "I loved it," Mom said.

Leaving Okanogan and moving back to Conconully in 1930 meant that my parents had to start over again to establish a cattle ranch. This time, though, was somewhat different from when they were homesteaders. Living in Okanogan and selling cars until I was age five must have been a good decision, because they had enough money to buy a house in Conconully, and they bought acres of ranch land up on a mountain, also. Eventually, the ranch I grew up on would consist of 180 horses (including some beautiful Arabians) and 400 head of Hereford cattle. While there were no daily horseback rides to get water for drinking, cleaning, cooking, and bathing like in 1910, much to Winnie's and Lois's disappointment, however, the toilet was once again in the backyard outhouse. Being the pampered child in the family, and a boy, I wasn't bothered much at all. There was no telephone at first. For light we used kerosene lamps. Later on we did have electricity, which was great when it worked, and a minor inconvenience when it didn't. Another welcomed convenience, and much more practical than a fireplace, was a wood stove to keep us warm in those cold months and to use for cooking, especially whenever the electricity was out. And if there was no power for the light fixtures, we had the kerosene lamps. We even had the luxury of a battery-powered radio to listen to popular tunes, like Ben Selvin's "Happy Days Are Here Again" and Harry Richman's "Puttin' on the Ritz." In addition to the smokehouse that kept our meat from spoiling, Dad built an icehouse. Every winter he would cut blocks of ice from the nearby frozen lake and put them in the icehouse. Sawdust was then spread over the blocks, which gave us ice all year long. We had milk cows and Mom was a pro at using the milk to make the most delicious ice cream. The butter and cheese she made were good-tasting, too. Growing up in Washington, my family was never affected when the economy suffered several recessions, or the Great Depression of 1929. When people living in major cities in other parts of the U.S. had to spend hours standing in bread lines because they were not working and had no money to keep food on the family table, those of us living in Conconully never were without an abundance of nutritious food.

That does not mean to say that ranching was easy. As true with most landowners my parents were land rich but sometimes cash poor. They prepared for these hard times, though, by being frugal; and every extra cent not needed to pay bills went into a bank savings account. One rainless summer could make a big difference in a rancher's income, for instance. If there was not enough water to grow the hay to feed the cattle through the frigid winter, then they had to be sold off prematurely, at a low price.

Mom was not satisfied living in the first house bought in Conconully, and she began to look for another house to buy, to "trade up," she said. Because there wasn't a big demand for lots of new houses to be built in Conconully, however, she had to wait until an owner was moving and wanted to sell. In the first six years of our return to the town we lived in three different houses. Mom was a master at painting and fixing up a house to make it more valuable, and she probably made money on every house she sold. Even though Dad was not around as much as Mom, he and I were close, and there were some really memorable times I can remember, like the night he got a call to take a string of horses up the mountain in Okanogan National Forest. It was an emergency, he had to go immediately. Mom was away, as were my sisters. Since I was a young child, he had to take me with him. I was spread over his horse, on my belly. He then strapped me down so I wouldn't fall off. Somehow, he got word to Mom because she arrived later in the family car. I can still remember Dad carrying me (I was half asleep) and putting me in the back seat. There were years when work took Dad away from home for several days at a time, and occasionally I got to go with him. At night we tethered our horses and prepared a campsite. If salmon were spawning in a creek, we caught a few for our dinner, and Dad would cook them on the campfire. He also made bantam bread. The dough was put in a cast-iron skillet and fried in oil or butter. There was nothing better tasting on these camping trips than eating bread and butter and beans (the can heated on the crackling fire), and fresh-out-of-the-stream cooked salmon. After a few hours of talking, gazing at the gorgeous moon and stars and enjoying the dancing shadows around the warm fire, I would spread my blanket over my pine-bough bed ... and hope that no snake would join me during the night.

There were lots of snakes in Washington, the timber rattlesnake, for instance. Dad was fearless; if a rattler crossed his path, he would pick it up by the tail with his bare hands and snap the head off. Mom, however, used a hoe to kill the occasional poisonous snake found in her garden. The good snakes, those helpful in keeping rats away, we left alone. There were times when I walked up the mountain to take lunch to my dad. In the winter there were unexpected blizzards to contend with; in the summer it was the snakes. Being short and skinny, when an unexpected blizzard struck I had to lie down flat on the ground, on my belly, my hands protecting my face, until the gust of wind had passed me by. And I preferred the blizzards to the snakes. I never have really hated anything, except for poisonous snakes. Walking or riding up the mountain trails also meant spotting a wild animal or two in those months they were active—a brown bear, for instance. There were wolves, although they were usually heard at night and not seen: they didn't like us humans any more than we humans liked them. The brown bears were mean, aggressive and dangerous, though. Dad was a hunter, and the wild game he killed was important to keeping food on our table or to keep us safe. I was taught how to shoot a rifle but never had the stomach for killing a deer, a bear or a snake.

Winnie, being fifteen years older than me, was not around much at the house after our move to Conconully in 1930. And, by 1933, she was married and living in Okanogan. Lois lived with Winnie, who took care of her, which meant there were no big sisters at home to help me with the daily chores. I had started school at age six in a small schoolhouse with only two rooms, and I stayed there from first to seventh grade. Being in school did not mean I had no chores, though. For example, there were the chickens to feed. We had lots of milk cows, and a milk cow has to be milked every day, twice a day. One of my chores was milking cows. Keeping a cow content so she will not kick over a pail filled with milk is one of the first lessons I learned. There's a fine technique to milking a cow. And with lots of coaching and practice I soon was a master. We had a barn cat whose job was to keep the rats away, and he often joined me at milking time. I got so good at milking that I could spray a stream of milk into his open mouth without wasting a drop. Not wasting milk was important because the extra milk not needed by our family was sold to businesses and individuals living nearby. After milking the cows in the morning, they were herded to open land so that they could graze throughout the day. My job was to ride my horse to herd the cows to a pasture in the morning and to find them in the late afternoon (the land was not fenced). Because I was a busy boy with lots to do every day, and saddling a horse takes a lot more time than I was willing to spend, I rode my horse bareback. Every herd of cows has a leader and the leader wears a bell. Once I could hear the tinkle of the bell, I could find the cows and then move them back to the barn.

Life in Conconully was not all hard work and sacrifices. Sure, the temperature would drop to below freezing in the winter months and could climb to 90 degrees in the summer. But neither the cold nor the heat was too bad because the air was dry, not humid. And while there was not a lot of free time for us kids to have fun and play, there was enough. We swam in the reservoir or lake in the summer, for instance. When the reservoir and lake froze in winter there were many fun hours ice skating. Family and community lunches or potluck suppers were a regular happening. Not only was there lots of great food to stuff our stomachs with, but we kids got to play games and run around chasing one another for hours.

Both my dad and mom had family living in the area or in the State of Washington, and the family got together as often as possible. Dad had three brothers and a sister. Mom had a step-sister and a step-brother, which meant I had cousins to play with. Mom's mother, however, was no longer living in Conconully. Soon after Mom and Dad married she had remarried and moved to Seattle. While none of us in my immediate family played competitive sports, supporting the local leagues was just something we did, and we attended swim meets and baseball games. There was a public park in Conconully, near a gorgeous lake. People would pitch tents and camp there. Occasionally, my aunts, uncles and cousins would meet us at the park for a family picnic. Also, there were times when some religious group would come to town and pitch a huge tent ("the Tabernacle," we called it) in the park for a revival. My dad's widowed mother was a hard-shelled Methodist—no drinking or dancing—and she was a regular attendee at these revivals. My parents didn't attend church regularly, nor did my sisters, but my grandmother did. Dad's mother had died when he was young, so "Aunt Emma," as she was called, was actually my step-grandmother. She was not

We had lots of pets around the house when I was growing up. Here I am with one of my many faithful companions at my home in Conconully, Washington.

especially child friendly, but, because she was my grandmother, whenever she asked me to go with her to church, I did.

Conconully did not have a movie theater, but Okanogan did and sometimes I got to see a movie there. Watching the Fred Astaire and Eleanor Powell movies got me dancing around our house. Theaters in those days had a stage. When the theater was dark it was rented out for parties, lectures and dance recitals. One day I would have my dance debut there. Because we lived in an agricultural area of the United States most farmers were members of an organization that held its meetings in a Grange Hall, located between Conconully and Okanogan. The building had lots of open space inside and was used as a dance hall on the weekends. These dances were quite a social event, with real musicians who were on tour, playing the golden-oldie ballroom dance music and the latest popular tunes. My parents loved to dance, and when I was a young child they would take me with them on a Friday or Saturday night. Couples began arriving at the hall about 7:00 p.m. A potluck dinner was part of this social event, and I stuffed my stomach with beans, meat, and lots of great-tasting desserts. There would be about 150 people eating and dancing. They came from all over, from both little and big towns. It is not bragging to say that my parents were excellent ballroom dancers. For hours I would watch them dance, such as the waltz and foxtrot. So huge was the makeshift dance hall that the dancers could perform group dances that required a caller, such as the "Big Apple." Fighting to stay awake, I'd watch as long as I could before having to lie down on a bench to sleep. While my parents were enjoying their ballroom dance parties my older sisters were off in Okanogan having their own fun dancing in a club. They preferred the popular dances to ballroom, though, and they were always willing to teach me the newest dances of the year. I remember turning on the battery-powered radio and dancing the Lindy Hop around the house. A forerunner of the Swing, the Lindy Hop came to be after Charles Lindbergh, nicknamed Lindy, was glorified in the press for his hop across the Atlantic Ocean in 1927. True, grandmother Aunt Emma didn't approve. But we danced anyway. When the Charleston was really popular Mom took time out of her busy schedule to make Charleston flapper dresses for my sisters to wear.

Even though Lois was patient (sometimes, anyway) when it came to teaching me the latest dances, that does not mean we didn't have our moments. We were typical siblings. We fought—sometimes a lot. Winnie, however, was like a second mother. One morning on my birthday, while lying in bed, she surprised me by walking in my room carrying a beautiful tricycle decorated with a big red bow. Later, when I was in high school, she bought me a car, a Model A Ford. She later played an important role in my schooling, too.

Elementary school was mostly uneventful. I never was sent to the principal's office for talking too much or clowning around in grades 1st through 5th. There were the few times when I had to stay after school to re-do my class assignments, though, when I didn't get the grade on an assignment or test that a teacher thought I should get. I didn't then, and still don't, like to be bored. If I was bored, I just did not do the assignments. I was one of those kids who was either a straight A student, if the courses were interesting, or an F student, if they were not.

I was about eleven when Mom and Dad moved to the town of Leavenworth in 1937. Because Mom and Dad had bought a small quaint and scenic mountain resort and didn't want to take me out of school during the school term to finish 7th grade, I lived with Winnie and her husband John and their baby Joanne in a three-bedroom house. John was the ranch foreman on one of the biggest ranches in the area; it was owned by the wealthy French family. Mom ran and maintained the resort. Dad took a job on a State of Washington government reclamation project to build a fish hatchery. Before the fish hatchery could be built, though, two lakes had to be joined. Not only was it a complicated project, it was dangerous. Joining the two water sources required digging a tunnel through mountainous, volcanic rock so that water from a lake created by a crater high up on the mountain flowed down to Snow Lake, where an artificial pond was being dug to put the fish hatchery in Leavenworth, Washington. The men lived at the campsite on Snow Lake while the project was underway, and Dad's job was to provide the supplies needed on the project, which included carrying food and equipment, for instance. He even carried the mail. The job was dangerous because everything, even the heavy equipment, had to be carried on a horse's back. Trucks could not be used because there was only a narrow trail up the mountain. A horse-drawn wagon was also too wide for the trail, nor could one safely negotiate the narrow, zigzagging, and rocky switchbacks, which is why Dad had to ride a horse and lead a string of six to eight horses carrying supplies. He had wranglers working for him; they followed, each with a string of packhorses, too. Winter months were particularly hazardous. A horse could slip off the icy, snow-covered trails. If one horse slipped and fell over a cliff, it took the others in the string with it. At least once Dad had to haul a big turbine up the mountain to the campsite. Thankfully, Dad never lost a horse or a turbine. Mom's job maintaining and managing the resort was less dangerous than Dad's, but it was still a lot of hard work and long days. The cabins were rented to tourists in the summer and hunters in the fall, which meant she cleaned cabins and supervised (or did them herself) the never-ending maintenance projects. Today it is a quaint Bavarian resort town with an interesting history. In World War II it was a

prisoner-of-war camp where captured Nazi soldiers were held. The prisoners were put to work protecting and maintaining the forests—fighting fires, building roads, and such—because so many American men were away fighting in the war. After the war the prisoners were released and sent back to Germany. A few, however, liked their prison enough to return to Washington and build a Bavarian-inspired resort. The resort was quite successful. And it is still so today, I believe. In the summer tourists hike in the mountains. In the winter they ski. The annual Oktoberfest is one of several popular events for both the locals in the nearby Washington communities and international tourists.

My parents' resort, although more modest, was a success with the tourists, too. They could fish in Icicle River or swim in the Wenatchee River. Dad rented his most docile horses to the tourists for recreational riding up and down the mountain paths to take in the breath-fresh mountain air and to admire the scenic views in the summer. Hunters rented horses in the fall. No matter one's preference—either a rifle or a bow—bobcats, deer, and bears were always around.

Dad and his men riding horses on the switchback to carry supplies to workers living in a campground on the mountain near Leavenworth, Washington.

In junior high I began working a part-time job, mainly in the summer months, in an apple orchard. It was an exciting day when I was handed my first paycheck ever. The excitement didn't last long, however, because I got very, very sick. It was lead poisoning from the pesticide used to kill bugs. Cherry orchards were not sprayed. Once I had recovered from my illness, I got a job picking cherries.

Boyish, mischievous shenanigans were not a regular happening when I was growing up. We teenage boys were busy with school, chores, and part-time jobs to get into too much trouble. Nor were illegal drugs and drinking a problem. While prohibition laws in the 1930s had caused crime rates to increase in major cities and big towns in various parts of the U.S., we were not affected in my town. That does not mean that we boys did not have a few pranks we liked to play. Cows generally sleep with their legs folded beneath them on the ground. But not always. So, there were the occasional times when my friends and I were walking through a pasture at night and where we might indulge in a little cow-tipping on an unsuspecting sleeping cow, who was surprised to find herself laid out on the ground. Then there were a few pranks when we knocked over someone's outhouse (only once was someone inside it). The most fun (and trouble that we got into), though, was decorating a big tree in front of a friend's house—with rolls and rolls of toilet paper. Parents were often outraged by the mess, especially if it had rained. Nothing deterred us, however. We teenagers saw our heroic effort on a late Halloween night as a grand tribute to honor a good friend.

High school was when I excelled in both academics and sports, and really had fun. In addition to owning the resort in Leavenworth my parents had bought a two-story house in Wenatchee, Washington, a town of about 30,000 people, located on the Columbia River. Because I was attending Wenatchee High School I moved into our house, and I lived by myself, at least during the week. Mom often checked on me every weekend when she came to town to buy supplies. Two doors down lived my mother's half-sister, Aunt Blanche, and her husband, Uncle Curt. At first Mom thought it her duty to iron my clothes on her weekend visits, until I complained about a wrinkle in a collar. She told me "Iron your own clothes if you don't like it." So I did: shirts, trousers, even my underwear. I learned how to cook, too. I liked to drive my stick-shift, black Model A Ford that Winnie had given me around town, which boasted a rumble seat to accommodate my friends. Being one of the few kids my age to have a car, I was very popular. I had to throw a blanket over the hood in the winter months to keep the engine from freezing. Paying for insurance was not something I had to think about, but tires did not last long, as they do today, and had to be patched or replaced often. Driving on the unpaved, rutted roads didn't help either. And gas had to be bought, too. To earn the much-wanted cash, I worked at a part-time job: first, as a bellhop at a local hotel. After about six months, though, Mom found out and made me quit. The job ended at 10:00 p.m. and she didn't like me walking home in the dark that late at night. Soon, however, I had a job working at J.C. Penney stocking tables and designing the windows.

Sometimes, I drove my spiffy car to high school, but usually I rode the bus. English literature was my favorite subject. My favorite English teacher was Miss Zeither (I don't know if she was married or not) and to this day I still like reading novels. I raced and high-jumped on the track team and won some competitions. I played tennis, until I wrecked a knee. Even though I did not play an instrument I knew how to do all sorts of fancy things with a baton, and I was elected drum major to lead the marching band. I never took any twirling lessons; it was just something I was able to pick up on my own. I was a member of an all-boys high school fraternity club, the Derby Club. A boy couldn't just voluntarily sign up; he had to be picked. And to be picked required that each candidate endure some hazing. Our designated uniform was a chic black sweater, and the stitched-on emblem over the front left breast was that of a black and white derby hat. It was a social club. One important high school social event was the Friday night dance, and we boys in the Derby Club took turns with the kids in the other social clubs decorating the gymnasium.

I had lots of good friends in high school, both boys and girls. There was one serious girlfriend—a couple, in fact. Some of my friends had summer homes in the mountains. Sometimes I was invited to visit them for the day, and sometimes I stayed overnight. As often as possible in those happy summers a group of us would ride our horses up a mountain and spend the afternoon swimming and picnicking at a popular lake.

Mom and Dad had lots of good friends, too. I still today have a belt that the wife of Dad's good friend Felix, a Northwest Indian, made for me. While my parents were not interested in federal politics much they voted, and they were active in community affairs. Daily life kept most of the farmers and ranchers too busy to spend hours chatting across a fence. But when an emergency occurred the neighbors were there to help. While we three kids in the Barnett family may not have had faddish toys under the Christmas tree or professional clowns to entertain classmates at birthday parties, we never thought ourselves deprived of things. Everything a kid required—food, clothing, shelter and love—was generously given. Maybe it helped not having a party-line phone or a television in my childhood and teenage years. Maybe it was good that I was not aware of what life was like for kids my age living in big cities throughout America. Certainly, such big cities may have had more goods to buy and fun activities to enjoy than Conconully or Leavenworth or Wenatchee. But in the 1930s, when those city folks (who called themselves "real Americans") were complaining about the invasion of aliens (immigrants) causing destructive changes to their once peaceful neighborhoods, and passing laws to stop it, our town was content to be diverse. In my part of America newcomers, no matter their ethnicity or origin or religious preferences, or whether they were born in the U.S.A., were welcomed. Also, luckily for me, neither my friends nor close family members (with the exception of Aunt Emma) ever teased or criticized me for dancing.

While I may have started life as a premature 2.5-pound infant with the odds of survival low, I was an active kid growing up. I did everything "on the run," Mom said. I was maybe four years old when she tried keeping me in safe view while she did her chores—she tied a rope to a strap of my overalls and hitched the other end of the rope on the clothes line. Running from one end of the clothes line to the other was soon boring, however, and I slipped out of my overalls and ran to the nearby pool hall, which was owned by a friend of my dad's. When Winnie found me, I was happily eating an ice cream cone. Because I liked to dance (à la Fred Astaire) around the small room in our house, when I was about age eight Mom enrolled me in a tap-dancing class. The trip to the weekly class required a drive of 18 miles one way to a town. The class was taught by a woman (probably a former B Hollywood hoofer) who drove to the town every Saturday to teach the one-hour class. Mom ordered my tap shoes from the *Sears & Roebuck Catalog*. While I danced she did her weekly shopping. After my class was over Mom and I would go to a café for lunch. I continued to take lessons through high school, and my teacher was Marta Cooper. She taught the one-hour Saturday class in a hotel ballroom, and I remember that the back wall was decorated with ceiling-to-floor heavy curtains that reeked of cigarette and cigar smoke. At age eighteen, after ten years of lessons and performances, I was really good. I was dancing solos, as well as dancing in ensembles, at local society club events, and in Marta Cooper's annual recital. Sometimes I performed on the small wooden stage at the local movie theater, or I tap danced on a concrete floor in some building where one of the town's social clubs met. The idea of what constituted a proper floor (less wear and tear on the knees) never entered my mind in those early years. I was invincible. Once, when my annual tap recital was performed jointly with another school's ballet recital, I got asked to partner a young girl, probably age twelve or thirteen, in a ballet piece. That one experience convinced me that I did not want to dance ballet ever again. I thought ballet might not advance my tap and theatrical training—that it might undo everything. I didn't like wearing the tights, either.

Neither my family, nor my girl or boy friends, ever showed any surprise at my tap-dancing interest. Some kids may have been jealous, in fact, because of my being picked to perform solos in dance recitals and to perform at local society-club programs, such as charity fundraising events. Mom made my costumes, including a pretty good-looking tuxedo. She bought my high-shine patent leather shoes and top hat. Dancing was a part of our culture both in the community and in my family. The Northwest Indians danced at their ceremonies. Mom and Dad loved the Hollywood musicals and they danced on weekends. Winnie and Lois went dancing at any local club popular at the time. There were regular dances at my high school. Perhaps, had it been ballet instead of tap some of my friends might have thought differently about me; or, if I had grown up in a state such as Missouri or Kentucky. But because Washington was not that far from Hollywood, California, and because we were living in an era when tap dancing was a big part of the movie musicals being produced, dancing was accepted. Indeed, many of us wanted to be like Fred Astaire, dancing in his signature tuxedo, top hat, and patent leather shoes, a beautiful lady in his arms.

Besides, even though I loved dancing, it was not going to be my career when I grew up.

While my parents chose not to get a high school or college degree they thought differently when it came to us kids. Part of their bank savings was meant to pay for college tuition, board and books. They didn't care what we studied as long as we got a college degree in something. Even so, being independent-minded (which my parents encouraged), Winnie did not attend college; she chose to manage her family's household affairs instead. But Lois got a degree in business, and her education proved beneficial when she opened her own hair-salon business. I, as well as most of my friends, definitely planned on attending college. Watching Fred Astaire and Eleanor Powell movies

Here I am in a fashionable coat and tie at age eighteen, the year I graduated from Wenatchee High School and enlisted in the Navy.

and loving the costumes the actors and actresses wore had inspired me to become a fashion designer. I even took design courses in high school, thinking that I would be better prepared to get a college degree in fashion design. I really liked my part-time job at J.C. Penney dressing the mannequins and designing the window displays. It never entered my mind to become a cowboy, or a railroad worker, or a businessman, or a Hollywood hoofer.

I was blond-haired and blue-eyed, had grown to a height of 5'5" and weighed maybe 120 pounds, when I celebrated my eighteenth birthday. High school graduation was a week or two away, and I was excited to be leaving home to start college. Excitement melted into worry, though, when an unexpected graduation present was delivered to me in the mail from the U.S. government—a draft notice.

Chapter Two

Military Service
and a Ballet Pre-Pro

In May 1943, I decided to enlist rather than await my orders, and I joined the Navy to serve my country in World War II. I am not sure why I chose the Navy over the Army or Air Force or Marines, but it may have been because I liked the uniform. The first day in this next chapter of my life started Thursday, June 3, 1943. Taking the bus to Idaho for my six weeks of basic training was the first time I had traveled outside of Washington. Military service would take me on my first international trip. Little did I know that traveling would become a regular part of my life.

I am looking sharp in my Navy uniform when I was stationed at Farragut Naval Training Station in Farragut, Idaho, for basic training.

Basic training was at Farragut Naval Training Station in Farragut, Idaho, and it was nowhere near the ocean. After the six weeks of basic training I was transferred to the Navy base at Port Hueneme near the town of Oxnard, California—it was a Seabee, a construction base. I was assigned to guard duty for about six months. Luckily, there were no security incidents. The rifle I carried was a fake. From Hueneme my orders took me to a Navy base in San Pedro for a short stint. From San Pedro I was transferred to Long Beach and from there to San Bruno, CA, where I was kept in limbo until I received my orders for the next assignment, which was the beautiful city of San Francisco. The base—Presidio Cavalry Barracks, a former cavalry base—had been built during the Civil War. It was located close to the Golden Gate Bridge. My job was to log every boat wanting to go into the harbor. Every ship and boat captain had to have a code to enter. Without the correct code the gate to the harbor would not open. Routinely, I had to send a report to San Diego and to Washington, D.C.

Surprisingly, being in the military did not stop me from pursuing my favorite hobby—tap dancing. I took a few tap lessons. Because of my theatrical experience I was invited to dance at some of the officers' clubs as part of the entertainment. On days when I had liberty and could get off the military base I took a bus to a nearby town. The buses were free, so I never needed to hitchhike. Often I walked miles of city streets studying the window displays, planning my future as a college student studying fashion design. When stationed in the Los Angeles area I sometimes saw a show at the Palladium or the Hollywood Bowl. On one of my leaves four friends and I took a bus to Hollywood. One of the guys was movie star handsome (later he would become a Catholic priest; another would become an executive for Sears & Roebuck). We were walking around Grauman's Chinese Theater when we

My parents and I (center), along with two Navy buddies (I do not recall their names), enjoyed some fine dining in a restaurant in Long Beach, California.

met a friendly family who owned an apartment building nearby one block off Hollywood Boulevard. We were invited into the house. They gave us snacks and drinks. We had such a fun time that we were invited to come back and spend the night. The guys and I went every weekend that we could. One of the daughters fell in love with my movie-star-handsome friend. The relationship didn't go anywhere, though. Maybe even then he planned on becoming a priest.

I entertained military officers and their guests at officer's clubs during my military career. This photograph was taken in Santa Barbara, California.

One day while walking alone down a street in Los Angeles I spotted a theater. The show was a touring ballet company. I recall it was Ballet Theatre, later known as American Ballet Theatre or ABT. Igor Youskevitch was the star. (Not only did he tour with Ballet Theatre, but he toured with Ballet Russe de Monte Carlo, also.) He probably was in his late 20s or early 30s and in the prime of his dancing career. The experience of seeing him dance changed my life. Watching Fred Astaire movies when I was growing up had influenced my decision to study fashion design; I really liked the clothing he and his dance partners wore. One's life, though, really is filled with surprises, an eventful journey of good and not-so-good experiences. I couldn't help but remember that time when I was a young boy and the not-so-good classical ballet experience I had had partnering a young girl in a local recital which made me decide that I would never dance ballet again. Now, as a man, watching Igor Youskevitch jumping, leaping and spinning across the stage, I changed my mind: as soon as my military service was finished I wanted a professional career as a classical ballet dancer.

Igor Youskevitch was born in Moscow in 1912. Because of the Russian revolution his family fled to Yugoslavia in 1920. In his early years Youskevitch trained as an athlete—gymnastics. Years later, I was told that he was performing in a circus when he met a man who would one day become an important figure in my dance career also—Anatol Joukowsky. At Anatol's urging Youskevitch began his classical ballet training in Paris with Olga Preobrazhenska. For one year, around 1934, he danced in Europe in a company that Bronislava Nijinska had formed. By 1938 he was dancing in the Ballet Russe de Monte Carlo, which toured the U.S. frequently. He and his wife, Anna Scarpova, decided to live permanently in the U.S. Youskevitch became an American citizen in 1944. I was lucky to see him perform before he voluntarily joined the U.S. Navy to fight in World War II.

Watching Youskevitch dance affected me emotionally. I discovered ballet (as it was correctly done) when I saw that performance. In later years I would see him dance again, partnering some of the greatest ballerinas in the world, such as Alicia Alonso in *Giselle.* Other dancers would inspire me as well. I remember Hugh Laing and Nora Kaye dancing in Jerome Robbins's work *Facsimile.* Nora screamed at the top of her lungs; it was part of the ballet. Still, I was so involved in watching, and she screamed so loud, that I jumped out of my seat. Another male dancer who would make an impression was Erik Bruhn. He was a principal in the Royal Danish Ballet and trained in the Bournonville technique. In the late 1980s, when I was artistic director at Atlanta Ballet, one of my students, Caroline Cavallo, would be asked to join the Royal Danish Ballet.

I stayed in California from 1943 into 1945 and spent most of that time on shore. When I was finally on a Navy ship for a lengthy period it was to leave San Francisco for Japan. There was a brief stop on an idyllic island

This postcard shows the area where I was stationed at the Yokosuka (also spelled Yokoska) Naval Base, about 50 miles south of Tokyo, Japan.

in the South Pacific for about two to three days. Finally, the ship docked in Tokyo Bay. I was in Tokyo Bay September 2, 1945, the day the Japanese signed the Document of Surrender on board the *USS Missouri* which was also in the harbor. While I was sailing across the Pacific Ocean an American B-29 bomber had flown over the Japanese city of Hiroshima on August 6, 1945, and deployed the world's first atomic bomb. About 80,000 people were killed. A second bomb killed about 40,000 Japanese people in Nagasaki three days later. On August 15 the Japanese Emperor Hirohito surrendered. While there may have been some talk among us on our ship about the possible effects of radiation poisoning, it was not something we considered seriously. I recall that most of us were relieved that the war was over. The end of the war did not mean the end of my military service, however.

From my ship I traveled by a small boat to Yokosuka Naval Base, about 50 miles south of Tokyo. I found my barrack, then my bed, and unpacked my belongings. Yokosuka had been an important Imperial Japanese military base before the U.S. Navy took it over. The Japanese must not have been happy about their eviction because on their way out they had slashed and destroyed any abandoned furniture, and the walls were marred. My stay in Japan did not get off to a good start: I got dysentery and was awfully sick. California had felt so foreign to me compared to my rural town in Washington, but that feeling was nothing compared to what I felt when moving to Japan. It was quite exciting actually. For one thing there were the distinctive smells. Compared to the lovely smell of the cottonwood trees in Conconully the smells in Japan were much more pungent. Not bad, just different. Despite the big difference in size of the population (and the smaller height of so many of the Japanese people compared to us Americans) and the culture, I loved living in Japan. It was so striking—all the exotic little streets. Early every morning there were horse-drawn wagons or trucks motoring down the busy streets carrying freshly caught fish and farm produce to local outdoor markets and shops. Surprisingly, living in Japan, a country that had just been defeated in the war, was not all that unsafe for an American soldier as long as one followed instructions. I did. But a few didn't heed the advice to stay on the American military base. Some sailors liked to go drinking in Japanese bars; a few were poisoned and died. Japan had gangs and the gang members were easily recognizable because their arms and necks were covered with tattoos. A confrontation between gang members and U.S. soldiers could result in the Americans being attacked and stabbed; a few were killed. I did not go off the base until it was determined safe enough to do so. Nor was there a need to; everything I wanted was on the base. And when my friends and I did start leaving the base we were watchful when on the streets, and really careful. We never put ourselves in a risky situation.

One good thing about getting off the base was that I got to see some excellent dance performances. Russian classical ballet training was not a rarity in Asia because, just as in the U.S., there were former Mariinsky (also spelled Maryinsky) Ballet or Bolshoi Ballet dancers who had settled in various Asian cities as a result of the 1917 Russian revolution. Some opened ballet schools. Some founded or taught in ballet companies. One Japanese ballet company I saw had some beautiful dancers. It was a performance of *Les Sylphides*. It was danced behind a scrim which gave it an airy, otherworldly quality.

I had learned to type in high school and, despite having to literally pound the keys on a manual typewriter, I could type 120 words per minute with almost perfect accuracy. So, I was a yeoman for several executive officers, meaning that I mostly was assigned to type letters and reports. I had to be one hundred percent accurate or type the letter over. Because I was pretty good at shorthand (learning the symbols was not a problem for me, and I was fast) I took dictation, too. I typed some of the military police reports. If a soldier was picked up by military police for being drunk, for instance, I was given a copy of the hand-written report which I typed up and put in the soldier's personal file. This was my job before I went into show business.

One of my friends told me about a theatrical production being developed by the U.S. Army Liaison Unit and that dancers were needed for the GI musicals. I auditioned for a Japanese choreographer, Michio Ito, whom the U.S. Army had tapped to direct and choreograph the shows, and I was hired. Even though I was in the Navy I was borrowed by the U.S. Army to do what I loved best—dance.

I took a train from Yokosuka to Tokyo which was a pretty long ride. I had already experienced riding the rails in Japan and knew that the typical Japanese traveler usually brought his own food—a lacquered box filled with sushi or eel. Because I wasn't into eating sushi or eel, and didn't like the smell, I rode in the baggage car. Riding the rails is filled with fun adventures. On a previous train trip I had met a Polish woman and her Japanese husband. He was a physicist who had earned a reputation for making fabric out of whale blubber. He had been a professor at the University of Chicago. On a visit to his native country, before the war, he and his wife were not allowed to return to the U.S. Stuck in Japan, for who knew how long, they had moved into a house in a picturesque resort community in the mountains. It catered to rich Japanese. There were hot springs, luxurious hotels, and stunning houses—the works. I know because I got invited to visit the couple. On one of my leaves a couple of friends and I checked out a jeep from the motor pool.

Arriving at the physicist's house late that night, we immediately went to bed. The rooms in the house seemed dark, unusually so. I remember seeing a huge porcelain stove (which made our room comfortably heated) but not much else inside the house. The next morning I woke to find my bedroom bathed in sunlight, as were the rooms in the rest of the house. The house had walls of glass and the view was spectacular. I learned that the house had panels that covered the glass windows at night, to keep the home cozily heated, and which were opened in the daylight. I met the couple's son, who was about twenty years old, and quite handsome. It was obvious that he was not one-hundred-percent Asian, although we heard no stories of him ever being bullied because of his mixed race. The family had a German housekeeper who was an excellent cook. Her apple strudel was outstanding. I visited the family more than once and met several of their good friends. One was a gorgeous Japanese princess; she was wearing a riding habit and leather riding boots. Although the illegitimate daughter of a Japanese prince, and incognito, her dad took care of her. That's the type of people, of that ilk, that I met. My experiences during my months living in Japan right after the war are much different than what is written in many of the history books.

This postcard is of Tokyo, Japan, where I performed in a GI musical at the Ernie Pyle theater, formerly known as the Takarazuka Theater. The dance director was Martha Graham's friend Michio Ito.

Arriving in Tokyo, I began the final phase of my military career tap dancing in the theater. Life presents unexpected opportunities, and these opportunities require that choices be made, and I have been very lucky in the opportunities and with the choices I made. Had I not met the artistic director and choreographer Michio Ito in Japan, I might not have followed through with my new career plan and taken ballet lessons, much less taken lessons from the renowned teacher Bronislava Nijinska. I might not have met David Lichine and danced with the Original Ballet Russe on tour in Spain and Portugal and North Africa. I might not have met George Balanchine and danced in New York City Ballet. I might not have met my wife, Virginia, fathered my two sons, and served as artistic director of the Atlanta Ballet.

Born in Japan in 1892, Michio Ito became interested in dance by seeing the dancers Isadora Duncan, Anna Pavlova, and Vaslav Nijinsky in performances. At age eighteen, in 1910, he left Japan. He moved to Germany where he studied Eurythmics at the Dalcroze Institute in Hellerau, Germany. It is said that Eurythmics inspired Nijinsky's choreography. It may have inspired Ito's, too. He moved to the United States in 1917. In New York City he was a dancer in Adolph Bolm's Ballet Intime company. Bolm had danced first with the Mariinsky Ballet in St. Petersburg, Russia, and then with Diaghilev's Ballets Russes, before immigrating to the U.S. with his wife and son. From 1923 to 1925, Michio performed in the Greenwich Village Follies where one of his fellow dancers in the Broadway production was Martha Graham. Later, Graham, Kirstein and Balanchine would become friends and collaborators. Michio had become friends with the sculptor Isamu Noguchi and introduced him to Graham. Noguchi and Graham's collaboration would become legendary. Noguchi would design the set and costumes for Balanchine's *Orpheus* that premiered in 1948. Michio had had a successful career as a modern dancer and a modern dance choreographer. He even had his own company. One of his dancers was Lester Horton, who, during the war, was playing an important role in America's modern dance evolution. Horton's technique and choreography would influence the modern dancer Carl Ratcliff, who would influence the professional dance career of my wife, Virginia.

After the outbreak of World War II Michio made several trips to Japan to visit friends and relatives. Apparently, some of his friends were in high-level government positions, or had friends who were well-connected to government officials, which caused the FBI to take notice and begin monitoring his activities. Michio was in the U.S. when within a day or two after the Japanese attack on Pearl Harbor he was arrested and accused of spying. He and his wife were deported to Japan in 1943 as part of a prisoner exchange. When I met him he recently had been hired by the American Occupation administration as the dance director for an entertainment center at the Ernie Pyle theater, formerly known as the Takarazuka Theater before the U.S. military took it over. Most of us in the company took Michio's appointment as an indication that he was unjustly accused of being a spy by the U.S. government and deported. Never again did Michio live in the United States.

Because of Michio Ito, dancing in the GI musicals was a remarkable way to end my military service. Also, he encouraged me to take ballet lessons, which reinforced my decision to pursue a career as a professional classical ballet dancer. I followed his advice. Having no interest in a long-term military career I mustered out (meaning that I had enough military points to be released from my military service obligation) of the Navy in June 1946.

After a short visit with my parents I caught a bus and went to California and stayed with an aunt and uncle in Pasadena. I couldn't drive my handsome Model A Ford, my gift from Winnie on my 16th birthday, because Dad had sold it when I was in the Navy. I was really upset.

My aunt taught deportment (manners) and fencing at Pasadena Junior College. She didn't know of any good ballet teachers in the area, but she sent me to the theater at the college where I talked to a woman in the box office. She gave me the name of a studio where a friend of hers was studying ballet. I got on a bus, then had to change buses at least three times, before I finally found the studio: It was two rooms above a movie theater. After walking up the wide steps of the stairway I got to the reception desk and told the receptionist—a friendly woman with teased, hairspray-stiff, bottle-blonde hair—that I wanted to study ballet. I was relieved to learn that my mature age of twenty-one did not prevent me from enrolling. In fact, not only was I eligible to study ballet at this studio, but because I had served in the military in World War II I was told that the GI Bill would pay for my lessons. The Servicemen's Readjustment Act of 1944, or GI Bill, was Franklin Delano Roosevelt's and the U.S. Congress' idea for helping us war veterans assimilate back into civilian life. It covered payments for Veteran Administration–approved loans for homes, farms or businesses; unemployment; and education and training, including dance education and training. By September 1946, I was officially enrolled in a ballet school. My teacher was the famous former Serge Diaghilev choreographer, Bronislava Nijinska. My journey on the path of a professional career as a classical ballet dancer had officially started.

Bronislava Nijinska was born in Russia in 1891, the younger sister of Vaslav Nijinsky. She received her classical ballet training at the St. Petersburg Imperial Ballet Theater school (now called the Vaganova Ballet Academy) where Enrico Cecchetti had taught until 1902. When she graduated she became a professional dancer in the Mariinsky Theatre Ballet, which the revolutionary Bolsheviks renamed the Kirov Ballet. Like so many other dancers, she fled Russia. In Europe she danced professionally and became celebrated as a choreographer, and not only because she was a rarity in the mid–1900s—a female, classical ballet choreographer—but because she was gifted. Serge Diaghilev recognized her talent and anointed her as the chief choreographer in his Ballets Russes de Monte Carlo. She also had developed a reputation as an excellent teacher while living in Europe. That reputation followed her to America when she moved to California.

Nijinska did not have a company when I took her ballet classes in California, so I did not get a chance to learn any of her works, such as *Les Noces* and *Les Biches*. Her important impact on my life was as my first classical ballet teacher, and I could not have asked for a better foundation. She followed the Cecchetti classical ballet technique-training method to the letter. During my years as one of her students I got to watch some of the greatest dancers in the world take her class (whenever they were passing through Los Angeles for various reasons): ballerinas such as Maria Tallchief, Marjorie Tallchief and Alexandra Danilova. It was common for famous dancers (those in touring ballet companies and from Hollywood) to take a private one-half-hour lesson before my ten o'clock class. Often, he or she stayed and took Nijinska's class—with me. I learned as much from watching them in class as I did from taking the class. It is because of Nijinska's teaching that I learned to jump high with my feet pointed and to turn sharp and fast. It is because of her excellence as a teacher that I would be hired to dance in the New York City Ballet. It is from her that I learned about proper class-etiquette rules: no matter how important a principal dancer you were. Once, when Marjorie Tallchief was leaning on the barre, Nijinska yelled at her, in Russian. Even though we students did not know exactly what she said, we pretty much figured it out when Marjorie quickly stood up straight.

While I was officially enrolled as a student at Bronislava Nijinska's studio, I actually took my first ballet lessons from her daughter, Irina Nijinska. A student could not just sign up to take a class from Nijinska; she picked her students. After about six months Nijinska watched a class, and I was honored when she picked me to join her specially-selected students. A uniform was required at the school, no exceptions. Every girl had to wear a black tunic just long enough to cover her tush. The sides were slit so that the legs had the freedom to move. A string wrapped around the waist and was tied in a knot in back. The tights were pink, and pink ballet slippers or toe shoes were the only proper footwear. Boys wore white cotton shirts, black tights, a dance belt, white socks and black ballet slippers. There were lots of dance supply stores in California, so I didn't need to order my clothes from the *Sears & Roebuck Catalog*. Even though I had looked at pictures in magazines of male dancers dressed in the typical ballet uniform (required as far back as the late 1800s), wearing the ballet uniform still took some getting used to. The studio had no air conditioning. I soon discovered that wearing the requisite wool tights to keep my leg and hip muscles warm was very uncomfortable in the California heat. I don't recall any awkward moments when walking into a dance supply store to buy the required uniform, not in California anyway, because there were so many male dancers living in the area—either studying dance or dancing at the Hollywood Bowl or in Hollywood films—that the store clerks were used to them.

Nijinska's class was every day, Monday through Friday, from 10:00 a.m. to 12:00 p.m. Thursday was pointe class for the girls. In center work they would have to stand on pointe while executing Cecchetti's eight positions of the body. The pointe class was brutal. Almost every exercise was done on pointe. Boys were in the Thursday pointe class, also, and we did the exercises on half-pointe. There were no partnering classes. It wasn't a big thing then. I don't remember any school, even Balanchine's School of American Ballet, teaching partnering classes. In the 1940s, it was something a male dancer had to learn on his own, usually from watching duets in rehearsals, or from

I am showing off my new classical ballet technique skills for this photograph in 1947. My esteemed teacher, Bronislava Nijinska, was Vaslav Nijinsky's sister.

being personally coached, either from a friend, a ballet master or the chore-ographer. Whenever we guys found a willing (a ballerina brave enough, such as Meredith Baylis) partner, and an empty studio, we would learn partnering techniques by trial and error, such as finger turns and fish dives and overhead lifts. In addition to ballet classes I took academic courses in music theory and French. Also required was character dance, on Wednesday. I took twelve academic and dance classes a week and was very serious about my training. I was twenty-one years old, and because of my determination to start dancing professionally as soon as possible I worked full tilt.

Nijinska was not a pretty woman; her shoulders were broad and square. But she was always immaculately groomed. Her hair, her clothing—her fingernails always looked as if they were professionally manicured. And usually she wore some expensive, beauti-ful turquoise jewelry that she had bought in Europe. To teach she wore a custom-made silk black pants and matching top outfit, the shirt buttoned up to the top of her neck. She wore black bal-let slippers. Her hair was always in the classical bun—hair parted in the middle, the bun low, at the nape of her neck. The story was that Nijinska had moved to Cali-fornia from Europe because of the weather and the glam-our of Hollywood. Because there were lots of professional dancers and want-to-be-professional dance students to study at her school, she had a lucrative business.

She smoked while teach-ing. One day she grabbed a male student's shoulders to pull them back (they were too

Dancing on the rooftop. Nijinska's studio was in the Los Angeles, California, area. Lots of Holly-wood stars and dancers from touring companies, such as Ballets Russes, who were passing through the city took her classes. This photograph was taken by a friend in 1947.

rounded for her liking). She got too close to him, though, and burned a hole in his shirt, blistering his skin. Undeterred, she continued the class. The poor guy never said a word. I only know about the blistered skin because I saw it after class when we were in the dressing room. Nijinska didn't use a cane to bang against the floor to keep time to the music or to push a leg higher up into the air, but she did keep a pointer in one hand. After two or three unsuccessful attempts to get a student to follow a correction she would use the pointer on an unresponsive leg. Nijinska could execute double tours, perfectly, always with a soft landing. She taught me to do double tours, and there were those really good days where I did triple tours, sometimes even four. She taught me pirouettes: sixteen, then a full stop, before I softly placed my foot on the ground. The whole thing was placement. It was good that her barre was always the same. She followed a set Cecchetti syllabus which really helped in my early training when the steps and movements were so foreign to me. The girls stretched in her class but the boys did not. She wouldn't let us: Nijinska believed that there was a tradeoff between flexibility and the explosive power necessary for jumping high into the air. Barre always started with a plié exercise. The second exercise was grand battement. The exercises in her center work were simple in structure, but hard to do. There were always four different petit allégro combinations; then, at the end of class, with the pianist playing the same piece of music, they were combined into one variation. She did it as a memory exercise as well as for learning the steps. We did exercises such as grande allégro, jeté en tournant, and grande fouetté usually in a circle. There were also some combinations on the diagonal, across the floor from one corner of the room to the next.

While the GI Bill paid for my classes and a cheap apartment to live in, I had to pay for food, transportation and clothing. And to earn money I worked at an insurance company from 7:00 p.m. until 10:00 p.m. My primary duty was that of a file clerk. Despite being frugal, occasionally I found myself short of funds at the end of the month. In those few situations, because my parents had saved money to pay for my college tuition and board, Mom wired me some money from my college savings account.

In addition to lots of long hours of hard work, the months spent studying with Nijinska were also a lot of fun. We students knew each other well; we danced together and with what little time we had we played together. After eighteen months studying with Nijinska I got itchy and wanted to perform somewhere. Because of the many Hollywood musicals being filmed in the 1940s, there was a big demand for dancers, especially male dancers, since so many men were still in the military service. When I heard about the Universal-International studio film *Up in Central Park,* I went to an audition.

The choreographer chose me for the film. We began talking about the terms of the contract and he asked me if I was in the union. No, I had to say. He said that he couldn't take me. If a union member did not have a job he or she got hired before a non-union member, even if the union member was not as talented or skilled. It would not have done me any good to join the union, either, because I would not have had the seniority status that was required. Disappointed, but determined, I then heard about a ballet company in Europe that needed dancers for an upcoming tour of Spain and Portugal and North Africa, and American union rules did not apply to companies in Europe. So my next audition was with David Lichine—a dancer and choreographer with the Colonel W. de Basil Original Ballet Russe company—who was in California recruiting dancers. A local dance teacher, Miss Frey, had a studio on Vermont

Avenue where Lichine was watching some of her classes. I took a class and got picked. A boy named Richard "Ricky" Adama, from Nijinska's studio, got picked, also.

While Nijinska trained me for a professional career in classical ballet it was David Lichine who launched my classical ballet career. David Lichine was born in Russia in 1910. His family had fled their homeland because of the 1917 revolution, and they settled in France. In Paris, Lichine had studied ballet with Lubov Egorova. By 1928, he was dancing in Ida Rubinstein's Les Ballets de Rubinstein where he studied with Bronislava Nijinska, who was the artistic director and one of the chief choreographers. When I met him he was married to Tatiana Riabouchinska, also a Russian immigrant. She was one of the

Here are some of my new classical ballet friends from Nijinska's studio. I am on the left, then Meredith Baylis and Ricky Adama.

three famous "baby ballerinas" discovered by Balanchine at the Paris school of Olga Preobrajenskay and Mathilde Kschessinsakaya in 1931. At my audition with Lichine in 1948, he and Riabouchinska were dancing with the Colonel's Original Ballet Russe. Lichine was choreographing, also. Probably his most famous work was *Graduation Ball,* which he had premiered in 1940. Thanks to David Lichine my pre-professional ballet training had ended. I was now officially a pro.

Lichine asked if I had a passport. "No," I said. While in the military I had not needed one. One other dancer hired did not have a passport either. Almost immediately I packed my few belongings, telephoned my parents to tell them good-bye, and left California. Along with my new friend we took a train to Washington, D.C., to quickly get a passport from the Department of State. From D.C. we took the train to New York City and met up with other newly hired dancers. Eight of us then went by ship to Southampton, England, including my friend Barbara Lloyd, whom I had met at Nijinska's studio. She was young, maybe fifteen or sixteen, and her parents were traveling with her. Despite her young age she had danced in the Original Ballet Russe previously, so she was the experienced one in our group. It took about seven days to sail across the Atlantic Ocean from New York to Southampton. We hit a patch of bad weather at least once and the ship rocked and rolled, but because of my naval experience I never suffered any sea sickness. Walking down the steep ramp and stepping onto European soil felt good. I was officially on my first European trip. We still had to get from the port to the city of London, though, which is about an hour and a half to two hours by train. Eager to keep going to Paris we all agreed not to spend time in London and went immediately to another train station. There, we got on the first train we could book to France. Too excited to let tiredness stop us from seeing the sights, that night we walked for hours admiring the luminous city. I have always had an interest in looking at jewelry in the store window displays, and there were some elegant displays in Paris. We had booked rooms in some little hotel for the night, and when we decided to return to the hotel to get some sleep we weren't sure how to find our way back. One of the girls—maybe Barbara Lloyd—got frightened. "Where are we?" she asked, as we all looked around the bustling street, trying to get our bearings. She thought we were lost. I have a pretty good sense of direction, however, and I assured her, and the others in our group, that we could find the hotel. First, though, we stopped at a quaint bistro-bar for one last drink and everyone calmed down. Leading the way, I followed the jewelry stores I had admired earlier in the evening, feeling some comfort in recognizing the shops and landmarks we had passed before. Eventually, we found the hotel. The next day we were on a train to Barcelona, Spain.

Francisco Franco was the dictator of Spain in 1948 and not a friend of the U.S. government. Thus, when our group went through immigration and customs the inspectors took everything out of our bags, searching for what I do not know; otherwise, we were not unduly held up and questioned. With our luggage in hand we went directly to the theater. My stay in Barcelona was expected to be about six weeks, so soon after arriving, I began walking the streets close to the theater to find a cheap place to live. I discovered the Pension Sussie (or Suisse), owned by a man who rented rooms on two of the building's upper floors, and the rent included meals. Ricky and I shared a room. Barbara and her parents rented a room next to ours. I considered myself lucky to have found the pension by pure chance. It was small but clean, offered meals, and was a close walk to the theater.

There were about forty to fifty dancers in the company (from Eastern Europe, London, Paris—all over) and those of us new dancers had to learn the whole repertoire, which included a lot of Léonide Massine ballets—original works and classics that he had staged. Massine had been a dancer and choreographer with Diaghilev's Ballets Russes de Monte Carlo and was considered one of the most important choreographers of the 1920s and 1930s. Massine had studied ballet in Moscow, and when Diaghilev was seeking a replacement for Vaslav Nijinsky he had hired Massine as both a dancer and choreographer. After Diaghilev's death Massine had danced and choreographed in a company formed by René Blum and Colonel de Basil; it was called "René Blum and Colonel de Basil Ballets Russes de Monte-Carlo."[1] (Ballets Russes, the plural of Ballet Russe, may have been used rather than Ballet Russe because it was a partnership.) By 1935–1936, because of a serious disagreement over the artistic direction of the company, Blum and de Basil dissolved their partnership. Both formed separate, competing companies. Massine and de Basil had had a fight over the right of ownership of the ballets that Massine had choreographed prior to his separation from de Basil's company. Eventually, the fight was settled in a court case. The jury had awarded Massine the rights to his ballets created before 1932 and after 1937, but ballets he had created between 1932 and 1937 were awarded to de Basil. While I wasn't knowledgeable about the court case when dancing with de Basil's company, or the current dynamics of de Basil's and Massine's relationship, we did perform some of Massine's works, such as *Les Presages*.

I began my professional dance career in de Basil's company beginning April 1948. While Colonel de Basil was always around in the year I danced with his company, I didn't get to know him well. In the hours and hours I spent riding on trains, traveling from one city to the next, de Basil was usually on the train, too, although he did not travel in the same train car as us dancers.

He was more interested in the business side of the company and left the artistic matters to people like Serge "Papa" Grigoriev, who was married to a ballerina in the company, Lubov Tchernicheva. They had a son who worked in the company as well. The company classes were taught mostly by Lubov Tchernicheva who had danced in Diaghilev's company, although occasionally her husband, Serge Grigoriev, taught. Grigoriev had danced with the Mariinsky Ballet in St. Petersburg before joining Diaghilev's company. He was Diaghilev's *régisseur* in 1929 when the impresario died. Being the manager for staging the company's productions was an important position and he had been well respected by, if not close friends with, Diaghilev.

After six weeks of rehearsing we boarded a train and started the twelve-month grand tour of Spain, Portugal and Spanish Morocco. The tour of all these fantastic cities would unite us dancers into a really close family. For me it would be a spiritual, thrilling experience that I feel lucky to have been a part of, and that I would treasure for the rest of my life.

Chapter Three

The Original
Ballet Russe Tour

The first time I heard about George Balanchine and Ballet Society was from talking to Richard Adama at Nijinska's school. Ricky was enamored with Balanchine and he couldn't stop talking about the man and his ballets. Almost exactly six months after our departure from the U.S., Balanchine and co-founder Lincoln Kirstein's Ballet Society would evolve into New York City Ballet. The launch of this company would be a world-changing event in the history of ballet in America. And as a first-generation New York City Ballet dancer I would be a humble character in this ballet evolution. But that was a year away. I had a tour of Spain, Portugal and North Africa to do first. While the Colonel W. de Basil Original Ballet Russe company may not have been of world-changing importance equal to that of Balanchine's New York City Ballet, it was certainly life-changing for me.

The story of how the Colonel W. de Basil Original Ballet Russe company came to be is interesting. And, as with so much of dance history in Europe and the United States in the early 1900s, it has a lot to do with the famous impresario Serge Diaghilev. Diaghilev was the creator of the first, the real original Ballet Russe company, the Ballet Russe de Monte Carlo (between 1909 and 1929 the company was sometimes called Ballets Russes de Monte Carlo). Although Diaghilev was brilliant at bringing together some of Europe's most talented visual and performing artists of the era, sometimes his judgment on what ballets to create and on programming missed the mark, and he was not so smart with the finances. The company, therefore, had its good seasons but also some bad seasons, even some financially disastrous seasons. He once fled London in the middle of the night when he was unable to pay the bills, including salaries, for instance. The dancers, musicians, stage crew, and many other employees awakened to hear the news that they were without jobs and stranded, not in their homeland, but in England. When he died, though, the company was somewhat financially solvent and artistically strong. He had suffered ill health for months, mostly complications from diabetes. Even so, his death on August 19, 1929, at age fifty-seven, caught his employees and close friends by surprise. Not only were they grieving but they were hustling to find new gigs. There were other European ballet companies around. Yet company directors, such as Nijinska, who was with Ida Rubinstein's Les Ballets de Rubinstein, could not possibly hire them all. Many of those unable to find work in small ballet companies or in music halls (the Folies-Bergère music hall in Paris usually had one or two ballet acts on a program) or in musicals or who could not find a willing partner to dance with on the European ballroom circuit, had no choice but to change their dance-career plans to eke out a living. At the time of Diaghilev's death the twenty-five-year-old George Balanchine, who had been on the outs with the moody, difficult-to-

One year I am dressed in a crisp, sharp Navy uniform and two years later I am wearing colorful pantaloons and dancing in the Colonel W. de Basil Original Ballet Russe company. The colonel purchased my costume from the Diaghilev company. I wore it in the ballet *Scheherazade.*

work-with impresario for a while, was struggling to earn a living freelancing as a choreographer and a teacher. He had even given private ballet lessons to the American black woman born in St. Louis—the often-bare-chested, banana-skirt-shaking, Folies-Bergère music hall darling—dancer-singer Josephine Baker. In the George Balanchine repertory is the work *Dances for Josephine Baker*, which was probably choreographed in 1932. (He admired the talented Josephine. She adored George but hated the toe shoes.) When Balanchine heard of Diaghilev's death he, along with two other former Diaghilev dancers, the Englishman Anton Dolin and the Russian Lydia Lopokova (who was married to the famous economist John Maynard Keynes), were in London filming the movie *Dark Red Roses*. It was a short-term gig and any hope Balanchine had had of returning to Diaghilev's company as a resident or a guest choreographer was not going to happen.

Two men not so devastated by the death of Serge Diaghilev were René Blum and Vasily Grigorievich Voskresensky, who had changed his name to Colonel Wassily de Basil. Seizing the moment that presented itself they formed a partnership to resurrect Diaghilev's internationally wildly-popular company. They even used the company's name so that devoted balletomanes would think the company had not died with Diaghilev, that, in fact, it was alive and well. The resurrected Ballets Russes de Monte Carlo was launched in 1932. Both men had fought in World War I. Both had a passion for the arts, especially the performing arts, although the fifty-four-year old Frenchman, René Blum, had much more job-related experience with opera and dance organizations than the forty-four-year-old Russian Cossack Colonel W. de Basil. In the partnership, Blum focused on the artistic side of the company; de Basil took charge of the administrative side, including the financial affairs such as writing the checks to pay staff and dancers. Blum hired George Balanchine to be the ballet master. Balanchine and Blum got along fine. Balanchine and de Basil, not so much. Their views on the company's artistic vision were too different. The Colonel wanted the company to continue performing the known and popular ballets that Diaghilev had produced, those that had a track record of providing enough money from ticket sales to pay the bills: maybe perform a few new ballets that were experimental and innovative, that would test the audiences' likes and dislikes, but not too many. Balanchine disagreed, and he did not appreciate the Colonel's heavy-handedness in telling him what he could and could not do. It was a clash of wills with lots of drama; historically, a common story in ballet companies. A Balanchine biographer, Bernard Taper, says that it was Balanchine's common-law wife, Alexandra Danilova who, even though she was not in the company (Balanchine had refused to allow the twenty-seven-year-old ballerina to join Blum and the Colonel's company because she was "too old"[1]), tipped him off that the Colonel was replacing him as ballet master with the more well-known dancer and choreographer at this time, Léonide Massine. Massine had contacted Danilova to ask her to join Blum and de Basil's company, "with top billing."[2] She telephoned George to ask why he was leaving the company. Willingly, or unwillingly, Balanchine left. He assembled a small troupe to perform in his own company that he called Les Ballets 1933. The company was floundering, maybe it had already folded, and Balanchine's ballet future a big question mark when Lincoln Kirstein made him the offer that he could not refuse.

This is a picture of some of the company members along with Colonel de Basil on the Colonel de Basil Ballet Russes tour, enjoying some rare, and much needed, leisure time. The colonel is center front, wearing dark glasses. I am on the far right.

Blum began taking a lesser role in the running of the company, and by 1936 the two men had dissolved their partnership. Blum formed a separate company, Ballet Russe de Monte Carlo, by hiring the former Diaghilev dancer Léon Woizikowski and many of the dancers in his small Les Ballets de Léon Woizikowski troupe. The Colonel launched Original Ballet Russe. As a result, Blum's and the Colonel's relationship changed from that of uncomfortable collaborators to that of fierce rivals. De Basil's company toured and performed in cities in Western European countries such as England and Spain, but also in Australia, South America and, occasionally, in the U.S. Blum eventually found a new partner, Sergei Denham, and the company toured internationally and throughout the United States. I joined the Colonel's Original Ballet Russe at the beginning of a one-year tour of Spain, Portugal and North Africa. While at one time there had been a few Balanchine ballets in Blum and de Basil's Ballet Russe repertoire, such as *Cotillon* and *La Concurrence*, I did not dance in any of them when I was in the Colonel's company. I never met René Blum. By the time I joined the Colonel's company Blum was dead, a victim of World War II. Adolf Hitler was anti–Jewish, anti-communist and anti-Black. Believing he could create the perfect political society, with the perfect people, he had the misfits—thousands of men, women and children—rounded up throughout Europe and imprisoned in concentration camps. Although Jews were the primary target Hitler's so-called misfits also included people of color and those whose political ideologies were not aligned with his. Josephine Baker, who was black, a Communist sympathizer, and Jewish (because of a husband she had married), was lucky. When the Germans invaded Paris she was able to escape. She hid out at her chateau-mansion in a French forest. It wasn't too long afterward that she agreed to become a spy for the French Resistance. In recognition of her work and bravery in the French Resistance, French president Charles de Gaulle had awarded her the Medal of the Resistance with Rosette in 1946. Blum, who was not only Jewish but a Jewish intellectual (intellectuals were considered a threat to Hitler's perfect society and therefore misfits), was unlucky. He was one of the thousands of men, women, and children rounded up during the war and herded into concentrations camps. Some were put to work; many were put to death. Blum died while either on the way to, or imprisoned in, Auschwitz concentration camp in 1942.

The reason for my lengthy explanation of the Ballet Russe de Monte Carlo companies of Diaghilev, Blum, de Basil and Denham is their importance to the evolution of ballet in America. These companies toured America extensively for decades. Highly-trained and experienced dancers performed in high school auditoriums, vaudeville halls and opera houses. These companies educated thousands of ordinary Americans living in small cities and rural towns about classical ballet. Many dancers settled in small towns and big cities throughout the U.S. and opened schools. Such teachers and schools were important to Dorothy Alexander's vision for the regional ballet movement, a movement that became an important part of my career. These immigrants—many of whom had received their training from the most highly-esteemed ballet companies in the world, and who had performed with companies such as the Paris Opera Ballet, Royal Danish Ballet, the Mariinsky, and the Bolshoi—taught American boys and girls the technique of Cecchetti, Petipa-Vaganova (now known as Vaganova) or Bournonville. It is because of these Ballet Russe companies touring the U.S., showcasing their excellent productions and well-trained dance artists, that so many of us American kids became inspired to become professional classical ballet dancers, too. Equally important, because of the excellent classical ballet technique-training we aspiring students received in America, we could not only get jobs with major ballet companies in the U.S and Europe, but dance as well as those who had been trained in the historically famous ballet schools in Paris, Denmark and Russia. Success often has its downside, though. The exciting growth of ballet in America because of visionaries and leaders in the regional ballet grassroots movement, such as Dorothy Alexander, would be one of the reasons that the last existing Ballet Russe company's popularity would begin to wane. In the 1950s, as more and more ballet companies were founded in the U.S., matured, and grew larger and became nationally and internationally known—New York City Ballet, American Ballet Theatre, Ruth Page's Chicago Opera Ballet, San Francisco Ballet and Atlanta Ballet, for instance—the last of the Ballet Russe companies, Denham's Ballet

Russe de Monte Carlo, became less known. By the early 1960s it would disappear. I owe a lot to the Ballet Russe companies. It was because of the Colonel's Original Ballet Russe that I was in Barcelona to launch my official professional career as a classical ballet dancer.

The Colonel's Original Ballet Russe had a history of financial struggles. When I joined the company, the Colonel was doing okay financially, although I did have some trouble getting my weekly paycheck from him in the beginning. We dancers used to sit on de Basil's doorstep to wait for our checks. He would ignore us if he did not have the cash, such as during those weeks of rehearsing. When we were performing, though, we got paid. Some of the company members regularly got money from their families, but I did not. The money in my college savings account was building, and I did not want to touch it. While I

I was twenty-four years old when this photograph was taken by one of my friends in Barcelona, Spain.

managed to live on what little salary I was paid, it was always a juggling act to pay the bills. Hotel rooms, food and our practice clothes were not covered, for instance, and I had to be mindful of every penny or peseta I spent. On the plus side, I never had to worry about gaining weight on the rich, starchy Spanish food. There were about forty to fifty dancers in the company, a lot from Eastern Europe, also London and Paris—really, from all over the world—and some were former Diaghilev dancers. There were also at least five to seven of us Americans. Even though there was a ranking system (and I was at the bottom) we dancers were close. A person's origins, or religion, or skin color, or political leanings never mattered. We spent hours together in classes and rehearsals and performances, our sweat, and occasionally a few tears, comfortably shared as bodies rubbed and bound together in duets and ensemble pieces, depending on the choreography. We spent hours on the twelve-month tour riding trains from one city to the next—elbows, knees, and shoulders touching as the train chugged and swayed along the miles and miles of track—each person offering dance-trade tips and dance history lessons. And we traded some gossipy secrets about favorite ballet stars, too. We shared stories about our families. During our few hours of leisure we walked the streets of the cities and shopped in small stores. Of course, I liked to look at the jewelry in shops, although I could not afford to buy much. In many towns there were street markets stretching for blocks and blocks along colorful wide promenades where we ogled at the goods displayed. As a group we stuck close to one another, navigating a path amongst the herds of humans crowding the walkways. United we strolled past the stalls and sniffed the delicious smells of fresh-cut flowers or held our noses and hustled past the stalls that stank, the girls especially not wanting to see the dead, plucked chickens dangling on hooks. Together our dance-family went to grande-parties given in our honor at embassies and in private homes, and where we all were treated like celebrities.

While watching Igor Youskevitch dance changed my career choice, dancing in the Original Ballet Russe in 1948 changed my life. Even though the nomadic life of touring (often one-night stands) was hard, it was never boring. In elementary school I made an F in any class I found boring. Never did I find a company ballet class or rehearsal boring. As a new, lowly corps de ballet member in this all-star group of experienced professionals, in my first professional job, I knew that I had a lot to learn, and I was determined to be an A student. My tutors were the choreographers, artistic staff, and dancers. One person who was especially important in teaching me the ballet-trade was Anatol Joukowsky. "Mr. J" as he was affectionately called, is not a widely known name in the ballet world, not today, anyway. He is known, however, in social folk dance circles.

According to the social folk dance website, Joukowsky was born in Poltava, Ukraine, on August 18, 1908. He and his family had fled Russia during the Revolution, and they eventually settled in Greece. Early in his life he attended a military school in Belgrade, Yugoslavia. For some unknown reason, at the age of fifteen, he began taking ballet classes. Anna Pavlova visited his school. As with so many kids who were inspired by the internationally famous ballerina, he decided to become a professional dancer, also. He studied at what was called a theater school and took classes in dance history, the history of costume, and dance technique, including ballet and character or ethnic dance. By year three he was taking additional classes at the same school in choreography, staging and stage design, lighting and spacing. After graduating he danced professionally in the State Theater company. In 1935, he was appointed ballet master and choreographer. In the summer months, when he was not working, he liked to hunt and fish, and he began to hike throughout the Yugoslavian countryside where he often watched the locals in small towns and big cities dance at weddings and festivals. Studying character and ethnic dance became a lifelong vocation, and his so-called dance research travels would make him an expert in ethnic dance. For a while in the mid– to late–1930s he even had a small professional ethnic dance troupe. The dancers and a few musicians performed wherever they could find a gig. Years later he would write a book published in 1980, *The Teaching of Ethnic Dance.*

We both joined Original Ballet Russe in 1948; he was a dancer, a choreographer and a stage director. Mr. J was thirty-nine years old and I was twenty-three when we met. He was married to the dancer Yania Wassilieva. The lessons I learned from my year with Mr. J were really important to my career. Despite the difficulty in communicating because of the language barrier, he taught me so much, such as how to apply the right stage make-up, and how to dance and act the role of a character so it became real. He taught me how to showcase a personality (without being a show off) that would move the audience emotionally; how to know the difference between dancing that would excite rather than bore an audience to death. I learned that if I danced steps technically correctly but without artistry, to dance as if I didn't care, that the audience wouldn't care either. These lessons are not as easy as they seem. A dancer, especially when dancing a character role such as the evil Merlin in *Picnic at Tintagel* (which I would one day dance at New York City Ballet), must strike the right balance—that is, showing a personality that the audience can believe. And you must not overact and tip to the side of mugging or they will see you as a phony. It is these lessons, and there are so many others, that I learned from my excellent tutors on the tour, such as Mr. J, and which I pass along to my students and the professional dancers I coach today.

After six weeks in Barcelona learning all the ballets in the repertoire—thank goodness we were quick learners—and getting accustomed to jumping, spinning and lifting my partners on the steep-raked stage (raked stages may be good for opera and theatrical plays, but not so much for dance), we toted our luggage to the central railroad station and leaped onto a train. Finally, the tour had begun. Although we did not perform any full-length ballets, there still were sets and, of course, costumes to transport from one city to the next. There were a few staff along, including a wardrobe mistress who was definitely needed. The Colonel had purchased some of the costumes once owned by Diaghilev, including ones from *Prince Igor*. The costumes that were hand-painted were works of art, but they were at least ten years old, and they smelled awful. (It was probably because of the egg whites the artists added to the paint.) We held our noses when putting them on and taking them off. The costumes had to be washed regularly and stiffened with something the wardrobe mistress used. Also on the tour was a pianist and a conductor, along with a few musicians. To complete the orchestra, in most towns local musicians were hired. Some were good, but some not so good, which made the tempo of the music at each performance unpredictable. In those months touring we danced in small towns and big cities in Spain, Portugal and Spanish Morocco. Most of the time the gig was a one-night stand (it was a luxury when we stayed a week in a city, such as Barcelona and Madrid), and therefore it was a physically and emotionally demanding tour.

Some stages were adequate for dancing, but some were not. In fact, they were hazardous, and we kept a hammer close at hand to pound nails deep into the floor. There was one stage where a cat could have fallen through the gigantic hole in the floor. Opera companies often used spikes which would tear up the floor, and we had to be mindful of every step we took, which isn't easy to do when spinning downstage on a raked stage. There were a few stages that still had footlights, which could be eye-ball blinding. Occasionally, we had to spray a really slick wood floor with Coca-Cola to make it sticky enough to prevent slipping and sliding and falling. Later, when I was on the international tours in Balanchine's company, he would refuse to subject us dancers to such conditions. In 1948, though, no matter the lack of heat or air conditioning inside an auditorium, no matter the possible perils caused by nails sticking their heads up above the stage floor (which made the ballerinas wearing pointe shoes paranoid), every theater was a new adventure for me and very exciting. Although I did use a lot of Tiger Balm, youth has its advantages, and muscle fatigue, injury, and sleep-deprivation-tiredness were not things I thought much about at age twenty-three. Also what helped keep me going was the adrenaline-high that offset the usual touring curse of travel fatigue, caused by the wildly applauding audiences showing their love and appreciation for our full-out efforts to please them. Only a few short hours later we would leave a theater and get back on a train. Arriving in a different city in the morning, we would rehearse or space, perform, then get back on a train or a bus and move on to the next city. It was only on those occasions when we spent a few days in a city that gave us a chance to walk the streets and experience the different cultures; at least when I wasn't trying to catch up on my sleep.

Touring today is not at all like it was in 1948. Unless invited to stay in the home of a local family, we dancers had to find our own lodgings. Because we had to pay for our lodgings, our rooms had to be cheap. A shared toilet and a bathtub in a room down the hall was typical and acceptable for me. What I usually looked for was lodging that was close to the theater and that included meals. In most towns I found what I wanted, until Burgos, where we stayed a night or two, and where despite a long search walking the streets I could not find a cheap, clean pension. I eventually had to settle on a tiny room with nothing more than a straw mattress on a dirt floor. That was really slumming. So fast-paced was the tour that I have little memory of most of the cities we danced in, except for Barcelona and Madrid in Spain, and Lisbon, Portugal. These I still today remember pretty vividly, but only because I would perform in those cities again with New York City Ballet.

After a performance in Barcelona we danced in Zaragoza, Pamplona, San Sebastián (where I enjoyed the luxury of spending a night with a family), Bilbao (which we dancers called Bilbo), Santander, Burgos, Valladolid, and Salamanca—these were cities and towns in Spain. Cities in Portugal were Porto and Lisbon. Then it was back to Spain where we performed in Madrid, Córdoba, Granada and Malaga. The two cities in Spanish Morocco were Tangier and Tetuen. The last two cities on the tour were Valencia and Mallorca, Spain, before returning to Barcelona. Today, I consider Barcelona one of my most favorite cities, not only because I danced there with New York City Ballet but also because my wife Virginia and I later returned to the city as tourists.

One responsibility we took seriously when performing was that of educating the audiences about classical ballet and its importance as an art form equal to opera, plays, and the visual arts. Because of ballet's centuries-old tradition of being a step-child of opera companies, many people in the audience had never seen an entire ballet program before. It certainly was rare in our travels to meet a balletomane. An exception was Bilbao. Not only was the man who made a point of introducing himself knowledgeable and an enthusiastic fan of ballet, but he was a very rich balletomane. Javier Ansar

owned a shipbuilding company, and he enjoyed all the luxurious perks that
came with having wealth, including a big, important-looking black limousine
and a driver. Javier began showing up in some of the other cities on the tour.
And the man fell in love with Barbara Lloyd. More than once he invited her
to his house or to dine with him at a restaurant or to drive around Bilbao, or
whatever town we happened to be in, so he could show her the sights. Barbara's
mom and dad were not about to permit their daughter to be alone with Javier,
however, so I, as well as some of her other close friends, got to go with them.
In Bilbao we visited his shipyard and his house. It was not surprising to see
that he lived in a huge, high-class house. What impressed me most was his
collection of items that had belonged to famous ballerinas such as Lucile
Grahn, Marie Taglioni and Fanny Elssler. It was a large collection and he
proudly showed us every piece, including fans, pointe shoes, and head pieces.
There was one excursion where he took us up in the mountains to a monastery.
When we walked into the church I was emotionally touched by a lovely sound;
the monks were chanting. An altar was lit with candles and behind the altar
was the black Madonna. She was made from onyx and housed in a glass case
except for one foot. I don't know how many years she had been hanging in
the monastery, but the foot was practically worn through because of the hundreds, if not thousands, of people who had touched it and kissed it. In San
Sebastián Javier took us to a restaurant that looked out over the sea. Dessert
was a tree of cream puffs, each dripping in caramel. Javier challenged us to a
game invented by the locals that tested our facility for eating and speaking
simultaneously: pop a cream puff in your mouth and try and say "Pamplona."
My usual diet was boiled eggs and bread (I carried a pot and burner to boil
eggs in my room), and I did skip a few meals to save money; therefore, gaining
weight was not a problem for me. Enthusiastically, I ate cream puffs and tried
to say "Pamplona" all night long. We were in Balboa when I began to suffer
from a lot of pain in my mouth. Javier sent me to his dentist. The problem
was a wisdom tooth that was inflamed. The dentist deadened the gum and
then cauterized the wound—the tool he used was a real flame. I didn't speak
Spanish and the treatment was unlike anything I had ever experienced before;
it was a little frightening even. But it worked. Neither my skin nor my hair
was set on fire and the pain went away. After I left the Colonel's company
Javier and I stayed in contact. Once he visited New York City when I was
dancing with New York City Ballet and I invited him and his driver to watch
a rehearsal. Even though Balanchine wasn't there that day and I couldn't intro-
duce them, the Spaniard thought he had died and gone to Heaven.

  Dancing in Original Ballet Russe, taking company classes with dancers
who had trained at some of the most well-known, elite classical ballet schools

Barbara Lloyd was a student at Nijinska's. school. She, Ricky Adama and I were on the Colonel's Original Ballet Russe tour together in 1948–1949. She joined Ballet Theatre (now American Ballet Theatre) and I joined New York City Ballet.

in the world, taught me what classical ballet was really about—both the technique required to master the craft and the artistry required to make audiences at every performance feel something. I learned that pretty feet, high jumps, or thirty-two fouettes does not cut it without artistry. Of course, continually taking technique classes is important, no matter one's age and professional stature. But to truly learn to dance, and to learn to dance well, one must perform on the stage. And I got lots of performing experience every night. Although we never met, I got to dance some of Massine's ballets that were in the repertoire, including *Les Presages* to Pyotr Ilyich Tchaikovsky's Symphony No. 5 (also known as Fifth Symphony). The ballet is in four parts and is about man's triumph over misfortune. It is one of Massine's symphonic ballets. In addition to Anatol Joukowsky, I learned a lot from David Lichine and Serge "Papa" Grigoriev. And there were the many older, more experienced dancers in the company who graciously took time out of their busy day to watch me rehearse a piece and critique my technique, to teach me how to partner, to help me to master the craft. They taught me stage manners and, most important, not only to have respect for the significance of your role as a dancer in the company but also to respect one another as individuals. In those months performing my muscles became stronger, my turns sharper, the power in my legs greater, my elevation higher, and my toes pointed whenever I soared in the air. I was promoted to soloist, a great privilege even if there was no increase in pay. The classroom is about learning to master technique. Performing on the stage before a living, breathing, high-adrenaline alert (hopefully not a sleeping) audience is about using that technique to master the role and to become an artist. Equally important on this tour were the friends I made and learning how to treat friends, no matter our peculiarities. A few were superstitious, for example (although I was not one of them). I saw at least one or two of my friends back out the door of the dressing room for good luck before going to the stage. Many of my friends are no longer with us, although Barbara Lloyd and I are still close friends today.

It was a great disappointment to all of us when the Colonel's planned twelve-month tour was abruptly shortened to ten months. He ran out of money. The American impresario Sol Hurok supposedly was managing the tour but was never seen. Nor was he well thought of among the members of our company. It seemed to us that he was more interested in managing prestigious opera companies and famous opera singers than ballet companies and dancers. While Hurok may have been competent in making a lot of money for himself, enough to become both wealthy and famous, he didn't provide much cash for the Colonel's tour. The company collapsed, and it was never restarted. Two years later de Basil would suffer a heart attack while in Paris and die at age sixty-three.

As a result of the company folding my good friends and I parted ways. Barbara Lloyd and her parents sailed back to the U.S. She was accepted into Ballet Theatre and lived in New York City. Her parents returned to their home in California. How her parents and Barbara managed their finances those ten months in Europe with no income other than Barbara's salary I do not know. Her parents were not financially well off, they were struggling, in fact, but they were not going to let their sixteen-year-old daughter travel unchaperoned in the Colonel's company. After returning to California her dad did become rich. He was an accountant. He started a business managing clients' money, and a lot of his clients were wealthy widows. Ricky Adama loved Europe so much he stayed. He was about 5'11" tall, with blond hair, and sharp facial features; he was a go-getter, an over-the-hill dancer. He became a soloist in the Grand Ballet du Marquis de Cuevas company before becoming a principal dancer in the Vienna State Opera ballet (now Vienna State Ballet). Ricky was an avid reader of dance history. Because he could read French he researched the Paris Opera Ballet's *Giselle* (1841) in the Paris Opera archives and said he discovered that in Act II the Willies danced up above the stage floor—wires were hooked to their costumes to ferry them across the stage and make them actually float like the ethereal creatures they were supposed to be. Years later I saw Ricky in Southern California. I was in Los Angeles teaching at a Cecchetti conference. He had returned to America to be with his family in Los Angeles but was not happy, and he eventually moved back to Europe.

It was with a great sigh of relief when almost immediately after the tour was cancelled David Lichine offered me a gig dancing in a film of his ballet *Graduation Ball*—in Paris. Along with several of my friends we took a train from Barcelona. In my one suitcase was the little pot and burner to boil my eggs. In my pocket there was maybe $50 and a few pesetas. I found my accommodations and then began to wait, and to wait, for the call on when filming was to begin. In the meantime, there were the streets of the beautiful city to explore. Compared to London there was little evidence that Paris had been in a war and occupied by the Germans. Because of the long wait to start filming, I finally had to contact Mom to ask for $100 from my college savings account, which she quickly wired through American Express.

When it became apparent that there was no definite date set for the filming, I spent a part of each day in my tiny room working out on my own. One of the principal dancers in the Colonel's company, Genevieve Moulin, did not believe exercising on my own was going to keep my technique up to standard, however. "Bobby, I want you to go to class with me," she said. She then told me about Lyubov (also spelled Lubov) Egorova, one of the most distinguished and important teachers in Western Europe. Egorova was also known as Princess Trubetskoy, a real Russian princess because she was married to Prince Trubetskoy. I told Genevieve that I did not have the money to take class. She took me anyway—to watch Egorova teach. The studio was small and cramped. Standing behind the piano, I squeezed into a corner, my back pressed against the wall, and watched this remarkable woman. The room had no heat and it was freezing cold. The tiny teacher sat on a three-legged stool and mostly used her hands to instruct. She gave verbal corrections in French, mostly, and not Russian, and she spoke little English. She wore a scarf on her head. The gloves she wore had the fingers cut out. She wore thick wool tights under a long skirt and was swathed in a sweater. She had the only heat in the room, a little pot-belly stove as close to the stool as safety allowed. At some point Egorova used her finger to motion Genevieve over. In French, the two discussed who that man was standing in the corner. I don't speak French or Russian, but it was obvious they were talking about me. Egorova said, "Tell him to come to class. He needs to come to class." When she found out that I had no money she graciously allowed me to take her classes at no charge. Egorova had received her early training from the great master teacher himself, Cecchetti, at the St. Petersburg Imperial Theatre School, and she had danced professionally in the Imperial Ballet in the Mariinsky Theatre. Not surprisingly, she later became a principal ballerina in Diaghilev's company. She was sixty-one years old when we met and internationally known. There were many famous dancers I saw walking the halls or taking class, such as the actress-dancer Leslie Caron. Thank goodness I had Moulin, because when Egorova corrected my mistakes Moulin would tell me what she said.

In addition to Egorova I took a few classes from Olga Preobrazhenskaya (also spelled Prebrajenskay); and she was even tinier than Egorova. Her studio space was not too far from Egorova's, and I got off at the same subway station whether going to Egorova's or Preobrazhenskaya's class. As with Egorova, Preobrazhenskaya was a popular teacher with the in-the-know crowd. Both taught the Russian technique method, and their classes were nothing like Nijinska's Cecchetti classes. Preobrazhenskaya had danced in Diaghilev's company in the early 1900s. Egorova had been considered a good soloist in the Mariinsky Ballet, but Preobrazhenskaya had been a star—a prima ballerina; until the day she fled her country. According to Jennifer Homans in *Apollo's Angels*, Preobrazhenskaya, "a dynamic technician with a demanding, irascible personality, had walked out of Russia in 1921, crossing the border into Finland on foot in the middle of winter."[3] She danced in major European cities whenever and wherever she could find work, even dancing in music halls, to earn a living. Preobrazhenskaya still was a dynamic force at age seventy-nine when I took her classes, and she had trained some excellent professional dancers, including Igor Youskevitch. She would continue to teach until about the age of ninety.

Living in Paris is not cheap today and it wasn't in 1949 either, and I was running out of money. Eating mostly bread and eggs boiled in my pot was getting old, and I needed a better diet to keep my weight up to at least 120 pounds. When I realized that there might be a lengthy delay before filming started, if it ever started, I decided to return to the U.S. I visited an American Express Travel office and learned of a ship that was sailing to New York City. The third-class ticket was cheap enough for me to afford, but the port was in Antwerp, Belgium, which meant buying a train ticket. The ship had been used in the war as an AKA (cargo) ship that was armed with guns and anti-aircraft weapons of various types. Then, after the war, it had been converted to carry passengers across the Atlantic Ocean. It was not a Cunard luxury liner. I lived in a hole deep down in the bowels of the ship. My bed was one of several hammocks stacked one on top of the other, so I spent most nights on an upper deck sleeping outside. We stopped only once, in Ireland. I met a group of Irish girls on the ship who were going to a seminary school in Texas. Also, there were some circus kids on board, and I watched them practice. The ship carried a lot of Jewish refugees. Before long I knew the captain and different members of the crew, those that spoke English. One night there was a terrible storm, and the ship pitched from side to side. The rocking was so bad it was difficult to walk without falling. Carrying a plate of food was extremely hard to do, although so many people were sick that the dining room was practically deserted. I was one of the fortunate to not suffer any seasickness. An elderly lady died, although I don't know the cause. The crew were able to contact her relatives, and, with their approval, she was buried at sea. The gigantic waves were so rough throughout the voyage that the ship suffered damage. Still, it got to New York, and it was a relief to disembark the ship at some unmemorable port—not Ellis Island. It was a good thing I returned to the U.S., because the film never was made.

Jay Lonergan met me at the port. He had studied with Nijinska but was more interested in musical theater than classical ballet. We had stayed in contact, however, and he had invited me to stay at his apartment. We took a taxi into the city. Sleeping on a couch or the floor was fine with me.

Despite Ricky Adama's constant talking about the brilliant George Balanchine, I was zeroed in on Ballet Theatre upon returning to the U.S. (the name would not change to American Ballet Theatre or ABT until the 50s). After all, Igor Youskevitch was a principal dancer in the company, as was one of his most famous partners, Alicia Alonso. Barbara Lloyd was there, too. Vladimir Dokoudovsky, who was a principal dancer in Original Ballet Russe, had told me to contact Edward Caton at Ballet Theatre. I did, and he let me take a class. Lucia Chase was in the studio watching. "I would love to take you, but I have no spots to fill," she said. The company had a good roster of dancers and no one would leave. The company was having some serious financial difficulties at the time, also. I reminded myself to be patient and to wait until a position did open up. In the meantime, I read *Variety* to search for auditions.

Chapter Four

The Muny in St. Louis

I arrived in the U.S. with $25.00 in my billfold. Staying with Jay Lonergan in his apartment was a big help with my disturbing financial situation. Still, those daily necessities, such as eating, made finding a job top priority—and fast. And now that any hope of joining my friend Barbara, and my idols, at Ballet Theatre wasn't going to happen—yet—the frustrating dog-in-the-urban-woods hunt for a gig began. In the meantime, conserving what little money I had was really important. I didn't mind saving money on food. There was the pot and burner to maintain my boiled egg and bread diet. Disappointing was being in the mecca of the entertainment world and not having the cash, and definitely no credit card, to see the fabulous plays, movies, Broadway musicals, or dance concerts that were everywhere. No matter how much Miss Temptation beckoned her finger, watching Moira Shearer dance in the movie *The Red Shoes* at the Bijou Theatre on West 45th Street and Broadway was not going to happen, even if the price of a ticket for the cheapest section in the theater was $1.20. Nor was it possible to purchase a ticket to Rodgers and Hammerstein's *Oklahoma* (Agnes de Mille was the choreographer), unless I could slip in through a side door unnoticed or charm an usher and get in free. There were small dance troupes performing at Carnegie Hall; but most of these were ethnic or modern dance performances and didn't encourage enough interest to splurge and buy an inexpensive ticket. Therefore, in those rare, few hours with nothing to do at night and on weekends but revere the sights, sounds and smells of the bustling city, because the buses cost about seven or eight cents to ride I hoarded the pennies in my pocket and walked. Most of my time in the late spring of 1949, though, was devoted to finding a job.

I guess there must not have been any forthcoming auditions publicized in *Variety* magazine for New York City Ballet. Nor was I interested in dancing in America's oldest opera ballet company, the Metropolitan Opera Ballet: "not very good," was the word on the dance-news-street grapevine. The ballet company was the step-child of the Metropolitan Opera, and no serious dancer wanted to be told to leap and jump and spin on a stage overwhelmed with massive sets, a mass of singers, and sometimes a real camel, an elephant, or a horse. Nancy Reynolds, who is the director of research at the Balanchine Foundation, wrote in *No Fixed Points: Dance in the Twentieth Century* (the coauthor is Malcolm McCormick) that in 1934 Balanchine's struggling-to-survive American Ballet company "found shelter as the resident troupe of the Metropolitan Opera, but three years later Balanchine left in disgust, complaining that the tradition of ballet at the Met was 'bad ballet.'"[1] I did audition for the *High Button Shoes* Broadway musical and received an offer. Jerome Robbins was the choreographer, although he was not at the audition. Taking the job was a lengthy commitment, however. Deciding that I did not want to get stuck in a musical theater career and labeled a "Broadway Gypsy," I declined. I then auditioned for a musical theater gig that was offering a short-term contract with good pay—a summer-stock musical show in Missouri. The audition was in a small studio crammed with about two hundred other got-to-find-a-gig-guys. I left with a contract in hand. Jay, who was born in Missouri and had family there, auditioned and was accepted, too. The gig was only sixteen weeks and paid so well it would give me enough money to return to New York City in the fall. Maybe this time Ballet Theatre would be hiring male dancers. The summer stock contract required every dancer to sign up with Actors' Equity Association union, which required using some of the last of my money to pay the initiation fee and annual fee. Also, there would be the dues to be paid, about two percent of the gross pay, but, fortunately, later. Unfortunately, the gig was not in any resort town close to New York City, such as in the comfortable Pennsylvania Poconos. I was going to live the sixteen weeks in hot, sweat-soaking St. Louis, where just walking on the streets for twenty minutes got pants and shirt wet enough to drive one to seek relief—to dry out—inside a store with air conditioning, which was not easy to find in those days.

In New York City the train departed from Union Station. A different Union Station, in the heart of downtown St. Louis, was the final stop. St. Louis is called the "Gateway to the West." Compared to New York City and its 7.5 million people, St. Louis, with 850,000 people, seemed small and a lot less noisy. After I left the station, step one was to find a place to stay; step two was finding The Muny amphitheater in Forest Park to start learning the eleven musical shows. Regrettably, there was no time to stop and admire the lumbering traffic of lazy steamboats slowly cruising up and down the mighty Mississippi River, the fancy-dressed ladies and gents playing bingo, gambling, dancing and singing "St. Louis Blues" and other popular tunes of the day played by jazz musicians on board.

Forest Park is so big that St. Louisans brag about it being larger than New York's Central Park (supposedly, Forest Park has five hundred more acres). The park offers lots of entertainment and educational choices: an easy-to-walk-around zoo, a Fine Arts museum, and a history museum. The park has an interesting history. The dedication ceremony was June 24, 1876, and it was a long carriage ride from downtown St. Louis, although there was a new train in operation, if one could afford to buy a ticket. For those couples and families who could not afford to take the train or a carriage and who walked from the city—carrying a picnic basket heavy with food—it probably took at least an hour. The St. Louis World's Fair in 1904 is what got the park spruced up by city leaders, and most importantly, gave the city international recognition. In the summer of that same year the city hosted and boasted the first Olympic games in America, another big international publicity bonanza. There are lakes, and boating is the thing to do in summer, whereas it's ice skating in the winter. The zoo is a popular attraction, which I did visit in my brief St. Louis stay, and I liked it a lot. But the really big draw in the summer months is the huge outdoor Municipal Theater, or The Muny. By the 1940s, summer-stock musical theater had become very popular in cities throughout the U.S. It is The Muny in St. Louis, though, that gets the gold star for being the oldest and the biggest. While it is likely that the park had offered theatrical productions back in the 1880s, the first official production dates back to the summer of 1917, according to the official MUNY website, the MUNY Saga. But it was mounted on a temporary stage. Because the summer productions were so well-attended by the public and profitable (even after accounting for those nights when rain caused a cancellation and money refunded), a plan was conceived to build a permanent theater. The Muny outdoor theater had its official debut on June 5, 1917. There were repairs and renovations made occasionally from 1917 to 1949, including the addition of a second-floor porch area for the actors and dancers to hang out and relax. Only a few years before my one and only summer-stock-dance experience, 2,000 seats (hard, no padding) were added, for a total of 11,950. Unlike many summer stock theaters in other cities, there was no lawn seating.

Jay and I found a cheap apartment within walking distance of The Muny. It was in the attic; the common bathroom was down the hall. We were in the room so little of the time that size and comfort didn't actually matter, though. We lived at the theater. That summer dancing was a physically and mentally grueling gig; there was a show every night, seven nights a week. We were supposed to have a day off now and then, but it did not happen because of being called in for dress rehearsal to get ready for the next show. Even though we had Equity contracts the union was not strong back then; there were not

This is a photograph of a postcard of the MUNY amphitheater in Forest Park, St. Louis, Missouri. The amphitheater had seating for about 11,900 in the summer of 1949. Unlike many summer stock theaters in other cities, there was no lawn seating.

as many rules. On those extremely long days living at the theater, when we were rehearsing a new show during the day and performing one that night, management had meals brought in to feed us. On those few occasions where we did get a half day off, Jay and I would eat at his mother's house. She was a good cook—a southern cook. At least once his cousins, aunts and uncles joined us for a home-cooked meal.

The Muny's choreographer was Pittman "Pit" Corry. His wife Caren Conrad was a dancer in at least one of the shows, maybe *The Red Mill*. She had studied with the Littlefields in Pennsylvania. (Catherine Littlefield, who founded Pennsylvania Ballet, had studied with Lubov Egorova in Paris.) Caren had danced with Ballet Theater and was famous for her incredible jumps. Years later Pit and I would meet again in Atlanta, both of us artistic directors of ballet companies in Georgia. The hoofer Ted Cappy was featured in every show's tap and jazz numbers. The rest of us did utility choreography. Opening night was June 9, *The New Moon*. Eleven consecutive nights later it ended on June 19. June 20 was *Bloomer Girl* for seven nights until June 26. *The Fortune Teller* started June 27 through July 3. The theater was not dark on Independence Day: *The Firefly* opened July 4 and ended July 10. *The Chocolate Soldier* was from July 11 through July 17, followed by *Bitter Sweet*, *Irene*, *The Vagabond King*, *Roberta*, and *The Red Mill*, each running for seven nights. *Song of Norway* was the longest show of the season. It opened August 22 and finished fifteen nights later on September 5. All the dance numbers were done so fast (we did one show and learned the following one at the same time) that most of the summer-stock experience was mind-numbing and truly forgettable.

At least one night off would have been appreciated. Not once did I get to go dancing in one of the popular Blue's clubs or to eat an Italian meal that the city is so well known for. And The Hill is the place to go to for the best Italian food in America, or so the citizens of St. Louis like to boast. The Hill is a neighborhood where this best Italian food can be found in abundance while relaxing in one of the small, quaint restaurants established years ago by Italian immigrants; the delicious smell of sizzling-in-the-pan garlic spicing up the humid summer day. This was the good St. Louis smell in 1949. The not-so-good smell was the stinky smog, the polluted air mostly caused by the coal burning in homes and businesses that was used for heat and power. It is a wonder that we dancers could breathe well enough to strut our stuff in front of the eleven thousand or more people every night, instead of having to call in sick because of a serious respiratory infection.

While the tourist-attracting Gateway Arch with its birds-eye view of the Mississippi River had yet to be built, there was the Fabulous Fox movie palace— one of a chain of theaters that movie mogul William Fox had built in big and small cities all over the U.S. in the late 1920s to showcase the Fox Film Corporation talkie films he was producing. The Siamese-Byzantine Fabulous Fox Theatre in St. Louis had its debut on January 31, 1929. The Fox in Atlanta, which I would one day know very well, celebrated its debut on December 25, 1929. The architecture and interior décor were basically the same in all the theaters: a fusion of mostly Persian, Egyptian, and Moorish influences. These movie palaces lived up to their reputation to symbolize a Far East temple. The Fox Theatre in St. Louis has about 4,500 seats and Atlanta 4,665 seats. Both had a magnificent pipe organ. With its more than 3,500 pipes, the "Mighty Mo" in Atlanta certainly lives up to its name. Long before Las Vegas had its artificial town-tunnels with their ceilings of silvery clouds, William Fox had his architects do it first in his Fox theaters. To this day the Fox Theatre in Atlanta entices thousands and thousands of people to gaze up in amazement at the enormously high domed ceiling, fascinated by the floating, wispy clouds and the twinkling, starry lights. Most of the Fox theaters erected in cities throughout America in the 1920s were demolished years ago. The Fox in Atlanta, Georgia, was doomed to the same fate but was saved from the wrecking ball at the last minute. It is still alive and thriving, and extremely popular and profitable. Beginning in the 1960s, the Fox and I would become closely associated.

Even with no time off to explore the city, there was a lot about St. Louis to appreciate, such as the stories told of the city's iconic Charles Lindbergh. Probably the one heard most often was his solo transatlantic flight. He took off from an airport in New York in 1927 to fly his custom-built single-engine monoplane (it was later named the *Spirit of St. Louis*) nonstop across the Atlantic Ocean to an airport in Paris. This historic first solo nonstop transatlantic flight captivated the attention of people all over the world. It took him only thirty-four hours to fly from New York to Paris. It took me about six long days to sail from Brussels to New York. I would never again dance the Lindy Hop without thinking of Lindbergh and St. Louis.

The first fourteen or so weeks dancing in St. Louis are a blur. But the last two weeks of The Muny season were special and memorable. I do not know if it was serendipity or fate, but the two stars of the musical *Song of Norway* were guest artists Maria Tallchief (George Balanchine's wife) and Herbert Bliss. Dancing with these outstanding artists was the start of what would become a close friendship. I had seen Tallchief before in Nijinska's studio. It was our two weeks dancing together in *Song of Norway*, though, when our friendship was officially launched. Based on the music and life of the Norwegian composer Edvard Grieg, *Song of Norway* is an operetta that debuted on Broadway in 1944. Balanchine was the choreographer. Neither Tallchief nor Bliss was in the original Broadway production, although Alexandra Danilova was. Taper would write in his biography of Balanchine that *Song of Norway*, *Rosalinda,* and *The Merry Widow* were three musicals that "allowed him more scope for dancing than the typical Broadway musical and which, incidentally, were extremely successful."[2] To this day whenever I hear Edvard Grieg's "In the Hall of the Mountain King" from *Peer Gynt Suite*, I recall leaping, spinning and running from wing to wing on The Muny stage, which has to be as wide as a football field. It was a cardio exercise marathon that was great for building endurance.

In all, the 1949 summer-stock season was eighty-nine consecutive nights of adrenalin-charging, exhilarating, and exhausting costume-sweat-soaking

Some of the MUNY dancers in St. Louis, Missouri. My one experience with a summer-stock season was eighty-nine consecutive nights of adrenalin-charging, exhilarating, and exhausting costume-sweat-soaking dancing. I am on the back row in the center.

dancing. It was impossible to keep the pancake face-makeup from melting and dripping down my steaming-hot-red cheeks, to my sweat-wet neck, to my costume. Indeed, costumes had to be cleaned often. Even my shoes squished because of sweat. Surprisingly, injuries were not a big problem; and, on the rare occasion when a dancer did need to be replaced, there were the extras—the swing dancers to call in. We did not actually need to warm up; our muscles were already warmed up just standing in the hot, humid summer heat. But oh, did we have fun. My frequent partner was Sue Ellen Fried. Years later I saw her in Kansas City. I was there for a memorial for the former New York City Ballet dancer Todd Bolender; the family asked me to come and speak. Afterwards Sue Ellen came up to say hello. It was happenstance that I should run into her after all these years. Not long after she brought her family to Asheville. She and her husband, the delightful Harvey Fried, rented a home and stayed for about two weeks. Sue Ellen and Virginia became good friends.

Dennis Brown wrote on the Muny website ("The Muny Saga: 1940–1949 'This Grim Business of War'")[3] that the total attendance for the summer season of 1949 was 898,000; the highest attendance on record. Two of the attendees were very special people—Mom and Dad. It was their first time to watch me dance professionally, and they stayed for about two weeks.

The Muny's 100th anniversary was celebrated in 2018. This for-the-people municipal theater continues the policy set forth in its humble, modest beginning in 1918—that of providing about 1,500 free seats to the public, albeit in the back of the theater. While these tickets are free, seating is first come, first served, and the waiting lines are long. For this 100th celebration one of the musical theater productions scheduled to be performed was *Jerome Robbins' Broadway*; the choreographer whom I was about to meet.

As much fun as I had dancing in The Muny in St Louis, coming home to New York City was a relief—like landing on a more civilized planet—definitely a more comfortable temperature, and a lot less humidity. It was not so much because of technology advances that made New York seem more civilized than other major cities in the U.S. Take radios, for instance. Most people, no matter whether he or she lived in a small town or big city, owned a radio in 1949. And I grew up in Washington listening to radio stations broadcasting everything from baseball games, to the news, to popular tunes of the day, to politicians preaching. What was certainly noticeable in New York City in the 1940s, and appreciated, was air conditioning. Sure, there were fans everywhere in cities and towns; theaters sometimes had gigantic ones blasting lukewarm-air from the wings. And loud they were, too. In homes there were small fans (more psychologically pleasurable than effective at cooling a perspiring body) in the living room and bedrooms in most single-family townhouses and mid-rise city apartments. But more and more theaters in New York City were starting to spend lots of money installing air-conditioning systems, in hopes of attracting more and more ticket purchasers. If a Broadway show or star was not attractive enough to sell out a performance, maybe the air-conditioning would.

Also becoming a big deal (a serious competitor to entertainment programs in brick-and-mortar theaters) was the boxy black and white television set—no color television for a few more years—that in a tiny loft apartment ate up a lot of valuable space; although, with no money for such an extravagant item, was not an issue for me. Returning to New York City was a jump into the Golden Age of television—New York City was the television industry control center as Hollywood was to the film industry control center. The increase in television sets available to buy caused an increase in the number of repair shops listed in the yellow pages of the phone book, which caused an increase in the number of repairmen being trained and available to come to a person's home to repair them. The popularity of televisions caused the new owners to demand more programs to watch, which caused an increase in the number of television stations being established. There was Columbia Broadcasting System (CBS) and its two main rivals, National Broadcasting System (NBC) and American Broadcasting Company (ABC), which caused an increase in the number of affiliate stations established. This in turn caused an increase in the number of programs offered to meet the public's demand. Had I owned a television I could have sat in my apartment laughing at the puppet and his master on the *Howdy Doody Show*; watching *Camel News Caravan* with newscaster John Cameron Swayze (who was required to hold a lighted cigarette in his hand); or watching a 15-minute news show. As it was, I was resigned to standing on the sidewalk shoulder-to-shoulder with a lot of other gawkers, looking through a window of the shop selling television sets to watch whatever show was on. Although there were not enough programs offered to stare at the big box in the corner twenty-four hours a day (unless one got a thrill from staring at a static test-pattern screen through the wee hours of the night), it was clear to the casual observer that the industry was booming. And variety shows were in really big demand. For example, *Arthur Godfrey's Talent Scouts*; Ed Sullivan's *Toast of the Town* with June Taylor and The Toastettes; Jackie Gleason's *Cavalcade of Stars* (June Taylor and the June Taylor Dancers joined his program in 1950); and *The Texaco Star Theater* starring Milton Berle. Even highbrow operas were televised. Balanchine got in the act choreographing ballets for the *NBC Opera Theatre* television program.

The idea of dancing on television had its appeal. Whether or not it would lead to becoming a celebrity, it was a job. My introduction to dancing in a television gig was on a Paul Whiteman show. Paul Whiteman frequently was referred to as the "King of Jazz." I don't know about him being the King of Jazz, but it seems that he did sell a lot of records and was popular on radio and television as well as in clubs and music halls when touring with his band. Some of his television shows in the late 40s and early 50s (he had a long career) included *On Stage America* for the National Guard and *Paul Whiteman Presents*. I auditioned for and got hired to dance in *Paul Whiteman Presents*. There was a choreographer who taught us dances to popular songs; it was all big-band music. It was a fun gig, except that it was terrible for my body because of dancing on a cement floor. The show was televised once a week before a live audience. I only performed three or four times before quitting. Dancing on the cement floor was just too hard on the joints and muscles.

It was my frugal spending habits and discipline in saving every possible cent (Mom taught me well) that got me through the months of October through December. Walking was my first preference of transportation, only taking a bus or subway if absolutely necessary. To stay in top physical condition I took classes from Tatiana Chamie. Born and trained in Russia, she had danced first in Diaghilev's company and then in Basil's Ballet Russe. Her school was located so near to the theater district that a lot of people took lessons with her. Her one tiny studio was in the same building where she lived in a walkup on 57th Street and 6th Avenue. The kitchen was off to one side of the dance studio, and Tatiana often walked back and forth between the two rooms teaching class and cooking at the same time. There was a class in the morning and another at 6:00 p.m. in the evening. I took the 6:00 p.m. class. She charged $1.00 per lesson. If you did not have the dollar you could take class anyhow. You kept track, and, eventually, when you did have the money, you paid her. The pianist was excellent, but certifiably crazy. She was so often seen downstairs at the entrance door shuffling through papers that had accumulated, that finally I had to ask Tatiana about this strange behavior. "She's looking for some papers she says she is expecting—for the last ten years," she said. The pianist had a thing about men, too. Maybe a fear of men. Whenever the boys' group danced a combination and got close to the piano, she cringed. Definitely a crazy lady.

I was reading *Variety* magazine when I saw the announcement of a forthcoming audition for a classical ballet company. Ricky Adama's most-talked-about company, Balanchine's New York City Ballet, was auditioning for one, possibly two, male dancers. The small apartment I rented was a walkup on the west side of Manhattan on 9th Avenue. On December 30, 1949, I began the emotionally-charged walk to New York City Center of Music and Drama—the stage door entrance, which was located on 56th Street between 6th and 7th Avenues. My gut told me that this was my big chance, that I had to do whatever it took to get this job. I absolutely could not mess this audition up.

Chapter Five

First-Generation New York City Ballet

The audition was in a studio on the 5th floor at New York City Center of Music and Drama, or just City Center. After signing in, finding the men's dressing room and changing into my practice clothes, I walked into the studio and began what seemed like a forever-wait-in-time moment, anxiously shifting weight from one leg to the other, wanting the instructions *now*, so we could get this drama started. There was only one or maybe two positions to be filled, and as usual there were about two hundred of us nervous guys auditioning. Across the room—calmly seated in those hard, uncomfortable metal folding chairs that, like barres and mirrors, are the typical equipment in every dance studio in the world—were our three judges: George Balanchine, Lincoln Kirstein and Jerome Robbins. The configuration of the room was a bit different from the typical dance studio: the chairs were on a raised, six-inch or so platform. There were stairs on either side. One set led to the men's dressing room. The other set may have led to the women's dressing room. Staring at myself in the mirrored wall behind the three men, I took a long, deep breath. The reputation of George Balanchine was well known to me because of Ricky Adama talking about him all the time. Lincoln Kirstein, however, not so much. Even though we had never met, Jerome Robbins was a popular dance-gossip topic because of his huge successes with Broadway musicals, including *Billion Dollar Baby, Miss Liberty, On the Town,* and *High Button Shoes,* which I had turned down after being offered a contract. For twenty-five cents one could read the Wednesday, December 14, 1949, issue of *Variety* about Jerome Robbins being the highest-paid choreographer on Broadway. There is good publicity, bad publicity and no publicity in theater and politics, or so public relations spinners like to say. And nobody out to make a name for himself in show business wants to fall in the "no publicity" category: No question about Jerry there. Controversy came in the Jerry-package. While he might be called "brilliant" and was a musical theater celebrity at age thirty, the Broadway-grapevine buzz on Jerome Wilson Rabinowitz, who was born in a Jewish hospital on October 11, 1918, cautioned that he was mean, bordering on cruel, to everyone on the team—producer, director, lyricist, composer, stage crew, wardrobe mistresses, actors, dancers. No one was spared. Ask my friend Lane Bradbury. She'll be glad to tell you all about her bad experience with him—the teapot debacle—in the Broadway musical *Gypsy.*[1] No matter one's ethnicity, origins, skin color, professional experience, star status, gender, sexual or religious or political preferences, he did not discriminate in choosing his victims. Still, Artistic Director George Balanchine must have liked the man, or at least respected him a lot, because when Jerry asked to join New York City Ballet, not only was he welcomed as a dancer, but he was also given the title of assistant artistic director. According to the Robbins biographer Amanda Vaill, it was after seeing Tanaquil LeClercq in *Symphony in C* that he wrote a letter to Balanchine asking to join NYCB as a dancer, a choreographer—anything. Balanchine sent his reply in a letter. To Jerry's delight the answer was "Come on."[2] Watching Jerome Robbins watch me at the audition … my anxiety went up another notch.

When called to begin the combinations in center floor, I marched myself up to the front row. Usually, I'm complimented for my mental facility to learn combinations quickly and to remember them. That is on a normal day, though, and auditioning for New York City Ballet was not a normal day. I was frightened that nerves would intrude, my memory failing me, my balance off and my famous sixteen pirouette turns down to two and my landing embarrassingly wobbly. Just because spinning turns across the floor was one of my strengths did not mean that I might not trip and stumble during the audition. Even though the two hundred of us were separated into several groups, I had to be light-on-the-feet, and on high alert, to avoid colliding with the other spinning and darting energetic males who were leaping across the room from one corner to the next, each trying to impress the judges. For every combination I made sure to be in the first group. Never before had I danced at an audition so aggressively. I was in excellent physical condition from dancing in St. Louis and because of my lessons with Tatiana Chamie. Still, like my friend Ricky Adama, I needed to show that I could be a go-getter, an over-the-hill dancer, also.

Two hours later I walked toward the men's dressing room to change into my street clothes. There were many well-trained and experienced men who auditioned on that Friday, December 30, 1949. But I was offered the position. While I was walking down the hallway, thinking about how to celebrate, someone on the staff called out my name. Robbins wanted to see me, in the same studio as the audition.

Waiting patiently in the studio was Barbara Walczak. She was my first friend and my first dance partner at New York City Ballet (NYCB). She was a wonderful ballerina and is a wonderful lady. And then I was with *the* Jerome Robbins—rehearsing. Barbara called him Jerry, so I called him Jerry, too. He was modifying *The Guests,* a ballet he had choreographed and premiered in January 1949, music by Marc Blitzstein. The twenty-minute ballet is a social commentary about two cliques: the highbrow popular in group and the lower class not popular out group. In the ballet both groups wear the same costumes. They dance on the stage together but never really mix. The out group has a star-shaped mark on their forehead to distinguish them from members of the in group. Blitzstein was a member of the Communist Party. Jerry had been a member since 1943,[3] as many true-blue Americans were in this era because of several reasons. One, because of a lack of faith in a capitalist system (caused by the 1929 stock market crash and the Great Depression of the 1930s); and two, because Communist doctrine advocated integration between blacks and whites at a time when U.S. politics' practices and laws were very much anti-integration. Even though the ballet's libretto did not trumpet-with-fanfare an obvious political leaning, the star on the forehead may have been Jerry's and Blitzstein's subtle way of showing they supported the cause to end segregation in America. During the ballet the star-shaped mark group puts on masks; and so do a few of the members from the in group. There is a pas de deux at the end of the ballet. The dancers take off their masks. The man is in the out group, the woman is in the in group. Hand in hand they run off the stage—despite peer pressure, two people from opposite social and economic classes romantically aligned. It is a theme Jerry and Leonard Bernstein would advance in what is today a classic Broadway musical, *West Side Story.* Maybe *The Guests* was the seed that launched the creation of this masterpiece?

It was not easy being in one of Jerry's ballets because every one of them was a work in progress. As I quickly learned, Jerry was always, always modifying his ballets. "Another version," we frustrated dancers would whisper to one another at rehearsals, He sometimes tinkered with the choreography up until the curtain was rising opening night. Union rules and practices were much different than now; a rehearsal could go on for hours and late into the night. A finger pointing up, then he changed it to down; the tilt of the head right then left, then back to the right or maybe up then down, then back to the original position; a plié of the knees deeper, then not so low to the ground. Nothing—not a gesture, a facial expression, a step, the twitch of the nose or an ear, or hairs on the head (natural or wigs)—escaped his attention. Nor was there ever a "please" or "thank you" uttered after his incessant demands.

We swore that with some of his ballets there were at least fifty variations. Balanchine's behavior when choreographing was always calm, and he could choreograph a thirty-minute ballet in two days or less. Jerry's behavior was frantically-feverish, if not complete panic at times. He never knew when to stop tinkering and let us polish one version before the opening night performance. It was crazy.

Thank goodness for Barbara Walczak my first day on the job. She was so tolerant of both Jerry's temperamental quirks and my inexperience in understanding what emotions he was trying to get me to express, what he wanted my movements and steps to say, and why. Once Jerry had left she stayed and taught me my part (which version I do not know). Thus, my first day, my first week, at NYCB was an adrenalin high—every day eventful and filled with drama. It was exhilarating. The next eight years would not be any different. Sixty-eight years later it is a privilege to pass along to anyone who asks what it was like in the early '50s to be an elite member of the first-generation NYCB. And I do get asked.

Thank goodness for Barbara Walczak. We learned a lot about partnering technique from each other and became good friends.

The official start date of my contract was January 1950, so my first paycheck as a NYCB dancer was in January. My first NYCB performance was Tuesday, February 21. It was the opening night of the NYCB winter season at New York City Center of Music and Drama. Then there were my first ballets with NYCB. The first Balanchine ballet I danced was *Symphony in C.* The first Jerome Robbins ballets were *The Guests,* and *Age of Anxiety.* And my first Frederick Ashton ballet was *Illuminations.* Freddy, who was choreographer-in-chief of Sadler's Wells Theatre Ballet (now Royal Ballet) in London, had been invited by Balanchine to create a world premiere ballet for NYCB. In Balanchine's *Symphony in C* I was learning a role already created; he had premiered the work on Paris Opera Ballet in 1947. But Robbins' *Age of Anxiety* and Ashton's *Illuminations* were world premieres, and it was a big honor to collaborate with these choreographers, to have these roles created on me.

In Balanchine's *Symphony in C* the music is by Georges Bizet, Symphony No. 1 in C Major. The ballet is about thirty-two minutes, and there are four movements. I was a demi-soloist in *Symphony in C,* second movement, and my partner was Barbara Bocher. The third movement is my favorite. It is an adrenalin-rushing, feet-never-stop-moving, fast-paced-tempo dance (at least my part was); and it was so much fun. The costumes were built by the legendary Barbara Karinska (there were a lot of Barbara's at NYCB in the early 50s), who had her own business but often collaborated with Balanchine. Jean Rosenthal was the lighting designer. The ballet is plotless; there is no story. But there is a different theme in each of the four movements. The ballerinas' white costumes were the traditional classical short tutu and some balletomanes were confused, and some overly critical, that they were worn in an abstract classical ballet. The women wore pink tights and pink toe shoes. We males wore white shirts, black tights, white socks and white ballet slippers. There is no spectacle-scenery, only a simple blue background. Such simplicity, the almost nude stage, was characteristic Balanchine, and it saved a lot of money, too. The ballet was something that some balletomanes found confusing—the abstract choreography unnatural, especially to those who liked the extravagant sets and exotic costumes of the ballets offered at the Met. And it showed in ticket sales. As Jacques d'Amboise said, in those early years there could be more dancers on the stage than ticket buyers in the audience at City Center.[4] Balanchine was determined, though, to do whatever it took to educate the public on ballet as an art form; that is, to what he believed classical ballet as an art form should be in American dance. Balanchine loved America. As historian James Steichen said about Mr. B and Lincoln's grand plan, it was "to reinvent the art form in a native idiom."[5] Balanchine wanted his ballets to respect his new country's free-range attitude. And he choreographed ballets that reflected America's youthfulness and playfulness, its fast-paced, enjoy-the-moment trademarks. He was intrigued with America's western cowboy and cowgirl culture. He sought to capture the essence of a people who welcomed new ideas and innovations, and most important, change. His plotless, no-narrative ballets were meant to make people feel something, and to think, rather than to tell fairy stories from centuries past. Certainly, there were a few ballets with the Russian and French-Italian traditional big tutus and fancy headpieces. But, as he explained to me, this was only done for those works that he considered "my bad ballets." Educating patrons to his way of thinking did not happen quickly. But little by little ticket sales had begun to increase as more and more people were learning to appreciate his bare sets, the often-simple costumes that resembled a dancer's practice clothes (leotards and tights), and his neoclassical choreography. He was following the path of the abstractionist painters. Lynn Garafola said it best, "In art, as in life, Balanchine had no use for nostalgia. He desentimentalized the past, viewing it through a prism of indifference."[6] No matter the number of patrons sitting in the theater, at every performance we first-generation dancers moved full out, dancing every step with heart and soul and a lot of sweat. We were determined to do our best to help him succeed in his quest to educate and to build an audience.

Dancing in Robbins' *Age of Anxiety* was quite different than Balanchine's *Symphony in C. Age of Anxiety* is based on W.H. Auden's poem "The Age of Anxiety." Leonard Bernstein composed the music, Symphony No. 2 for Piano and Orchestra. Tanaquil LeClercq, Todd Bolender, Francisco Moncion, and Jerry were the leads. Because students from Kirstein and Balanchine's School of American Ballet (SAB) frequently danced in NYCB performances, there could be as many as thirty to fifty dancers in a piece. There were forty-four dancers in *Age of Anxiety.* I was in the corps de ballet for the premiere. Later I would dance a demi-soloist role. The ballet is about four strangers meeting for the first time and their discussion on the life of man from birth to death. Together, they begin the journey through life, which is shown in the ballet through seven variations. The corps wore red leotards and masks. Since we were unable to show facial expressions, our movements—gestures and steps— in each of the seven stages had to depict whether we were an obstacle to man's journey through life, or a walkway to help him on his journey through life. It was my first experience rehearsing in a studio in one of Jerry's new works. The NYCB dancer, Barbara Milberg Fisher, said that she was often cast in and then cast out of Jerry's ballets "sometimes more than once, for reasons unfathomable to anyone but himself."[7] So far, he and I had gotten along very well—no insults and no drama. I had witnessed the tirades and verbal attacks, but there were no shameful, cruel insults slung at me. The ballet is a gloomy, pessimistic-on-the-state-of-America statement that was not out of sync with the economic, political and social conditions of the time. The world premiere was Sunday, February 26, 1950. While small in number, the audience enthusiastically approved. We all were really pleased.

Meeting Frederick Ashton for the first time was an exceptionally momentous happening in my career. I joined him in a studio to learn a part in the ballet he was creating, *Illuminations.* The world premiere of *Illumina-*

tions was Friday, March 2. It is a one-act ballet based on the poems of Arthur Rimbaud with music by Benjamin Britten. The sets and costumes were designed by Cecil Beaton. The NYCB website lists four people in the lead roles for the opening night: Nicholas Magallanes, Robert Barnett, Tanaquil LeClercq and Melissa Hayden. I danced the role of "The Dandy" in the first section. The choreography was very contemporary in 1950: the steps and movements were fast, and there were a lot of turns. In the second section I danced the "Drummer," and the "Coachman" in the third. It was a thrill to collaborate in the creation of these three roles with a master choreographer who understood my body type, and my way of moving, and who chose me out of the twenty-five or so principals and soloists in the company for the lead role of "The Dandy." I remember running onto the stage, dancing past the girls dressed in white costumes sitting on the floor. My variation of "The Dandy" took place in center stage. I wore white pancake makeup, white gloves, a white hat, a tuxedo with white tail coat and white pants; everything was white. When I danced the "Drummer" in section two, I wore a small drum that was held in place by a belt around my waist, and while dancing around the stage I pretended to beat it with the drumsticks in my hands. In the role of the "Coachmen" I wore a top hat and got to crack a whip. The costume changes between my three roles were really fast.

John Martin's review, published in *The New York Times* March 3, 1950, said that the ballet was "a work of rare and delicate poetic beauty, a ravishingly romantic ballet…" The article concludes by complimenting Ashton for choreography that "besides its strong, if finely spun, central line, is filled with delights—with movements and phrases that are touched with wit, with feeling with true theatrical invention. It is a work one wishes to return to at once for a second seeing."[8] The poet's two loves were represented by Tanaquil LeClercq and Melissa Hayden. Tanny danced the role of the beautiful one, the innocent and sweet good girl. Four bare-chested men accompanied her in the ensemble. Melissa was the bad girl, the whore. She danced a pas de deux with Nicholas Magallanes. She wore only one toe shoe. Her other foot was bare, perhaps Ashton's acknowledgment of the mixing of classical ballet and modern dance that was occurring in a few (but very few) private dance studios throughout America, including Balanchine's School of American Ballet, where Merce Cunningham was teaching, and Dorothy Alexander's Atlanta School of Ballet.

Years later I would be at Joffrey setting a ballet for the second company when Bob Joffrey interrupted me. In another studio a répétiteur was setting Ashton's *Illuminations;* it was the Dandy's variation. Bob Joffrey did not think it looked right and he asked me to come and take a look. He was right: It was nothing close to the version I had danced. Whoever had staged the "The Dandy" for Joffrey's company had him coming in from the wrong side of the stage—stage right instead of stage left, and on a diagonal. Because the dancer was not downstage, where he was supposed to be, it just wasn't working. And the steps were nothing close to what Ashton had choreographed, not when I danced it anyway. "I watched you dance it many times and I just knew it wasn't right," Bob said. He asked me to fix it. I did not know if I could recall the choreography after so many years. Then I heard the music. I got it fixed.

In 1952, Ashton would create the role of the evil "Merlin" for me in *Picnic at Tintagel.* At our first rehearsal together, he said "you studied with Nijinska, didn't you?" I said "Yes. How did you know?" Freddy said that he had known her in Europe when he had danced in Ida Rubinstein's company and Nijinska was the artistic director; and "there was no one better for teaching or choreography." He told me about sitting in a corner and watching her, trying to learn. "What she does with the corps is amazing—her patterns." He described her as being a strict disciplinarian. "She was just incredible in every way," he said. I had to agree. *Picnic at Tintagel* was quite a bit of dancing, although my variation was more acrobatic than conventional ballet steps. The night *Picnic at Tintagel* premiered Jerry came running up to me when I was in my dressing room changing costumes. He said, "I never saw you dance like that. You were absolutely fantastic in the role, and I didn't know you could do it."

Another important person in my career at NYCB was Lew Christensen, the ballet master and a choreographer. His wife, Gisella Caccialanza, had danced in Kirstein and Balanchine's ill-fated Ballet Society. The couple had one son. Gisella, although born in San Diego, California., in 1914, had studied with the world-renowned teacher Enrico Cecchetti, in Italy, who was so taken with the young American girl that he legally became her godfather. Lew cast me in a principal role in his classic ballet *Filling Station.* While on a tour of Europe, he then honored me with another important role in a Balanchine ballet. It was early, really early, one morning when Lew called me. I had to get out of bed to go into the hallway to answer the phone. He asked me to come to the theater, immediately. A principal dancer, Harold Lang, was ill, and Lew, who was the ballet master, wanted me to dance Lang's role in *Bourrée Fantasque,* which was being performed that afternoon. Balanchine had set the work on Jerome Robbins. Jerry was not on the tour, though, and Lang, a dancer at Ballet Theatre, had been hired as a guest artist to fill in. There was a pas de deux in section one with Tanny LeClercq, who was at the theater when I arrived. Not only did I learn the role and dance it in the matinee a few hours later, I danced it for the rest of the tour. Nancy Reynolds describes the ballet as "Melodious, colorful, full of comic touches, dash, high spirits, elegance, lots of difficult dancing, and massed effects created by a horde of dancers on stage...".⁹ It was all that and, at one memorable performance, much more. In the first section Tanny is supposed to kick me in the head, not hard of course, and I am supposed to fake being dazed by her kick. In one of our performances there was no faking, though. Tanny misjudged the distance between us and because of her flexibility her foot went all the way over my forehead; she actually kicked me—hard. So hard that not only could it be heard a block away, but I was semi-dazed for a few minutes. Even though partners usually did not make comments to one another when performing because it caused a loss of concentration, Tanny was so distressed that she whispered an apology, again and again.

Here I am dancing with the wonderful Patricia Wilde in *Bourée Fantasque* (author's collection, *Bourée Fantasque*, choreography by George Balanchine © the George Balanchine Trust).

That first season performing at City Center in 1950 was an experience never to be forgotten. In addition to dancing new, exciting original ballets by some of the best choreographers in the 20th century, I was making a lot of new friends. We were a family. Members included Maria Tallchief, Nicholas Magallanes, Herbert Bliss, Ronald Colton, Helen Kramer, Jillana Zimmerman, Melissa Hayden, Janet Reed, André Eglevsky, Tanaquil LeClercq, Roy Tobias, Todd Bolender, Francisco Moncion, Diana Adams, Yvonne Mounsey, Vida Brown, Arlouine Case, Charlotte Ray, Eddie Bigelow and Betty Cage, and there were many others whom I stayed in touch with until they were no longer with us on this earth. Today, there are my good friends Jacques d'Amboise, Barbara Walczak, Barbara Milberg Fisher, Patricia Wilde, Allegra Kent, Janice Cohen, Ann Crowell Inglis, Una Kai, Victoria Simon, and Barbara Horgan. And then there was George Balanchine.

Georgi Balanchivadze was born in Russia in 1904. At age five he started his formal training as a musician, specifically, as a pianist. He also took courses in musical theory and composition. In 1913, he switched to dance and studied at the Imperial Ballet School in St. Petersburg. He made his dancing debut with Russia's esteemed Imperial Russian Ballet at the age of ten as a cupid in *The Sleeping Beauty*. He joined the company, in the corps de ballet, in 1921. He created one work for the company, *Enigmas*. Balanchine liked choreographing and he wanted to experiment, to create works that were different from the traditional classics, such as *Swan Lake* and *Sleeping Beauty*. He formed a small troupe. It seems his experimental ballets did not receive the required stamp of approval from the government authorities, though, and the troupe was threatened with dismissal if they continued to perform these kinds of nontraditional works. In the summer of 1924, Balanchine and three other dancers in the troupe—his first wife, Tamara Geva; Nicholas Efimov; and Alexandra Danilova— requested permission to tour Western Europe. They were granted permission. Nervously, they waited, and waited, at the Russian border to have their travel documents approved. Finally, they were allowed to cross. They did not return.

I was fortunate to have danced with many excellent partners at New York City Ballet, such as Allegra Kent. To our right are Barbara Fallis and Herbert Bliss. The ballet is *Interplay* (by William McCracken, from author's collection, choreography by Jerome Robbins © the Robbins Rights Trust).

While Balanchine's experimental, modern works may not have impressed the Bolshevik authorities, these ballets did impress the famous impresario Serge Diaghilev. He, too, had left Russia because of the Bolshevik Revolution, never to return. He hired Balanchine and the other three members of the Russian troupe to dance in the Ballets Russes de Monte Carlo. Also, he let Balanchine choreograph, who was permitted untethered creativity. Bronislava Nijinska was a chief choreographer in the company. She and Diaghilev were having some disagreements, though, and when Balanchine's works began to take precedence over hers, the frustrated Nijinska departed. She was hired by one of Diaghilev's former dancers, Ida Rubinstein, who had formed her own company, Les Ballets de Rubinstein. Balanchine eventually left Diaghilev's company, also. He formed a small company, Les Ballets 1933, and Lincoln Kirstein saw a performance in Paris. Kirstein wanted America to have a ballet company equal to the Bolshoi, Kirov, and Paris Opera Ballet. The story I heard was that Kirstein's first choice was Léonide Massine, but he refused. Kirstein then met with his second choice—Balanchine. In their meeting Kirstein pitched his plan to start a company in New York City. Balanchine was interested: "Europe had become a museum; in America he sensed the promise of new possibilities."[10] "But first a school," Balanchine said. In fall of 1933, he arrived in New York City. The School of American Ballet (SAB) opened its door on January 1, 1934, at 637 Madison Avenue. There were twenty-five students enrolled, and three were males. The students from the school performed in Balanchine and Kirstein's newly established ballet company: American Ballet. The Balanchine and Kirstein partnership would last for fifty years. The early years, however, were not without a lot of trauma and disruptions, some caused by financial failures, one caused by World War II. Despite the difficulties, the two men never abandoned their dream.

Balanchine's first original ballet choreographed and performed in the U.S. was *Serenade*. The music is Tchaikovsky's Serenade in C Major for String Orchestra. The opening performance was June 10, 1934. It was performed outdoors on the estate of Kirstein's friend, Edward Warburg, near White Plains, New York. The ballet, with four movements, has no narrative. When asked what the ballet was about, Balanchine replied that it was suggestive of different emotions and human situations. "…this plot, inherent in the score, contains many things—it is many things to many listeners to the music, and, many things to many people who see the ballet."[11] In the summer of 2017, I staged the ballet on students at a school in Hawaii. Balanchine would have been pleased with their performance. I have known, and still know, a lot of talented artists in the performing arts. I have never known, or know, anyone like George Balanchine.

Jerome Robbins also deserves praise and thanks for my wonderful professional career. I think Jerry was the reason I got into the company, because I was the type of dancer he liked to cast in his ballets. He used me as a guinea pig, a lot. He would call me into an empty studio to work out various roles in a new ballet he was creating—whether I was going to be cast in the role or not—just so he could try it out, to put it in his head, to see what he might do with it. One night one of the male leads in Jerry's ballet called thirty minutes before the start of the performance to say he was too ill to dance. Jerry immediately ran into my dressing room and asked me to dance the part. Although I had helped him set the ballet early on, lots of changes had been made since then. Thus, I did not know the steps. The curtain was held for fifteen minutes while Jerry, Tanaquil "Tanny" LeClercq and I worked on the choreography in a hallway. That is the kind of performance a dancer has nightmares about. Still, I liked working with Jerry, although not many people did. He had problems. He was often depressed. But he was brilliant. One person, besides me, who escaped his cruelty was Tanny LeClercq. It was obvious that he loved her. There was talk of Balanchine being in love with her too, and she was certainly a muse. But in 1950 he was married to Maria Tallchief.

Lew Christensen taught company class. And so did Balanchine, and it was quite an experience. He did not teach the usual barre class that was followed in the traditional classical ballet technique syllabi—Cecchetti, Vaganova or Royal Academy of Dance (RAD), for example. Balanchine had only one lung that functioned normally, a consequence of tuberculosis. Even so, he demonstrated more often rather than talking us through a combination or a correction, rarely showing signs of extreme tiredness. His classes were not conventional. He did not waste time starting barre with a plié combination to warm up the muscles gradually, for instance. There was no time given to stretching, either. We dancers had to be warmed up before taking one of his classes. He was famous, or infamous, depending on one's perspective, for his repetitious, tedious tendu exercises. His tendu combinations (it seemed that there were at least one hundred tendus in every combination) could be muscle-fatiguing slow, using every muscle in the foot as it massaged the floor, or very quick, the accent in, not out. He demanded that the hip of the working leg not move; you always took the emphasis from under the butt. The tendu was pushed forward, always with the heel of the foot first. When the foot returns to fifth or first position the pelvis stays lifted, to pull the working leg under you. There were many days that my muscles were sore, but boy did those tendu exercises work. It bothered me that my feet were not flexible— a bit stiff; they were not banana feet. Although my elevation on jumps and leaps was impressive, my feet were not perfectly pointed in the air. I remember asking Mr. B to give me a specific exercise to stretch my feet but to also keep them strong. He said, "Bobby, tendus, tendus, tendus ... tendus in your sleep." Another thing he was known for was his plié. He taught the plié as a connecting step; it was not an end in itself. In his grande plié the heels had to come down at the last second to propel the body back up. He drilled us on pirouettes, also. He repeatedly told us not to lay an egg; meaning, don't sit, don't pause in a fourth or fifth position before pirouetting. A lot of his variations were at a really fast tempo, so fast that there was no time to put your heels down between steps. People often ask me about the Balanchine technique. There is no Balanchine technique; there is the Balanchine style. Barbara Walczak said in the book she co-authored with Una Kai that Balanchine's classes should not be given to most dancers, especially young students.[12] I have to agree.

It was obvious to us all that Balanchine loved America, and he was especially partial to anything that reflected the western part of the country. He usually wore a western shirt to class and often rolled up the sleeves. I believe it was because he was now married to Maria Tallchief, who was a Native American (Osage Tribe), that he wore turquoise jewelry. He was mildly superstitious and wore a turquoise bracelet for good luck—always. As much as we dreaded his tendu exercises there was an energy in the room whenever he taught. We called him Mr. B.

In a couple of performances I got to watch Mr. B dance. I remember an ensemble movement in a piece with four boys and four girls, and Balanchine was one of the boys. It was a character dance; it was really authentic—the costumes, the orchestra and everything. It was performed for a couple of nights and was fascinating to

Here I am in a photograph for Balanchine's *Western Symphony*, **third movement (by William McCracken, from author's collection,** *Western Symphony*, **choreography by George Balanchine © the George Balanchine Trust).**

watch. Mr. B used to do innovative things all the time. What I learned from Mr. B's choreography is that not every ballet has to have a story—the why and the how. A ballet does not have to have a plot—the what. Take *Serenade,* for instance; it is just a gorgeous ballet. The patterns and everything. There were some movements and sections, specific steps, that were added in his ballets to the choreography because of things he had seen on the city streets or things that had happened within rehearsal; a particular dancer's way of moving that he liked, for instance. Mr. B did not expect a balletomane to ask the question, what does a ballet mean? Rather, he expected each person to leave the theater thinking about how the ballet moved her, made her feel, made her think. And every individual might have a different emotional response. While I think about it now, at the time my thought about a Balanchine ballet was that it wasn't up to me to think why we were doing it or not, or whether there was a purpose. I just did what I was told.

Of the triumvirate, Lincoln Kirstein was a curiosity, a mystery-man. While he was always around, even on the national and international tours, I never got to know him well. He was seen but not heard, and he did not talk to the dancers much. Luckily for the company he knew a lot of New York City leaders, politicians and corporate CEO's, and his significant role was raising money to keep the NYCB financially stable and growing. From what I could tell Balanchine, Jerry and Kirstein seemed to have a mutual respect for each other. Kirstein and Mr. B had their moments; he didn't always approve of what Mr. Balanchine was doing. But if there were times when a really serious disagreement caused them to not speak to another it was never obvious to us dancers. What was obvious is that Mr. B was like a big hero to Jerry. And Mr. B had respect for Jerry's talents. Jerry had such a great reputation for Broadway shows and theater. He was a little kooky—sometimes he would create an awkward situation just for the fun of it, and he could be a SOB. Nevertheless, I liked him, a lot. He was not a teacher, and he did not teach any company classes that I took at NYCB or teach any student classes in SAB. He might coach a dancer in a role. But teaching a class was not his thing. Kirstein, Balanchine, Robbins, they were such an outstanding team. Together they overcame economic recessions and depressions, and McCarthyism. Together they launched the neoclassicism movement that was so significant in the progression of ballet in America. Together, they created a ballet company that today is ranked in the top five worldwide. It was such an honor, and a wonderful experience, to be a New York City Ballet dancer in those early years of the company's beginning.

I made about $87.00 a week when I first joined NYCB. The dancers were paid for the hours spent in rehearsals (except for my many un-official hours with Jerry) and performances. Costumes were paid for by NYCB. Anything we used for rehearsals (practice clothes, for example) we had to pay for ourselves. The women did not have to pay for toe shoes. Soloists got paid more than those of us in the corps de ballet, and the principals even more. In the early years the seasons were short, there were many weeks off when we did not receive a paycheck. I spent a lot of hours standing in line applying for unemployment benefits.

Even so, frugality and money from my NYCB salary and the U.S. government's unemployment checks allowed me to find my own apartment. After thanking Jay for letting me stay in his apartment rent free, I moved to the eastside of Manhattan—a tiny one-room walkup on 9th Avenue. It was a brief stay. I soon traded up to an apartment nearer City Center; it was on the west side of Manhattan, near Central Park. The location was closer to Tatiana's studio where I continued to take classes. I would move a lot, always trading up to an apartment with more conveniences (such as a washer and dryer), and slightly larger, and in a better neighborhood. Packing my goods didn't take a lot of time because there wasn't much to pack. I am happy to say that I did have a boxy black and white television to move and the essential rabbit ears for reception. It was while living in a nice garden apartment that Mom and Dad came for a three-week visit. Although I kept my apartment tidy and clean, Mom couldn't help herself. She rearranged anything she could find to organize in my drawers and cabinets, and she scoured and scrubbed everything in the apartment, probably even the walls.

In addition to collecting unemployment checks, in NYCB's off season I found other gigs on occasion, such as dancing in the Agnes de Mille production of *Brigadoon* in May 1950. It was a short-term gig at City Center. I suffered painful shin splints for weeks caused by the Scottish folk dance steps in her choreography. I did not teach at SAB and did not take classes there during the off season. I stayed in shape by doing classes on my own or taking from Tatiana. In the summer I usually went to Washington to visit my family, unless NYCB was lucky and we got to tour. We got lucky the summer of 1950. Ninette de Valois, the director of Sadler's Wells Ballet, invited NYCB to perform in London.

Chapter Six

Triumphs, Tragedies and Tours

It didn't take long to feel at home at NYCB and to get to know all the people. There were so few staff that I soon knew them all really well. Initially, it was mostly one person who kept us all organized, and in line, so to speak: the unflappable Betty Cage. She was everywhere; taking care of us all. I did play a part in helping her find a capable assistant: Barbara Horgan. Barbara was working part time at a record store when the two of us met. Recognizing me as a NYCB dancer, she introduced herself. Our second meeting happened when the two Barbaras, Walczak and Milberg, and I were walking 56th Street between 6th and 7th Avenues, and we saw Barbara Horgan. I invited her to join us for lunch. First, though, we had to stop by the office to see Betty Cage and get our paychecks. Betty was looking for a secretary. Horgan was hired. Including Barbara Horgan, there were maybe three administrative staff, and they had to juggle a lot of roles and responsibilities.

NYCB's new home theater, City Center, was an okay place to dance. NYCB was the resident ballet company and shared the theater with the resident opera company. There were five floors of dressing rooms in the building. Maria Tallchief and André Eglevsky each had their own private room. There was a huge dressing room for female corps de ballet and soloists to hang out, apply makeup, and do what dancers do to perform their pre-show rituals, to get psyched up for a performance. The girls wore robes when walking down the hallway to the costume room to change. I shared a dressing room with three guys. No walking down a hallway wearing robes for us, however; our costumes were in our room. If not in the building located on Madison Avenue for company class and rehearsal—or later in a building on Broadway and 83rd Street—we were at City Center, either in the studio on the 5th floor or on the stage. City Center was my home theater for eight and one-half years.

While the stage (width and depth) was smaller than Mr. B wanted, having a permanent home theater was very important; it just made performing easier than if we had had to move from one theater to the next throughout a four-week season. If any dancer complained about City Center, Barbara Milberg Fisher, who had been with Balanchine since 1946 when she danced in his Ballet Society, did not withhold her schoolmarm words in telling us newbies how good we had it compared to those days when performances moved from one stinky high school auditorium to another, and where she danced on tiny stages not designed for ballet. Actually, it wasn't so bad at City Center in those early years because the productions usually did not require much in the way of sets or props, and we dancers quickly learned how to adjust our spacing to accommodate the stage's width and depth limitations. Our biggest concern was those empty seats in the 2,000-plus theater. Often, there were more dancers on stage than patrons in the audience. And at the most, there were fewer than forty to fifty of us dancing on the stage. It is almost certain that not all of those patrons bought a ticket, either. One had only to charm an usher on a day when the theater was mostly empty seats and his chance of being invited to sneak in through a side door was pretty good. I know, because I did it. "In its first year at the City Center, New York City Ballet gave but twenty-four performances. "[1] Eight weeks of dancing annually at City Center was not going to prevent bankruptcy. More money was needed to keep the company in business and us dancers employed, and the best option was to tour nationally and internationally.

In 1950, the company made its first tour to England at the invitation of Sadler's Wells Ballet (later Royal Ballet) artistic director, Ninette de Valois. My new friend, Freddie Ashton, was the resident choreographer. The contract was for six weeks in London followed by short gigs in Manchester, Liverpool, and Croydon. Leon Leonidoff, who had known Balanchine back in the Diaghilev years, took a big leap of faith that the tour would be financially profitable and handled the arrangements. In London, on our drive from the airport into the city, we were surprised, and emotionally affected, by the visible consequences of World War II. There were the burned, bombed-out buildings, the rubble piled high and wide, in what had once been people-friendly neighborhoods filled with parents and children happily smiling and calling out good-greetings to friends and strangers passing by. There were the minor inconveniences caused by the war that we had to get adjusted to, such as knowing how to use the ration coupons we were issued: bacon, meat, butter, cheese, sugar, tea, and even soap were only a few of the items on the list. Dancers who could exist on a diet of potatoes and fish and chips without gaining ten pounds were lucky. Those who were having to carefully monitor their weight had it tough because fresh fruits and green vegetables were not easy to find. In addition to the ugliness caused by the German bombs, because coal was the primary source of fuel, the buildings were covered with black soot. London definitely was not a pretty city back then, as it is today.

I had to find my own accommodations in London, and I found what was called "digs" in a building near Piccadilly Circus. I shared the flat with two other dancers, and we each had our own bedroom.

My first NYCB tour was filled with a lot of fantastic firsts. Not only was it my first international tour as a company dancer, but it was my first time to sit in the first-class section of a humongous plane. Furthermore, it was my first time to dance on the Covent Garden Opera House stage in London. On opening night, when the curtain parted, I can remember the feeling of electric excitement and the thrill of seeing the theater completely packed from the orchestra stalls up to the last row of the highest balcony with enthusiastic patrons. These were only some of the many exhilarating, wonderful, can-life-get-any-better events that I experienced on this first international tour. But life is a roller coaster, and it was on this first international tour that I had my first bad Jerry experience—our first fight. It was a humiliating, mind-numbing upsetting experience that I will never forget.

The ballet was *Age of Anxiety*. As usual Jerry was changing the steps—at a final rehearsal. The choreography called for me to be thrown up in the air by some of the boys. Jerry began experimenting with different ways for me to be thrown, and then rolled off the stage. The boys and I worked for one-half hour and nothing suited him. When a step or movement didn't work it was never Jerry's fault; he blamed the dancer. I was new and I was going all out to please him. No matter what I did, though, I could not give him what he wanted. Finally, he blew. He let me have it in front of the other dancers on the stage. There were no curse words; it was the volume and the tone of his voice. "Mr. Robbins," I said when he had finished talking, "I've got the bruises to show that I have been working my butt off to make this work. I don't know if it is me, but I know it is you." And then I walked off the stage. Bone-tired, I walked slowly to my dressing room, took off my dance clothes, and then I went downstairs and stood for a long time in the hot shower trying to wash away the fatigue and worry. I weighed about 126 pounds soaking wet; so, it was no surprise that I had red marks on my arms and bruises on my hips. I was nerves-shaking upset. Less than seven months in the best job of my career and I was about to be fired. When I returned to my dressing room Jerry was waiting. Not knowing if he was going to blow up again, or fire me, or probably both, my already sky-high-soaring anxieties jumped up another notch. He talked, and I listened. Calmly, he apologized, and he offered to take me to dinner. Because I had already promised some of my friends that I would go out with them I politely declined. I thanked him for the offer, though. Fortunately, this was my first, and last, Jerry Robbins fight. Never, ever, did he blow up at me again. Later, he even suggested that I dance in some of his musicals. But I always said no. Some of the boys at NYCB went with him to dance in *West Side Story,* but it didn't interest me. That fight with Jerry taught me a valuable lesson: that some people are more bark than bite. From that day on, if at a rehearsal Jerry was in one of his terrible, infantile moods, I refused to let it bother me.

Except for my one gut-cramping drama with Jerry, that first tour through England was a lot of thrilling-good experiences and a triumphant success. In the Colonel's Original Ballet Russe getting paid at all, much less on time, was a constant worry. Balanchine and Kirstein made certain that we got our paychecks on schedule. They made sure that we dancers sat in first class on the plane, round trip. There were no one-night gigs. Where they found the money, I do not know. But such treatment made us dancers feel special, and respected.

A dancer's life on the road, or the rails when in Europe, is not easy. A few cannot take the frequent moves from one city to the next or the weeks, sometimes months, of being away from the familiarity of home. I loved touring; the journey and its adventures suited my personality. On buses or trains some members of the company made use of the downtime to write letters to friends and family back home, played poker or worked crossword puzzles. The ladies often darned the tips of their toe shoes with pink satin thread. They had to sew on the pink satin ribbons, too. There were those who read a book (and I was one) or who stared out the windows enjoying the scenery. Traveling gave us the time to chat and to gossip and to learn more and more about each other's likes and dislikes. Touring is what made us so close—a real family. A real, typical family: "there were the inevitable complaints, clashes, petty rebellions, snits and grumps—plus the occasional temperamental explosion."[2] These grumps and occasional explosions were not unusual. In fact, they were normal. Touring is hard on the body emotionally and physically and being out of sorts comes with dancing a lot in a few short weeks, all out, and with few days off to rest. Each theater had its own peculiarities and challenges: the temperature, the dressing rooms, the wings and the stage floors, for instance. The steep raked stage in Barcelona was exceptionally challenging, and Balanchine rehearsed us to death. Trying to execute piqué turns and châiné turns up stage and down stage is no easy feat on a raked stage. I thought for sure I would end up down in the orchestra pit. I had the dubious honor in Jerry's *Interplay* of doing the four consecutive double tours. On my own I practiced for hours. Finally, I discovered that what I had to do was to forget the stage was slanted, to think it was flat, to focus straight ahead, that it didn't matter what you landed on. Touring made me appreciate City Center and the benefits of performing night after night on the same familiar stage.

These tours, as hard as they were, helped our dance-family to understand our role in fulfilling the company's mission, which was to achieve a big-name reputation internationally and, if successful, to make us better appreciated (increase ticket sales and monetary donations) back home. Given Balanchine and Kirstein's lack of success in establishing a financially profitable company before NYCB was inaugurated, we knew that the company's odds of survival were not high. The empty seats at our City Center performances were a real big hint that the New York City patrons who were more familiar with the Met's preferred offerings of the ballet classics, such as *Swan Lake,* and *Giselle,* were not overly excited about Balanchine's neoclassical ballets. Balanchine was doing his best to educate them, though. He was very generous with his time talking to newspaper and magazine journalists, to almost anyone who wanted to interview or to debate him. He talked about the history of ballet in Europe and his vision for NYCB. Most important, however, was his explanations on the ins and outs of modern classical ballet: What is it? Why is it important to the art form of dance? Journalists, academicians and patrons debated whether abstract classical ballet was real classical ballet. Balanchine patiently replied that he did not create *abstract* ballets; his modern classical ballets were plotless. "He did not see how anything performed by living human beings could be called 'abstract.'"[3] The term "neoclassical ballet" was being mentioned more and more, only instead of being associated with the Diaghilev era (Mikhail Fokine, Léonide Massine, Vaslav Nijinsky and Bronislava Nijinska, for example), it was being attached to Balanchine and NYCB. Tirelessly, he continued to explain, to answer their questions, to educate. As the debate by journalists in the media and academics in the lecture halls continued, we dancers did our part by working our tails off, dancing full out at every performance to educate and to entertain. We danced when ill, and we danced when injured. Everyone in the company was determined to do whatever possible to keep NYCB going and growing. Our role model was Mr. B, who, despite his one fully functioning lung, was everywhere on those grueling tours. He taught company class; he was with us in rehearsals; and he was always standing in the wings for every performance. Thus, once the first international tour in England had concluded there was a collective sigh of relief that the European newspaper and magazine dance critics' reviews were predominantly positive. As a result, there were more international tours planned.

By the mid–1950s, it appeared that Balanchine and Kirstein's decision to tour was paying off at home in New York City, literally: Box office receipts were increasing. The heady triumph of gaining the notice, if not yet the respect, of the revered, centuries-old companies in Western Europe, such as the Royal Danish Ballet, the La Scala Theatre Ballet, and the Paris Opera Ballet, made us first-generation NYCB dancers proud. Jacques wrote that the "reports and reviews from the big European cities—Paris, London, Berlin, Hamburg, Milan, Amsterdam—drifted across the Atlantic and illuminated the New York audiences and critics to the jewel they had in their midst."[4] The company's growing international and national recognition and its financial stability made us think that this time Kirstein and Balanchine's dream was going to survive; that NYCB would be around for a long, long time. Then the bomb dropped. It happened on the European tour of 1956. Mr. Balanchine was married to Maria Tallchief on the England tour of 1950. On the tour in 1952, they were divorced; he and Tanaquil LeClercq were married. The tour of 1956 included the cities of Munich, Frankfurt, Brussels, Antwerp, Paris, Cologne, then Copenhagen and Stockholm. Parties and receptions had become a regular occurrence, a perk the dancers looked forward to (especially the opportunity to save my per diem by gorging on really good free food). In one of the cities on the tour Tanny borrowed my mohair scarf to wear to a reception given by the cultural attaché. A few days later, she had not given it back. I remember thinking it unlike her not to at least mention having my scarf, but if she liked it so much she could keep it. In Cologne, Germany, Virginia Rich and I were walking along a street window shopping when we met up with Mr. B, Tanny, and Diana Adams. Tanny confessed that she had lost my scarf and that she was searching the shops trying to replace it. I said, "Don't worry about it. It's just a scarf." Mr. B invited us to join him and Tanny for dinner at a restaurant in their hotel. Without hesitating, Virginia and I accepted. The four of us were enjoying a relaxing evening together when Tanny said that she was not feeling well and that she needed to go to her room. Having no clue that it was anything more than a twenty-four-hour stomach virus or painful headache, Mr. B, Virginia and I took our time eating, drinking fine wine, and talking. When we got on the train to travel to our next gig, Tanny seemed to be okay. Opening night at the Kongelige Teater in Copenhagen was October 26, 1956. Twenty-seven-year-old Tanaquil LeClercq danced in *Swan Lake*. The next night I arrived at the theater and learned that Yvonne Mounsey was substituting for Tanny in the Mozart *Caracole*. I was not performing that night and was eating in a restaurant in the theater when Mrs. LeClercq, Tanny's mother, came to my table. She asked me if I had seen Mr. B. I said yes, that he was on stage rehearsing Yvonne. She said, "Well, I need him, because Tanny is very sick." The hotel's on-call doctor had been called and Mrs. LeClercq wanted Balanchine to talk to him.

The two of us went inside the theater to find Mr. B. Mrs. LeClercq found him first, and they quickly left the theater. The doctor, whose full-time job was at the local polio clinic, immediately diagnosed the problem: polio. Tanny was rushed to the city's polio clinic. She was in a coma. She woke up in an iron lung. It wasn't until we were on the train to Stockholm that Betty Cage walked from car to car to tell us about Tanny's polio. Her case was so bad it was not known whether she would live. Not only were we scared for Tanny, but we were scared of contracting this insidious disease, too. We were told that the U.S. army was sending the vaccine to inoculate us all. A few of the company members, including Virginia, had been vaccinated before starting the tour. I had not, however. When I was in the Navy Jonas Salk had not invented the vaccine yet. I got my shot in Stockholm. It was such a frightening time. Because we were at the end of the tour everyone suffered from some sort of physical ailment: fatigue and, what was most worrisome, muscle pains. In one performance Ann Crowell Inglis was having a lot of pain in her shoulders. It was so bad that she had to make a supreme effort to throw her arms up in the air over her head. We thought for sure that the pain and loss of muscle control was caused by polio. Thank goodness, it wasn't. The only remedy required was rest.

Back in New York the sadness we felt for Tanny, the fear that one of us might get polio, and the increasing anxiousness of not knowing when Mr. Balanchine would return to NYCB caused morale to plummet. We dancers felt leaderless. Jerome Robbins was not a leader. We knew that Kirstein was around, but he must have been hiding in his office. When the couple did return to New York City Tanny was admitted to Lennox Hill hospital, and Balanchine still was not seen at NYCB. Tanny was then moved to Warm Springs, Georgia, for further rehabilitation. And Balanchine went with her. As one month after another passed, there was talk that NYCB might fold. A rumor spread that Mr. B was not coming back. Some of the dancers wondered if they should start looking for another job.

In 1956, when tragedy struck in Copenhagen, Balanchine was determined that Tanny would dance again. He got her the best treatment. He personally spent hours moving, exercising the muscles in her arms and legs. Eventually, she did regain the use of one arm and partial use of the other. But never again could she stand on her own or walk. Every basic need—toileting, getting in and out of bed, moving from one room to the next in her wheelchair—required an assistant. It was only after twelve very long months, and only after realizing that Tanny would never walk, much less dance, again, that Balanchine finally returned to NYCB. Tanny and Balanchine remained married for another ten-plus years, divorcing in 1969, although they maintained a committed friendship. Polio may have claimed her body, but it did not crush her spirit. She taught classes for Arthur Mitchell at his ballet school in Harlem. She went out with friends. Jerry, who had been devoted to Tanny before polio, was still devoted after. He would bring her to the theater, sometimes carrying her in his arms, and gently place her in a seat. Eddie Bigelow and Diana Adams were two other friends who remained close, who were there to assist with whatever Tanny needed. It is often said that experiencing a tragedy can make a person stronger. I think that experiencing the tragedy of 1956–1957 made NYCB stronger. For one thing it showed how committed we were to Kirstein and Balanchine's dream.

There were two notable tragedies that affected me directly, and, no surprise here, both happened while on a tour. The first occurred the year that I decided to save some money by subleasing my apartment to a SAB student. The apartment was on East 59th Street between 1st and 2nd Avenues. My tenant's mother came to spend the summer with him. She liked to spend evenings in one of the neighborhood bars drinking and meeting new friends, and one night she and a young man ended up in my apartment. Her body was found by her son. She had been murdered, in my apartment. I could never go back. Not even for one night. Upon my return to New York City I immediately found another place to live.

Having to quickly search for a new apartment because of a murder was disturbing, but not as frightening as the second tragedy I encountered. In addition to the European tours there were the national tours—Los Angeles, San Francisco, Baltimore, Washington, D.C., Seattle, and Chicago, for example. I danced in lots of cities throughout the U.S. with NYCB, except for cities in the Jim Crow South, which Balanchine avoided. It was on a tour in the U.S. that my personal tragedy occurred. I blew out my knee. Injuries are a part of a dancer's life. It is almost certain to happen. One just hopes it will not be career-ending, that the rehabilitation and recovery will be for a few days and not months, or years. I was dancing eight shows a week in one city after another. The most demanding, technically difficult dance was "Candy Cane" in Balanchine's *The Nutcracker*, a divertissement that requires toomany-to-count jumps and leaps around, over, and through a hula hoop. The tempo is really fast and there are lots of quick steps and changes in direction. The soloist must have excellent agility and versatility. It requires exceptional physical stamina to end the divertissement without the soloist huffing and puffing, without the lungs audibly gasping for air. Early in the tour I had asked Mr. B for an understudy; reluctantly, he finally agreed, although the understudy only danced in a few matinees. My disaster happened in Chicago. I was on the stage getting prepared, making certain my muscles were good and warmed up. I pranced in place to get my feet going; did a few easy petit allégro jumps. Then I did what I had done thousands of times in my years of training and performing: I bent my knees in a deep plié. I could not get up; the right knee was locked. The pain was piercing and frightening. There was no discussion on how bad the injury was, on whether I should ice and rest; immediately, Mr. B flew me back to New York City. I went for a consult with Dr. Jordan. He was chief of staff at Lennox Hill Hospital, and he was an orthopedic surgeon. The diagnosis was a ruptured meniscus. I pretty much had all the symptoms: swelling and unbearable pain and difficulty bending and straightening the leg, especially if the knee locks up, as mine did that night on the stage. With a meniscus tear a piece of cartilage that cushions and stabilizes the knee joint tears or a piece of cartilage may shred, break loose and catch in the knee joint. If this happens, the knee can lock up. Dr. Jordan operated on my knee. I worked with a physical therapist as part of my rehabilitation. Now began the worry over whether I would be able to dance again, and if so, whether I could dance at the same level of technical proficiency as before the injury. Would I be able to dance "Candy Cane"? Six weeks later I was back on stage dancing. I felt so lucky. The many hours worrying that my career had ended were for nothing. Or so I thought. Within a year the meniscus, in the same knee, ruptured again. This time, though, I was in New York City.

I was really, really worried this second time when I took my re-injured knee back to Lennox Hill. Dr. Jordan said, "Well, I thought you'd be back sooner. I didn't want to do everything on your injured knee that needed to be done the first time because you would lose so much muscle." He did the second part of the operation. Dr. Jordan's wife was a therapist, and I worked with her to rehabilitate my knee. The company was touring cities on the West Coast, and six weeks after the second surgery I flew to Seattle to join them. The next night I danced in *Interplay*. I guess it was good for my career that Dr. Jordan decided to do the surgery in two parts, because otherwise I might have been in rehabilitation for months, not weeks, which might have caused me to quit dancing for good. It is a question without a definite answer. What I do know is that because of Dr. Jordan I was able to continue my "Candy Cane" divertissement as if there had never been a meniscus tear. Barbara Milberg Fisher is most gracious when she wrote in her book *In Balanchine's Company* about my injury and return to dancing:

> Balanchine set the hoop dance for Bobby just as it had been passed down to him, step for step. Bobby had chronic trouble with his left knee, an old injury from his high school days, but you'd never know it to see him in *Nutcracker*. What a jump he had! In his red-and-white striped costume, Bobby expertly leapt in and out and over his

hoop as he whirled and twirled at 200 rpm—a peppermint candy-cane spinning as dizzily as a top. A visible explosion of energy. Wild applause every time, especially from the kids in the audience.[5]

Tragedy to triumph to tragedy to triumph: It was such a relief to get back to dancing the way I wanted and in the works I loved. Although I liked dancing "Candy Cane," my favorite Balanchine ballet was the Third Movement in *Symphony in C*. It was so me—strong technically but also very lyrical. It really moved, fast. Another great memory is dancing with Tanny in the first movement of *Bourrée Fantasque*. Balanchine choreographed a duet for a tall girl and a short boy. Tanny was a little taller than me when not on pointe; therefore, the two of us were the perfect fit. Because of her height when standing on pointe, I had to hold her wrist on what was usually a finger turn. Indeed, there are only wonderful memories of all my partners. I never had to dance with a partner that wasn't strong—Tanny, Melissa Hayden, Janet Reed, Barbara Walczak, Patricia Wilde and Allegra Kent are just a few. There was one time when my partner was a little off pointe on a pirouette—her pointe shoe was caught in a crack on the stage floor—but it was simple for me to make an adjustment and put her back in the proper placement and on balance. There are a couple of almost-tragic moments, such as when Tanny kicked me in the head and almost knocked me out. The worst, though, happened in *Interplay*. I was dancing with Janet Reed, and she accidentally kicked me in the crotch. I thought I was going to die the pain was so bad (almost as painful as that first meniscus tear), but I had to continue dancing. It was the finale of the ballet and I never stopped moving. Because we were such a small company in the early 1950s, we dancers danced a lot compared to dancers in most companies today. It is astonishing, actually, how lucky I was not to have suffered more serious, debilitating injuries from over-worked tendons, ligaments and muscles or because of jumping and landing wrong. There were the dancers I knew who did suffer career-ending injuries. But I was not one of them. In all my years of dancing I was very, very lucky—not even one obvious (not obvious to the audience, that is) partnering embarrassment, not even one humiliating fall.

One learns from both the good and the bad experiences. I was fortunate to have mostly good experiences at NYCB, but learned a lot from the few bad ones as well. I took every opportunity possible to watch how Mr. B taught classes and choreographed, even if it meant sitting quietly in a corner because I wasn't scheduled to be in a class or rehearsal that day. I learned so much from the two major roles he set on me: "Candy Cane" in *The Nutcracker*; and, in *Stars and Stripes*, the Second Campaign, *2nd Regiment,* "Thunder and Gladiator." Not only was he a master craftsman (his preferred term) at choreographing, he was an excellent coach. I remember one combination that gave me a lot of trouble, because I was trying to do it academically. He said, "Bobby, you just have to attack it; make it happen." He was telling me to stop over-thinking the technique, which I did, and it worked. Unlike Jerry, Mr. B had specific ideas about what he wanted in his choreography, and he always came to the rehearsal well prepared: he knew both the musical composition and the steps and movements he wanted to set. Then, whether setting a solo, duet, or small ensemble section, he would make adjustments based on one or more dancer's personality type and body type (or maybe based on a jump or a leap he had seen his cat make earlier that day). That's why

George Balanchine set the "Candy Cane" variation on me in his 1954 premiere of *The Nutcracker*. It was fun to dance, even after knee surgery (by Radford Bascome, from author's collection, *George Balanchine's The Nutcracker®*, choreography by George Balanchine © the George Balanchine Trust).

he worked so fast, why he could choreograph a thirty-minute ballet in three days. He was incredibly disciplined. And so was I. It was from watching him for those eight great years at NYCB that I learned how to direct a company.

America has benefited so much from Balanchine and Kirstein's dream. They had the best partnership, which they maintained for many, many years. Balanchine was the man in the spotlight, standing on the stage, while Kirstein was always out and about—growing the network of dedicated supporters, always looking for the money and resources to fulfill their plans and vision. I never got to know Kirstein; he seemed shy. If he saw one of us dancers coming down the hallway, he would turn and run the other way. Rarely did he attend the company's parties. He only went to those parties where he felt comfortable with his close friends, such as the Roosevelt family. Yet he did so much for NYCB. It is because of him that Lincoln Center was built, which includes a theater designed specifically for ballet, the theater that Balanchine badly wanted. Equally important, Kirstein and Balanchine created an outstanding NYCB team. It is because of all these wonderful people they hired—artistic staff and administrative staff and the dancers—that NYCB progressed in those difficult, early years and became the iconic company it is today. NYCB is of major importance in the history of ballet in America. It also is of major importance to me. It is because of NYCB that I met my wife. It is because of marrying Virginia Rich, that the two of us would move to Georgia to take on the jobs of principal dancers and associate artist directors of what is now the oldest continuously operating company in America, The Atlanta Ballet.

Chapter Seven

Virginia "Ginger" Barnett

Labor Day weekend. Ginger and I stand outside the front door, waiting for the automobile to make its way up the road to our home in Asheville, North Carolina. After passing through the gate, the car takes a couple of minutes or more to arrive at our house. It is a slow drive on the single-lane, narrow-paved road that is bejeweled by hundreds of brilliant emerald-green ferns. Along the way our guests can admire the gently rippling water of the Swannanoa River that runs along the periphery of our forty-eight acres of forest property. There are the miles and miles of flora to gaze at with wonderment—a real-life painting of the green earth-land and the crystal-clear blue sky of the Blue Ridge Mountains. Often, there may be wild life to appreciate—perhaps a doe and her baby or a flock of wild turkeys strutting across our driveway to remind us that they really own the place. Labor Day weekend is the annual NYCB reunion, a tradition started around 1996, a nostalgic, fun three days with about eleven close friends. Ginger and I have made all the arrangements, including transporting guests to and from the airport, determining who will sleep where in the house and organizing excursions—arts & crafts shops and art exhibits, plays and concerts, for instance. During our three days together, the walkers stroll on the soft-spongy nature trails each morning on our property, the average temperature a perfect 65 to 70 degrees, and take in the glorious dogwood, spicebush, Virginia creeper and beech trees, as well as the evergreens, such as the American holly and white pine. The more adventuresome hikers spend hours walking through the gentle country mountains, taking in the smells, captivated by the sight-intoxicating exposure to the birds, animals, plants and trees that are in the Blue Ridge Mountains. Those who prefer wheels and the comfort of an air-conditioned automobile take a slow drive on the Blue Ridge Parkway. Some guests visit the mansion and garden-grounds of the most popular Asheville tourist attraction, George Washington Vanderbilt II's Biltmore House. The house, all 175,000-plus square feet with 250 rooms, is the largest privately-owned castle in America.

To prepare for our NYCB reunion, Ginger and I have been cooking for a week. She specializes in the vegetable dishes; my specialties are the meats and desserts. Over lunches and dinners, we will reminisce about old times, and share new experiences—both the good, the funny, and the sad. For so many reunions the usual guests included Patricia "Patty" Wilde, Melissa Hayden, Helen Kramer, Vida Brown, Arlouine Case, Ann Crowell Inglis, Una Kai, Charlotte Ray, Barbara Milberg Fisher, Ronald Colton and Todd Bolender. Before she published in 2006 her memoir *In Balanchine's Company*, Barbara Milberg Fisher—who after ending her ballet career had become Dr. Fisher, a professor of English at City College of New York—brought chapters she was writing. When she was reading aloud, a chapter or three at several reunions, our little NYCB family spent stimulating evenings correcting her errors on important dates, on who was what on where and when; critiquing her prose; laughing and crying at the memories her beautiful writing summoned on those wonderful experiences we had together as NYCB's first-generation dancers. As she says about the book, and which I can now fully appreciate, "A memoir, it turns out, is all about other people."[1] Ginger and I were honored that some of those special "other people" visited at our home for the annual NYCB Labor Day holiday reunion weekend.

For several years the reunions were at our home in Waynesville, North Carolina, where Ginger and I lived for ten years after leaving Atlanta in 1996, two years after I resigned my position as artistic director of The Atlanta Ballet. We built the house from scratch, and it was on top of a mountain. Looking across our property of 600 acres, we could admire five mountain ranges. In 2006, we moved to Asheville. Ginger had a passion for the arts—the folk, visual and performing arts, especially—as I do, too. After our professional dance careers had become less time consuming, we sought a much slower pace in a city that promoted and supported local artists, and the arts are practically worshipped, in the Asheville community. The Asheville population in the city limits is about 89,000. While small in the number of residents compared to Atlanta or New York City, Asheville fit our requirements to live in an artists' colony. Ginger was first a performing artist and then a folk artist. She specialized in creating beautiful, satin-ribbon decorated pillows that add the finishing designer's touch to our sofas and chairs. The pillows she made were of such artistic quality that she could have owned a successful business. Lovingly, she gave them away to friends and to family. She sold many at the New Morning Gallery, and she donated the proceeds to the Asheville Art Museum. Living in Asheville gave us more time to travel together, such as the many trips to Europe we took, a photograph safari expedition in Africa, and trips to Washington to visit my relatives. There was more time to enjoy family events. Ginger had her gardens to lovingly nurture. We both had more time to telephone old and new friends, former colleagues and students, people we had stayed in touch with (some since childhood), and with whom we could talk to more often now. There was more time for those special, big celebrations that Ginger and I had time to organize and to pull off so well that our results earned lots of compliments and praise from the hundreds of guests in attendance. And, there were those very important more private, personal celebrations, also, such as our 50th Wedding Anniversary in 2007 with the family.

Virginia Gleaves Rich and I officially met in 1955 on a NYCB West Coast tour which included Los Angeles, San Francisco, and Seattle, before finishing in Chicago. Prior to the start of the tour, Mr. B had needed to quickly replace four female company dancers, and he got the replacements from SAB. One of the dancers picked was Virginia Rich. Our meeting happened in Los Angeles, where the company was performing at the Greek Theatre. I had a rental car. One day, after a rehearsal, I saw these four ladies walking along the street and from just looking at their posture, their well-toned ballet legs, and their attitude as they laughed their way down the street, I knew they were from the company. I stopped and offered them a ride. Three of the women were chatty, we talked and talked. Virginia, sitting in the back seat, did not say one word. The five of us went to lunch together, and Virginia was the quietest of the four ladies. I was definitely intrigued by her beauty and her aloofness, and I wanted to get to know her. Fate then intervened. I walked out the stage door after a performance one night and a woman stopped me on the street. It was Mrs. Virginia Gleaves Lazarus Rich from Atlanta, Georgia (mother and daughter had the same first name). She and Richard H. Rich were in town to watch their daughter dance. She told me that I should meet her daughter; she said enough to confirm that Virginia had been one of the ladies I took to lunch. At company class, rehearsals, in a backstage hallway, anywhere, I began to seek opportunities to talk to Virginia Rich; maybe even to ask her out. A cabaret show featuring Lena Horne was the opportunity I needed. I was friendly with Lena's daughter. She saw *The Nutcracker* in San Francisco. Afterwards, she told me that her mother was performing at the Fairmont Hotel, and she invited me to a show. She said I could invite seven other guests, too, and I included Virginia. I guess you could call it our first date, even though we were not alone. It was probably a Monday, and we had the day off. That night, at some point during the show, Lena Horne sent a note to the table inviting us to her suite when the performance was over. To give Lena time to wind down and to take off her makeup, the seven of us had a drink in the hotel bar first, and then we went to Lena's room in the hotel.

There she was, curled up on a corner of a couch, dressed in a Chenille robe. She was so warm and friendly, and not at all arrogant or putting on airs. We stayed for about forty-five minutes. Virginia and I started officially dating from that night on. In Seattle my parents met me at the train station. And they met Virginia. My dad was 5'11" tall, and Mom about 4'6" short. Virginia was 5'5", medium height. The three of them got along great. By the time Virginia and I got to Chicago, we were pretty tight.

Virginia was born in Atlanta on April 16, 1934. Her mother was a gorgeous, sophisticated Southern lady, who was a patron of the arts. Virginia's father, Richard H. Rich, came from a family of businessmen. His grandfather founded what had become named Rich's department store in Atlanta, Georgia. Richard "Mr. Dick" Rich had risen from bundle-wrapper and stock boy at Rich's—summer jobs he worked at during his teenage years—to a full-time employee in 1924, and on up the Rich's corporate ladder to vice-president in 1937 and to president in 1949. He was a hardworking man. He had gone to college, earning a degree in economics from the Wharton School of the University of Pennsylvania, and he had done post-graduate studies at Harvard University. He was disciplined, and over the years he had sacrificed some precious hours of fun times with the family to make life better, not only for his family—his wife and three kids, Sally, Virginia and Michael—but for his employees and their families, and the Atlanta community, too. He had a strong work ethic, believing that a leader treated his employees fairly and with respect. For example, up until the 1960s, company Christmas parties were segregated. Mr. Dick, as his employees affectionately called him, did not support segregation. Still, he believed it was his civic duty to abide by the local, state, and federal Jim Crow–era laws. Mr. Dick, therefore, paid for two parties: one for whites and one for blacks. Dick was Chairman of the Board of Rich's when I met him, and he had recently started expanding, opening Rich's department stores in other states, such as Knoxville, Tennessee, and Birmingham, Alabama. There would soon be two locations in Atlanta—one downtown and the other in Buckhead.

Ginger started her formal ballet training at Dorothy Alexander's School of Dance around 1940. The one-room, tiny studio was in the basement of Dorothy's Ansley Park home. In addition to owning a ballet school, Dorothy was a full-time employee in the Atlanta Public Schools where she was responsible for developing the dance curriculum and for teaching young boys and girls to dance. The public-school job was her major source of income. She earned some income from her ballet school but did not take a salary from the non-professional regional ballet company she had founded. Miss Dorothy, as her students affectionately called her, taught ballet classes in the evenings,

Monday through Friday. Saturday was dedicated to rehearsing the company dancers or performing. Dorothy never had any children; her students were her children, she said. There were some she nurtured more than others, though, such as Ginger. By her teenage years, Ginger showed the discipline, the talent, and the ambition necessary to become a professional ballet dancer one day. She auditioned, and she was accepted, in Dorothy's Atlanta Civic Ballet. Dorothy mentored Ginger. She advised her on where to study ballet in private schools in New York City. Ginger spent one summer studying at Sadler's Wells Ballet school in London, and two of her teachers were Monica Mason and Margot Fonteyn. One night, while riding in a taxi to see NYCB perform at Covent Garden, she heard on the radio that America was at war with Korea. Alarmed, Ginger debated whether she should cancel the ballet performance or immediately return to her hotel to pack and fly home. Thank goodness for me that the ballet won. She got into her seat just as the curtain parted. There stood the dancers in the iconic pose of Balanchine's classic ballet *Serenade*. It blew her away. This providential performance was NYCB's opening night in 1950: It was my big debut at Covent Garden Opera House, and although I did not dance in *Serenade*, I did dance a demi-soloist role in *Symphony in C* that night. When Ginger decided to do something, she did it. She decided that she wanted to dance with NYCB. After graduating from high school in 1952, she moved to New York City and took as many classes as she possible could at SAB. While waiting for the opportunity to join the company, she danced in a ballet company at Radio City Music Hall, in Rockefeller Center (the ballet company was separate from the Rockettes). Following Dorothy's example, she took some modern dance classes. She studied the most with Anna Sokolow, a former dancer with Martha Graham's company. One day Anna said, "I don't know why you want to be a bunhead. You'd be the most spectacular modern dancer."[2]

In 1955, Ginger accomplished her goal: she was accepted into NYCB. On a national tour, she and Janice Cohen roomed together. Betty Cage had promised Janice that she would love rooming with Virginia Rich, and, as always, Betty was right. As a result of rooming together on the tour, Ginny (that's what the dancers at NYCB called her) and Janice became very good friends. Ginger was living in her parents' New York City apartment on 54th street, near the Warwick Hotel, and Janice was a frequent visitor. Not only did Janice get to know Ginger's mother and father, sister and brother, but her grandmother DearMa. Janice and I became good friends, too. The three of us often joined the NYCB dancer Herbert Bliss in going places together. He was a fabulous cook, and we liked to go to his place for some fun meals. Herbert was a good technician and a good partner. He had a recurring problem,

though—a bad back. He frequently had to telephone and cancel a performance at the last minute because of the severe pain.

On our tours, Mrs. Rich often mailed presents to her daughter, and to
Janice, also. That's the kind of lady Mrs. Rich was. She and I were very fond
of one another. Still, while Mrs. Rich approved of my friendship with her
daughter, she did have some reservations where it was leading to, though,
when she realized that our relationship was serious. She wanted Ginger to
return to Atlanta, to have babies that she could dote on, not now, but one
day. I was a soloist in NYCB, a company that was on its way to becoming as
well-known as the inimitable Mariinsky, Royal Danish and Paris Opera ballet
companies, or so we hoped. Therefore, the idea of my moving with her daughter to Atlanta at some point in the future just did not seem like a possibility
to Mrs. Rich. But Ginger and I were in love, and Mrs. Rich did come to appreciate the relationship her daughter and I had, especially our devotion to each
other's happiness.

Ginger's second mother was also very interested in our relationship. My
first time to meet Miss Dorothy Alexander was probably in 1955, the year
Ginger had joined NYCB. Dorothy Alexander and co-owner of the Atlanta
School of Ballet, Merrilee Smith, had flown to New York to watch Ginger
perform. Most likely we met at Dorothy's favorite restaurant, the Russian Tea
Room. It took only a few minutes to recognize that Dorothy Alexander was
a visionary with a cause: that is, to have a dance company in Atlanta that was
nationally ranked; and also to broaden dance appreciation and education
throughout the Atlanta community. Her mission was not only to enrich and
inspire audiences with performances that provided a high-quality standard
of classical ballet training and artistry, but to offer dance training and performance experiences that enabled her students to reach their professional
and personal goals, whether as a professional dancer or a teacher of dance.
There would be no poorly trained classical ballet dancers or bad dance teachers released into the world under her watch. It was a vision and mission that
I would one day share with Dorothy Alexander.

By the time Ginger joined NYCB, I no longer had to spend hours standing in line to collect an unemployment check. Nor did I have to look for part-
time gigs to supplement my NYCB salary. Balanchine was making progress
in his quest to educate the New York City community, and beyond. His plotless ballets were becoming accepted critically. Financial support was increasing. At our City Center performances, there now were more patrons in the
audience than dancers on the stage. There were our two seasons at City Center, one in the spring and one in the fall. There was the international tour in
the summer, and there were tours to cities throughout the U.S. Thus, NYCB

was keeping me extremely busy; there was not a lot of time to relax and play. Ginger was very busy, too. But as busy as we were, we did have some leisure time to enjoy dates together. Besides, our relationship had reached the stage of such importance that we would have found the time to be together as much as possible. Indeed, everyone at NYCB now knew that our relationship was serious. The person responsible for spreading the big news about Ginger and me was probably Jacques d'Amboise. If a man carried a lady's suitcase, it was a sure sign that the couple were dating. On that first tour together in 1955, Jacques noticed that I had started carrying Ginger's suitcase. Ginger and I went to restaurants to eat. We sat in the now air-conditioned theaters to watch popular Broadway shows. There were meals and parties with our NYCB family. There were movies to see in a theater on 42nd Street. Ginger and I liked to go to see a midnight movie, usually after one of our performances. There was one night when we walked out of the theater and into a blizzard. There were no autos, no taxis, no nothing on the streets except ice and snow. Because the sidewalks were too icy to walk on without risking a slip and a fall, we walked in the middle of 7th Ave, then in the middle of 54th Street to her family's apartment where she lived. I saw her safely to the front door of the building. My toes were numb by the time I got to my apartment on 59th Street, by the 59th Street bridge, the same apartment that I later sub-leased and abruptly moved out of after the tenant's mother was killed.

Sadly, during those years dating Ginger between 1955 and 1957, I did not get to enjoy spending much time with her mother. Mrs. Rich had cancer. For two years, despite multiple treatments and consultations with various oncologists, the cancer continued to spread throughout her thin body. Ginger's mother was born in New Orleans, Louisiana, on April 17, 1908. She died on January 8, 1957, at the age of 48. Virginia was with her. She had taken a leave of absence from NYCB back in the fall of 1956, missing the annual Christmas *The Nutcracker* performances, to care for her mother in Atlanta. Bittersweet was the year 1957. Mrs. Rich died; Mr. B and Tanny still were dealing with her health crisis; Ginger and I bought our wedding rings.

"Dancers to be Wed: Robert Barnett and Virginia Rich of City Troupe Engaged."[3] The announcement of our engagement was published in *The New York Times,* Friday, April 19, 1957. Sweet Melissa Hayden threw us our only engagement party. Her father-in-law was a prominent attorney in New York City, and he let us have the party in his luxurious penthouse apartment. The building had a tower that you could walk up to the rooftop and then step outside. There were benches and chairs to sit on where we could gawk at the twinkling city lights and listen to the familiar hustle and bustle on the streets below. The food and drink at the reception were catered. There were too many guests for me to count, including many we had never met, and many gave us gifts. Ginger wrote lots of thank you notes. Melissa and I had a close brother-and-sister friendship. We just hit it off the first time we danced together. I would be invited to teach classes at Melissa's school when she was no longer dancing. She and Ginger became close friends, too. They would one day take a vacation trip to Puerto Rico together.

The Sunday July 28, 1957, edition of *The New York Times*, "Two Dancers Married: Robert Barnett Weds Virginia Rich—Both of City Ballet,"[4] proclaimed our marriage. The ceremony was performed by Rabbi Jacob Rothschild at Ginger's home in Atlanta on Saturday July 20, 1957. The wedding party was small. Ginger's sister, Sally, was her only attendant; her brother, Michael, was my best man. The month of July can be too hot, and rainy and awfully unpleasant; or it can be gorgeous. Because the reception was out-

NYCB dancer Melissa Hayden hosted an engagement party for Virginia and me in 1957. Melissa is in the center and Virginia is behind her. The man standing behind me on the left is Michael Maul. I wish I knew who is kissing Virginia.

doors, Ginger worried that a tent might be needed to protect the guests and the food from the weather. Luck was with us, though. No tent was required. It was not so hot that the ice-sculpture swans floating in the swimming pool melted; the hot hors d'oeuvre—conveniently placed on tables set up on the tennis court—were good tasting and thoroughly enjoyed by our guests. In fact, the weather was photo-snapping perfect. The celebrity black musician Graham Jackson strolled the reception area playing his accordion. Tables and chairs for the sit-down dinner were on the tennis court—the table settings artistically beautiful. There was a separate table for the wedding cake, although my excitement level was so high that I do not remember what it tasted like, much less

Melissa Hayden's engagement party for Virginia and me was at her father's apartment in New York City in 1957. From left to right are friends: the dancer and the wife of Jacques d'Amboise, Carolyn George; me; Ruth Sobotka; Virginia and Jacques d'Amboise.

what it looked like. I do recall that the catering department at Rich's department store did everything first class to make our wedding day exceptionally special. My parents flew in from Wenatchee. Lois and Winnie came, too. Dorothy Alexander attended. Mr. B came with Tanaquil LeClercq's mother. They were on their way back to New York City from Warm Springs, Georgia, where they had visited Tanny.

Before going on our honeymoon Ginger and I drove down to Warm Springs to say hello to Tanny. The last time I had seen her was in Copenhagen, when she danced in *Swan Lake,* and I was really excited to visit her. She was in this little room, in this little single, old-fashioned brass bed. The room, the sheets on the bed, everything in the hospital, were white. There was a black male orderly with her—a gentle giant of a man—and he stayed the whole time we were there. It was fun being with Tanny: she could move her head; she was talking and smiling. She decided that she wanted us to go outside, to soak up the radiant summer sunshine. The orderly picked her up carefully, with as much dignity as possible, holding her fragile body securely against his chest. Her head, her arms, her legs—they dangled. She had no control. The sadness of seeing her like this, so helpless…. I lost it. Tanny was a joy in every way. I adored her, as did so many others. She was special. She always had to dance the role her way, such as in *The Cage:* everybody wore these wigs, but not Tanny. She took her hair and braided it and used egg whites to stiffen it, like tentacles growing out of her head. She was exceptionally creative. And she was beautiful: her proportions, and facially she looked like a fashion model. She was so gifted that I believe she could have been one of the top ten most famous ballerinas in the twentieth century. Even today, as I look at films of her dancing—nobody could touch her. Despite the enormous sadness seeing her unable to control her body that day in Warm Springs, Georgia, I was glad to have had the chance to talk to her, and to share the memories of those times we danced together.

The next day Ginger and I flew to Jamaica for our honeymoon. We rented a car and drove to the hotel, which was on the other side of the island from where the airport was located. The road was awfully narrow and winding. We would drive around a corner and, suddenly, I would have to slam on the brakes to avoid hitting a bunch of chickens blocking the road. It was a wild experience driving on dusty rural roads in this foreign country. We stayed for about a week before returning to New York City to begin rehearsals for the September season at City Center. Also, we had to move, into Ginger's apartment. My cold-water apartment was about 900 square feet. Ginger's was

In the late spring of 1958, NYCB began a tour first of Asia and then Australia. On a day off, Virginia and I got up close and personal with a koala bear at a zoo in Sydney.

much, much bigger, and nicer. It was close to City Center and to the Museum of Modern Art, and very accessible to our favorite restaurants and theaters. We lived there for the next twelve months.

In the late spring of 1958, the company began a tour first of Asia and then Australia. It was a physically demanding three-month tour. Ginger, especially, was feeling the fatigue of traveling and dancing. Finally, it got so intolerable that when we arrived in Melbourne, Australia, she consulted a physician. The rabbit test killed the poor animal: Ginger was pregnant. The doctor predicted that the baby would be born on April 4, 1959. We were relieved that there was a joyful cause for both her tiredness and her thickening waist. She never suffered any nausea, although she did crave Coca-Cola, which was not always easy for me to find in Australia. She kept dancing for the remainder of the tour, and the accommodating costume mistress kept enlarging the waists and bodices of her costumes.

A baby, arriving in spring 1959: The thought of how life was going to change with the birth of our baby was something Ginger and I discussed often. We wanted to be the best parents we could be. The one big question we kept coming back to was: Did we want to raise our child in New York City? We had two opportunities that landed in our laps to consider: an offer from Lew Christensen, who was with San Francisco Ballet, for me to join the company as assistant artistic director. And an offer from Dorothy Alexander. She wanted Ginger and me to be principal dancers and associate artistic directors in Atlanta Civic Ballet. This opportunity was most welcome, as Ginger's dad was gripped with grief from the death of his wife. By moving to Atlanta, we could provide the attention he badly needed; and he would get to know his grandchild. Ginger and I were still in Australia when I broke the news to Betty Cage of our forthcoming resignation; that Ginger and I were moving to Atlanta. Betty asked me when I was going to tell Mr. Balanchine who was in New York City and not on the tour. I told her that I wasn't going to tell him. I left it up to her to break the news.

Upon our return to New York City, we packed up our things as fast as we could. Our friend Herbert Bliss had resigned from NYCB before the tour of Asia and was living in California. Thus, of all the men still in the company, I was truly going to miss the two principal male dancers that I had known the longest—Moncion and Magallanes. Francisco Moncion was a beautiful man inside and out, who lived in a beautiful house filled with beautiful artwork. He was not a strong technician; his talent was in making his partner look good. Nicholas Magallanes, who was not a particular strong technician either, was another principal whose talent was partnering. These men had all preceded me at NYCB; they had seniority. Yet they never engaged in any one-upmanship; they were never arrogant. In fact, they were always ready to jump in and help any newcomer to the NYCB family, even if he or she was just starting out in the corps de ballet. Of the women in the company there was Victoria Simon, who regularly was one of the six Candy Cane girls dancing upstage, their role primarily to add some color and cuteness to augment my solo divertissement in *The Nutcracker*. There was Patricia Wilde—a strong technician and a beautiful artist. There was Ann Crowell Inglis, who was from Atlanta and knew Ginger when they were both young, as both had studied with Dorothy and Merrilee. After leaving Atlanta, Anne had studied at the school of San Francisco Ballet, before moving to New York City to dance with NYCB. There was Una Kai, who would become a regular attendee at our annual Labor Day reunion. There were Janice Cohen, all the Barbaras, Betty Cage and so many others. Last, but not least, was Allegra Kent. She was a phenomenon. She was about sixteen years old when she joined NYCB, but people broke their necks watching her dance. It was hard saying goodbye to all these close friends.

When Ginger and I started our move to Atlanta in late summer 1958, Dorothy and her dancers in Atlanta Civic Ballet were at Jacob's Pillow—the first classical-ballet regional company in America to be invited to perform at Ted Shawn's annual summer dance festival. Some of the other famous dancers on the schedule included Erik Bruhn with Nora Kaye, and André Eglevsky with Mia Slavenska. The drive in the rented bus from Atlanta to Lee, Massachusetts, was long. Nevertheless, everyone had to dress up throughout the long ride—hair, makeup, and dressy suits; no pantsuits were allowed in those days, much less blue jeans or shorts. When the bus stopped for breaks and the girls stepped out to stretch their legs, they were ambassadors representing the Atlanta Civic Ballet, and Dorothy expected them to make a good impression.

Ginger and I flew on Eastern Airlines from New York City to Atlanta. The flight was uneventful; our arrival, much more memorable. As we carefully made our way down the portable steps to the tarmac, the hot Atlanta sun hit me like a blowtorch. And walking from the plane to the terminal wearing what today would be considered dressy, and not necessarily lightweight, clothing, quickly had me soaking wet. Nor was the terminal air-conditioned; there was absolutely no relief from the heat. Dorothy Alexander and Merrilee Smith were waiting, and they were both dressed to the nines; not one hair out of place. Their dresses were looking crisp and dry. Southern ladies don't sweat, they perspire; but there was no sign that they were suffering from any perspiration discomfort. Riding inside the car to a restaurant was not much of an improvement. While the ladies kept their windows up to keep their hairdos from being messed up, I rolled mine down. After lunch, we drove to Ginger's home—27 West Andrews Drive, in Buckhead. I had not been back since the wedding, and the big house was so quiet with only Ginger's fifty-seven-year-old father living there. After a few days of looking for our own place to live, Richard H. "Mr. Dick" Rich (I now called him "Dick") asked us to move in with him. At first we voiced our objections. He insisted, however. He began meeting with an architect and builder to add a suite of rooms to the house, a wing that would give him his own private space. Dick, Ginger and I lived there for about eighteen years.

One reason Dorothy had asked us to join her in Atlanta was her ill health. Dorothy had cancer, and the treatments were as debilitating as the malignancy that had invaded her body. As a result, she had decided to initiate a succession plan. In addition to dancing as a principal in the company, teaching company classes, learning to manage and run the day-to-day operations of the company, Ginger and I both began teaching at the Atlanta School of Ballet. The co-owner, Merrilee Smith, was responsible for directing the school. Dorothy did some teaching, depending on her health, but she was mainly involved in running the company, and she was very involved in the regional ballet movement that she and Anatole Chujoy had started in 1956. Neither Ginger nor I received a salary from the company—not as dancers, associate artistic directors, or administrators. Our only income came from teaching at the school, and teachers were not paid a lot. I could make money performing with other companies in America as a guest artist, but I needed a partner. Although we had danced together, including in some musicals, it was not aesthetically practical to partner with Ginger in a classical ballet pas de deux on a regular basis. At 5'6" in height, I was one inch taller than her. But when standing on the tips of her pointe shoes, she was three to four inches taller than me. Also, I did not want to be away from home too much during Ginger's pregnancy. Therefore, to supplement my income from teaching at the school, I began working at Rich's department store. I would continue working at Rich's until assuming the position of artistic director of Atlanta Ballet in 1962.

The stories of women spending hours in pain in the delivery room are endless. Ginger, though, had an incredibly easy delivery. We had returned to the house one night after playing bridge at the home of a friend. We got into bed and her water broke. There was a nurse staying at the house to assist if Ginger needed help, and she prepped her for the delivery. We then drove to St. Joseph's Hospital, which in 1959 was downtown. After checking in at the admissions desk, I was told to make my way to the visitor 's waiting area. Fathers were not yet welcomed in the delivery rooms. The last time I saw Ginger she was lying on a gurney. I had not yet gotten to the waiting room when my name was called. "You have a baby boy," some man yelled out. Ginger had had one contraction, one big push, and Robert James Barnett, Jr., made his grand entrance—on the gurney. A group of friends and family had placed bets on the date of our baby's birth. I chose April 4, 1959, the date given by the doctor in Melbourne, Australia. I won the bet. The $1,300 was the seed for a fund we set up to be used for college tuition. The easy-delivery-story was repeated on March 11, 1962, when our second son, David Michael Barnett, was born at St. Joseph's Hospital. I believe Ginger's deliveries were quick because of her well-toned, strong abdominal muscles that dancers develop. When Robert (or Rob) and then David were born, hospital practices required that mothers stay in the hospital, in bed, for several nights. On one of those nights with David, I was dancing in an Atlanta Civic Ballet performance. A friend of Ginger's, Teena Stern, came to the hospital. Together, they snuck out, watched the performance, and then snuck back in. If the nurse-nuns suspected anything, they tactfully never said a word about an AWOL patient.

Ginger took her roles and responsibilities of wife, mother and daughter seriously. In addition to her professional dance career and teaching, Ginger was busy driving first Rob, and then Rob and David, to school, to ice-hockey, soccer and any other activity the boys wanted to participate in. Dick asked a lot of his daughter's time. If he wanted to invite a few businessmen to the house for a dinner meeting, he did not hesitate to call Ginger to make the necessary preparations, sometimes with only a few hours' notice. Ginger would stop what she was doing, sometimes leaving a rehearsal, to make a fast trip to the grocery store to buy food, then drop it off at the house for the cook to prepare. Organized and efficient, Ginger could have written a best-selling book on how to be a great project manager. Whatever her family needed, she was there to provide. And she never complained. She even took on an incredibly big project, co-founding the Southeast's first professional modern dance company. Ginger, the bunhead, was pregnant with David when she saw Carl Ratcliff, a modern dancer, audition at Dorothy's studio for a job. "I want to do that," she said. So, after David was born, she started working with Carl. He not only taught modern dance classes at the school, but choreographed modern ballet works for Atlanta Civic Ballet. Ginger took Carl's classes, and she began transitioning from classical ballet to modern dance. Her final classical ballet performance was Lilac Fairy in *Sleeping Beauty*. After the performance, she tossed her toe shoes into the metal trash can and lit a fire. She never wore pointe shoes again. Ginger, Carl Ratcliff and Teena Stern founded the Carl Ratcliff Dance Theatre. Ginger was officially a barefoot dancer. She would continue to dance professionally until the age of sixty, retiring the year I resigned as artistic director of Atlanta Ballet.

Virginia and I struck a pose for this photograph probably around 1958–1959.

While the arts in general, and dancing particularly, were really important to both Ginger and me, so was maintaining a close relationship with the family. During the summer months we took the boys to Washington to visit relatives. We usually drove, taking side trips to places such as Disney Land, and to historic sites. There were the annual holiday celebrations in Atlanta. Thanksgiving, for instance, was a big day of feasting and fun with family and friends, including dancers and staff from the company. To celebrate our 50th wedding anniversary, we went back to Jamaica and took all the kids. The boys were married—David, to Jackie; Robert, to Elizabeth. David and Jackie brought their only son Aaron. Robert and Elizabeth brought their only son Ryan. Elizabeth was pregnant, so grandson Austin can claim that he was in Jamaica, too. We rented a house, which came with a cook and a laundress and a maid upstairs and one downstairs. Another momentous occasion was the huge celebration for my 85th birthday. I never suspected a thing. All of a sudden people started showing up at the house in Asheville, dropped off in chartered buses. People came from all over; it was such a shock. Ginger arranged the whole thing with the help of our friend Kathy McBeth Hutcheson, somehow miraculously keeping the fabulous party a surprise.

In spring 2016 Ginger had her annual physical. The test results were excellent. She did mention to the physician that there was a lump on her neck. They decided to do nothing, but she was told to come back if any changes occurred. It wasn't long before Ginger was back: a second lump had appeared. In April 2016, Ginger was diagnosed with lung cancer. It had metastasized to other parts of her body. Briefly, she underwent radiation treatment in Atlanta. Then she decided to stop further treatment. She wanted to go home to Asheville. Ginger died eleven days before our 60th wedding anniversary, in her bed, surrounded by the family.

Everything was exceptional about Ginger: the way she looked; the way she treated her friends and her family; her honesty. She was not necessarily a Southern belle. And you couldn't walk on her; or take advantage of her. There was nothing phony about her, either. Not only was she a wonderful mother, grandmother, friend and wife, she was a beautiful dancer. And she had a distinguished professional career, both in ballet and modern. She served on the Dance Panel for the Georgia Council for the Arts, Fulton County Arts Council, and Atlanta's Bureau of Cultural Affairs. In 1975, the American Association of University Women gave her an Outstanding Leadership Award. In recognition of her contribution to the arts, she received the Georgia Governor's Award in the Arts in 1984.

In total we spent sixty-one years together, and we were never bored. As I walk through our house, I feel my Ginger when touching the art we collected—the hundreds of pieces of pottery and the statues. There are her pillows she created for me to stroke and to hug. I step outside, onto the deck. The sweet smell of pine-scented trees in the scenic forty-eight acres of forest surrounding out home offers comfort, a peaceful warmth, a reminder of the many times we sat together and watched the sun rise, and set.

Chapter Eight

Atlanta Civic Ballet

In 1958, entering the Atlanta airport building to get our luggage was like stepping into a Quonset hut—a functional facility but without that warm-southern-welcome feeling that the South and its people are known for. Ginger and I, though, were too excited about starting this new stage of life to be bothered much by this omission in southern hospitality. It was such a privilege to be principal dancers and associate artistic directors of what was at this time in dance history America's oldest civic ballet company. This Ginger and I knew prior to our move to Atlanta. What I did not know was how much I would learn from the fifty-four-year-old Dorothy Alexander. Dorothy was born the same year as Balanchine, in 1904. Like Balanchine, who believed it important to start a school before starting a company, and did so in 1934 soon after his move to America, Dorothy did, too, although she was first, in 1922–1923. Furthermore, Balanchine and Dorothy had established schools that were somewhat administratively and financially separate from their companies. In the beginning, Dorothy was the company. She traveled in her car, along with her pianist, and sometimes a male partner, from one gig to another in Atlanta and nearby cities, sometimes dancing in private homes (indoors or outdoors in all sorts of good and bad weather conditions) for all sorts of events and celebrations. It was only after her school enrollment grew and once she had a few well-trained dancers that she started the Dorothy Alexander Concert Group. The company's name would change several times between 1929 and 1943 when it became Atlanta Civic Ballet (ACB). No matter the name of the company, though, her vision would remain the same: that her students must get the highest level of classical ballet training possible; that they would have the performing opportunities to use the art mastered; and that they would give free performances to the public—as a gift. Dorothy's mission statement was "To further Dance Art; to help Dance take its rightful place with the other arts fostered in Atlanta and the South; to serve as an instrument of Education in its aim to direct youth into recreative, enlightening and ennobling pursuits; to offer an opportunity for advanced dancers to continue their work as an avocation; to give experience to dancers interested in professional careers."[1] Prior to her establishing ACB a talented, ambitious ballet student from Georgia had to move to New York City or San Francisco or Europe to get the classical ballet training needed for a professional career. Because of the times this was not much of an option for young girls who were barely in their teens since moving to one of these so-called scary, big American cities—or, heaven forbid, across the ocean to some foreign city, such as London or Paris—without a chaperone was strongly discouraged, if not strictly forbidden. Consequently, few young women considered a professional career in classical ballet. But then Dorothy Alexander in Atlanta, Georgia, decided it was time for a change, and she began shaking up America's cultural mores making it happen. By 1955, her success in Atlanta was noticed by the writer and dance critic Anatole Chujoy, who resided in New York City. He asked her to lead the charge to initiate a grassroots regional ballet movement throughout America. Dorothy accepted the challenge. On April 13, 1956, America's first regional ballet festival was held in Atlanta, which launched the nation's first regional ballet organization, the Southeastern Regional Ballet Association or SERBA. This weekend festival was a critical and financial success. There were a lot of curious nonparticipant-observers at the festival from ballet schools and companies all around the U.S. Impressed and motivated, directors of other civic ballet companies were soon organizing regional associations, following Dorothy's model. Eventually, there would be five regions: Northeast, Southeastern, Southwest, Midstate and Pacific. Dorothy was front and center in guiding them, making certain that her standards were met and maintained. She expected every dancer performing in the annual regional festival's public-attended gala to be well-trained technically, and every student had to be taught and coached on artistry. The choreography had to meet a standard of excellence, too. Weaker companies performed, but not in the one premiere festival performance that was open to the public. To make certain her requirements were followed, an adjudicator—icons such as Alexander Danilova and Ted Shawn, for instance—was paid to visit participating civic ballet companies a few months prior to the spring festival. The adjudicator picked the best five or six companies to perform at the public performance, usually held on a Saturday night. Because of Dorothy's educational objectives, the weekend festival included lectures to help administrators become better managers and to help teachers to become better teachers. There were classes on diet and other subjects pertinent to dance. There were dance classes taught by dance masters to teach students how to become better dancers. I began teaching master classes and lecturing at the regional festivals, as did Balanchine, Danilova, Ted Shawn and lots of others who supported Dorothy's grassroots movement. Dorothy made certain that the mission of the movement was known to the general public by giving lots of interviews in national newspapers and magazines, including *The New York Times*. For Dorothy, the cultural arts were a necessity to promoting and nurturing a civilized society, and she wanted ballet to take its rightful place among the fine arts, theatrical arts, and symphonies that had existed for centuries throughout Europe and the U.S. Historically, ballet in America had been a step-child of opera. However, she believed that ballet could stand on its own. To do this she used the regional ballet movement to raise awareness of ballet as a worthy art form in America, to showcase it as a place of leadership in the national dance world. Furthermore, Dorothy preached that regional companies had a civic duty to offer performances for free or for nominal ticket prices as a gift to their communities. It was her way of building community support and for giving back. Examples of ACB civic performances included Trail Club, Music Group of Studio Club of Atlanta, Atlanta Dogwood Festival, Russian Moonlight Concert for St. Luke's, Uncle Remus Memorial Celebration, Poetry Society of America, American Legion, Civitan Club, Lions Club, Junior League and Shriners. The company often performed with other local arts organizations when asked, such as the Atlanta Opera and Art Institute. One notable event was the Art Institute Beaux Arts Ball. There was lots of touring, also. ACB averaged six to twelve out-of-town performances per season. There was the Dancing Masters of America convention in New York City, and a lecture-demonstration at the National Physical Education Association convention, for instance. Dorothy's civic ballet model was similar to that of youth symphony orchestras in cities throughout America, many of which had evolved, or were evolving, to professional status. Indeed, Dorothy had generously given the net proceeds from ACB's 1946 annual spring concert to the Atlanta Youth Symphony to help the organization become a professional orchestra. The Atlanta Youth Symphony had prospered, and it had become a professional orchestra, the Atlanta Symphony Orchestra. Dorothy and I wanted to do the same for ACB. When I joined the non-professional company as a principal dancer and associate artistic director it was in its 29th year and had been recognized by the major dance magazines for its importance in American dance.[2] By joining Dorothy and ACB, I was joining the historically important grassroots regional ballet movement, too. The regional ballet movement was part of a much broader subject being talked about throughout the U.S.—that is, the purpose and role (if there was a role) of the arts in society. While journalists and university scholars debated whether the arts were "good for people,"[3] Dorothy and I knew that it was, and that "arts" included ballet.

Upon my arrival in Atlanta, from my first step on the tarmac, I was running to get everything done that I wanted to accomplish. My life at NYCB had kept me busy. But my life at ACB was like being in hyperkinetic motion, especially in the first year when there was a lot to learn. Miss Dorothy was so sick when I arrived that a lot of the job-related responsibilities for managing the company were on my shoulders. Also, I had to stay in shape to dance the principal roles, and I had to teach at and to assist Merrilee in running the school. Merrilee Smith, a former ACB dancer, had become co-owner of Dorothy's Atlanta School of Ballet in 1945. Running a school is not easy. There is always so much to do besides teaching, such as collecting tuition in a timely manner from parents so that the bills can be paid. The school had received accreditation, which meant that we had the required government approval to admit foreign students, and there was a lot of paperwork involved to get the required visas approved. Once a

Dorothy Alexander, founder of the oldest continually operating ballet company in the United States, and her associates, in Atlanta, Georgia. From left to right are Hildegarde Bennett, Merrilee Smith, Hilda Gumm and Dorothy Alexander (by Marion D. Ware, courtesy Anne Burton Avery).

student arrived in Atlanta, a lot of time and effort was then needed to assist her in finding housing, learning how to use public transportation or to buy a car, with grocery and household shopping needs, and much more, including how to speak Georgia-drawl English. Thank goodness there were some great volunteers on the ACB team, including Hildegarde Bennett and Hilda Gumm, because my time and effort had to be directed to running the company, time and effort that I was glad to shoulder. By shifting most of the company duties to me, Dorothy had more time to recover from the energy-sapping treatments she was receiving for cancer, and she could concentrate on the regional ballet movement she was leading, which was progressing so fast that it was decided a national organization should be established. Once again, significant people in the dance capital of America, New York City, pointed their fingers at Atlanta. Dorothy had become chairman of a committee to create the National Association for Regional Ballet (NARB). Committee members included Ben Sommers, president of Capezio, Ballet Makers; Alice M. Bingham of Capezio; Anatole Chujoy, founder/editor, *Dance News;* Doris Hering, associate editor, *Dance Magazine;* Lydia Joel, editor, *Dance Magazine;* and P.W. Manchester, author and managing editor, *Dance News.* At least Dorothy was no longer working a full-time job with the Atlanta Public Schools; she had retired in 1952. Nor was she dancing. She had retired in 1947 at the age of forty-three.

There was so much to do in this new phase of my professional ballet career that I had almost no time to get quickly settled in Dick's house: the upcoming fall ballet-performing season and resuming the school after the summer break were a threatening thunder-booming storm cloud looming above my head. Thus, Ginger and I split up the duties that required our immediate attention. She got us settled into our new home and began preparing for Robert's birth. In addition, she taught at the school and took dance classes to stay in good physical conditioning. We were burning the candle at both ends.

Dorothy and Merrilee had two school locations, the tiny one-studio room in Dorothy's Ansley Park house, and the second in a building in Buckhead—3215 Cains Hill Place—which had two studios, one on the ground floor and one on the second floor. The walls on the first-floor studio could be opened up. Chairs were set up in the parking lot and the studio became a sort of workshop theater—a stage for a school performance and even for a company performance when a larger theater was not required. The architect who developed the plans to renovate the building into a dance school, a la theater space, was A. Thomas Bradbury. He was married to Janette, who was ACB Chair of the Board of Trustees. The couple had a son and two daughters, and the two daughters, Lane and Lynda, had been students at the Atlanta School of Ballet. Lynda was in ACB when I arrived, but Lane had become a professional dancer-actor and was living in New York City. In addition to being a well-known architect in Atlanta, Tom had a law degree. What was most unusual for the times is that Janette had a degree in law as well. (Thomas Bradbury would become famous in the late 1960s as the architect for Georgia's new Governor's mansion on West Paces Ferry Road.)

There was so much to learn and to do that first year at ACB that my brain was spinning like châiné turns endlessly circling the stage. And I quickly developed an appreciation for what Betty Cage, Barbara Horgan, Mr. B and Kirstein were doing to keep SAB and NYCB running smoothly and growing.

For example, I had to learn how to prepare budget reports and other reports to present to the board of trustees. Dorothy had a bookkeeper and Merrilee was running the school, but I ran the company, which meant choosing the ballets, casting them and running the rehearsals, for instance. Then there was my initiation into the role of a choreographer. Add in injuries and dancers who were of high school age in a non-professional company … it made me have to be especially flexible in scheduling my day. There was the annual SERBA festival every spring and the final year ACB concert to prepare for. There was the artistic staff (mostly volunteers from the Atlanta community) that I had to supervise to arrange the lighting, sets, and costumes required. There were the accompanists and, for those really special occasions, the conductor of the Atlanta Symphony Orchestra to work with, which required tactful discussions and negotiations, especially if we disagreed on tempo. There were lots and lots of meetings to attend. Thank goodness I inherited Mom's high-energy DNA. Because my roles at ACB were done without a salary I was working at Rich's department store during the day and teaching at the school in the late afternoons and evenings. My day started early and my usual time to get home was about 10:00 p.m. At Rich's I coordinated all the merchandise, saw that all the clothing, shoes, hats, for instance, went to the right departments in the store. My boss encouraged me to give up dance and find a career at Rich's. It was certainly a more secure job, and the offer was tempting. I would think about it a lot for the next four years, weighing the pluses and minuses.

Soon after my new ACB job started, I received a significant letter from Mr. B. It was permission to stage any of his ballets that I could remember, without a royalty fee. I immediately jumped at this great opportunity. My second year at ACB I staged "Snow" in December and all the divertissements through the second act of *The Nutcracker*. I recall that ACB was the first company in the nation Balanchine allowed to do his *The Nutcracker*, and his generosity made us famous in Georgia. It gave us national awareness, and it saved ACB a lot of money. When I arrived in 1958 the budget was $16,000. Dorothy's practice was to put all the revenues from performances in the bank and to never use it until absolutely necessary. We always had money coming in, but we only spent what we had. The budget was small because almost everyone associated with ACB was a volunteer. The Board of Trustees was a working board—literally. Those members who could sew made the costumes, for example; and almost everyone served as ushers at the performances. The fifty or so trustees served on committees, which were: social, property, wardrobe, costume, studio, bulletin board and contact. Other committees were formed, on a temporary basis, as needed. Many trustees also were members of the

Atlanta Civic Ballet Guild, whose primary responsibility was organizing fundraising events, such as the annual ACB ball and annual luncheon. In addition to the small tasks, such as writing copy for the flyers and newspaper ads and stuffing envelopes, we all helped to build the sets: hammering nails and painting, for instance—doing whatever it took to make the productions look as professional as possible.

Because Dorothy was well-connected in the Atlanta civic community there were many requests to dance at social and fundraising events. Some of what Dorothy viewed as the company's civic-duty-responsibility performances occurred at less than ideal venues, though. We danced on cement floors in the lobbies of municipal buildings; on carpeted or tiled floors in hotel ballrooms; on grass or on not-always-the best-for-dance temporary stages in parks, or at the Atlanta's Women's Club on a small stage. Some buildings did not have air conditioning, and it could be horribly hot. In the winter months dancing on a cement floor could be tendon-tearing cold. Yet I was having so much fun in this new chapter of my professional ballet career that never once did I think: What have I done! I was ambitious. I wanted to get ahead with my career while I could still do it, and I believed that ACB was my ticket for getting what I wanted. I knew that Dorothy and Merrilee were outstanding teachers—I had only to look at Ginger and at the dancers in ACB. But it was only soon after moving to Atlanta that I became aware of ACB's excellent reputation throughout the U.S., and that Dorothy's nationally recognized reputation was extraordinary for someone residing outside New York City or San Francisco. As far as Ginger and I were concerned, leaving New York City when we did was the perfect decision. Sixty years later, there are no regrets. I would make the same decision again today.

Dorothy's reputation was well-earned. Her standards were high. She had very, very strict rules and she enforced them. Students from the Atlanta School of Ballet had to audition for a position in ACB; the minimum age was thirteen. An Audition Board—directors and the teaching staff—was responsible for determining which students were accepted and which were not. Once a student was accepted into ACB, she (rarely was there a he) had to sign a contract that was for three years—from high school up until she graduated and either went to college or became employed. Dorothy did not push the importance of marriage to her young ladies as much as a lot of people did in the 1950s. She wasn't against marriage; she just didn't believe that a woman's sole role in life was to be a wife and mother. If a woman chose not to work, that is, to stay at home and raise her kids, that was okay. What she did push, however, was that no matter one's chosen path, it was one's moral responsibility to give back to the community as a volunteer in local civic organizations—a lesson she preached and preached and preached to every student in her school and to dancers in the company. The contract company members signed had nothing to do with money, as the dancers were not paid. It was a contract of agreement on Dorothy's rules, a lot having to do with proper behavior. If a dancer was absent from any rehearsal three times (in the three-year contract period) without a satisfactory excuse, she was excommunicated. Permanently. If an absence was caused because of sickness, she had to provide a written letter from a physician justifying the absence. No letter meant an unexcused absence. It didn't matter if you were a star or at the end of the totem pole: three unexcused absences and you were out. "No social obligation is considered excusable," Dorothy wrote in "The Atlanta Civic Ballet Company By-Laws." And since most of the twenty-one to twenty-five company dancers were in high school—which meant that rehearsals and performances were scheduled for Friday night, and then all day Saturday through Saturday night—a teenage girl's usual social highlights, such as dates with a beau, were practically impossible, except during the summer. If a company member was absent from a rehearsal, at any time, without first notifying the director, co-director or managing director, the dancer could be dropped from the ballet being rehearsed, or, if the offense was considered really bad, ejected from the company. Being a dancer in the company was expensive. She had to take at least two classes during the week at the Atlanta School of Ballet, and classes were scheduled in the late afternoon. Because company class, rehearsals and/or performances were Friday night and Saturday, Sunday was the only day off. Dancers, or in most cases their parents, had to pay for almost everything—classes, pointe shoes, practice uniforms (black leotards and pink tights) and character shoes. Also, there were the expenses for transportation, meals and lodging for out-of-town gigs. About the only thing a dancer did not have to pay for was her costumes. Dorothy often said, "If a dancer misses even one rehearsal, she is causing the other dancers who do attend to be inconvenienced." It was from Dorothy that I learned to be strict, but fair, one of my principles that I pass along today. Joey Carman, a former student at the school and a company dancer, who is now a distinguished writer, credits our Atlanta Ballet culture with teaching him an important lesson: "The ballet world is a tough one, but I never forgot how important it is to treat people well."[4]

On April 4, 1959, Robert James Barnett, Jr., was born. I beamed with pride the first time I saw my son. He was so beautiful. Soon after Robert's birth, Ginger was back in class and at rehearsals and teaching full time.

Balanchine came to visit America's oldest ballet company in 1959, the year of ACB's 30th anniversary. In the early 1950s, the name Balanchine was not well-known outside the New York City area. That was changing, however, and his visit had the Atlanta arts community grapevine buzzing. The Guild of the Atlanta Civic Ballet had invited him to be a featured guest at an ACB fundraising event. Balanchine was aloof and standoffish with most of the dancers in NYCB when I was there. He might pass you on the street or in a hallway and never make eye contact, never speak. It's not that he was rude to me; he just often seemed distracted. Once I was no longer dancing in NYCB, though, Mr. B treated me like a good friend. He loved Ginger. He was charmed by her personality, and he liked her long neck. While in Atlanta he saw me dance. My partner was the sixteen-year-old teenager, Anne Burton, who had grown up in the Atlanta School of Ballet, enrolling when she was age six. So impressed was Mr. B that he offered Anne a Ford Foundation Scholarship to study at his School of American Ballet. Anne moved to New York City. Before there was a National Endowment for the Arts in Washington, D.C., or any significant federal government subsidies (other than the former Works Progress Administration subsidies during the Great Depression era of the 1930s), serious support for the arts was mainly available from a few major corporations, such as the Ford Foundation. It was started by Edsel Ford in 1936—the son of Henry Ford, the founder of the Ford Motor Company. According to the Ford Foundation website, the resources, such as grants, were to be used for scientific, educational and charitable purposes to promote the public welfare. Support was given to all types of institutions and organizations, and because Edsel Ford was passionate about the arts and humanities, the arts were included. Luckily for Kirstein and Balanchine, the Ford Foundation relocated its office from Michigan to New York City in 1953. Kirstein's networking talents and skills obviously were successful, because by 1958 SAB and NYCB had become major recipients of what would over the years total millions of dollars in benefits. San Francisco Ballet was another major beneficiary, also. For example, the support provided by the Ford Foundation enabled well-known individuals from SAB (such as Mr. B) and San Francisco Ballet School to visit dance studios east and west of the Mississippi. These people were on a search to recruit the most talented students to study at SAB and San Francisco Ballet school from one to three years. The idea was for those students who lasted in the scholarship program to have the opportunity to be picked to join NYCB or San Francisco Ballet. The regional dance movement also benefited from the beneficence of the Ford Foundation, as many of the recipients selected for a Ford Foundation scholarship were from a regional civic ballet company. Anne Burton was only one of many examples; it established her career as a professional classical ballet dancer and, later, as a teacher. Soon after she moved to New York City to train at SAB on a Ford

Foundation scholarship, she was asked to join NYCB. She would stay through 1963. She toured with the company to the Soviet Union, which was quite an emotional experience for Mr. B and, therefore, for the company: It was his first time to return to Russia since 1924. After leaving NYCB, Anne moved to Utah to get a bachelor's degree in ballet at the University of Utah. While there she danced principal roles with Willam Christensen's Utah Ballet, which is now Ballet West. Willam was my friend Lew Christensen's brother. P.W. Manchester in her *New York Times* article "Dance: Regional, Nonprofessional Ballet Companies Hold Lively Spring Festivals," who was writing on the status of the regional movement in 1961, said, "Proof of the high standard that some of these dancers attain is that today all of our professional companies contain members who were formerly with a regional group, many of them having made the transition from nonprofessional to professional status without any additional training."[5] In addition to Anne Burton, Balanchine invited one other ACB dancer to enroll at SAB on scholarship in 1959: Caroline "Carol" Todd, a dancer in the corps de ballet. Like Anne, Carol danced with NYCB. She stayed several years longer than Anne, though. Then she danced with American Ballet Theatre (ABT) until her retirement.

In 1960, Dorothy was one of the distinguished annual Dance Magazine Awards recipients. The two other recipients were Fred Astaire and George Balanchine. Dorothy was honored for her outstanding work as founder and director of ACB. I did not attend the ceremony; I was too busy running the company to have the time to take off. Famous attendees in the whose-who of the dance world included Alexandra Danilova, Carmen de Lavallade, Merce Cunningham, Ruth Page, George Zoritch and Igor Youskevitch. The award ceremony was at the New York Athletic Club on May 6, 1960. The same day as my 35th birthday. Ted Shawn presented the award to Dorothy. In his remarks he said,

> Here is a woman so beautiful, so warm, so gracious, such a true Southern lady it's hard to realize that she had done some of the most grueling of pioneering. Her looks are deceptive, because hers is such determination, such courage and indefatigable devotion that she has gone through hell to achieve what she's done.[6]

While the cancer had to have been taking its toll on her body, anyone meeting Dorothy for the first time would not have known how much she suffered. Her battle with cancer would continue off and on for many years. Yet she always maintained her poise, her grace, her beauty. When I met her she was slim and 5'4" in height with striking blue eyes and gorgeous silver-streaked hair pinned up on top of her head in a trademark dancer's bun. Standing tall, with her ballerina-posture always perfectly erect, she was an inspiration to us all.

Another big event that same year was the SERBA festival. Once again it was in Atlanta. There were at least twelve ballet companies participating, as compared to eight in 1956. There were attendees from non-member small companies throughout the U.S., as well as important people from the big dance cities, to see how this regional movement Dorothy was leading was doing. Mayor William B. Hartsfield proclaimed the week of March 27, 1960, "Ballet Week" in Atlanta. Alexandra Danilova was the adjudicator that year, and ACB was one of the SERBA companies she picked to dance in the open-to-the-public festival performance. Ginger and I danced a pas de deux. The performance was at the Tower Theater on Peachtree Street. It's too bad that the Tower was demolished, the bare land paved and used as a parking lot. It was a perfect theater for dance, and the interior was just as elegant as the Fox's. It had about 1,800 to 2,000 seats; there were three balconies. It had a good-size stage for dance productions, and the Tower was perfect for ACB. The Atlanta Symphony Orchestra used to play there, also. I have a lot of wonderful memories: Our first *The Nutcracker* was performed there; *Serenade* was performed there. I loved that theater.

Because I had Mr. B's permission to stage *Serenade* I asked a friend, Una Kai, to set the ballet on ACB. Una and I had been in NYCB together, and she

Students and staff at our summer program at Mt. Pinnacle Dance Camp in North Carolina in 1961.

was currently an assistant ballet mistress at NYCB. Despite being neoclassical, the ballet was well received by the southern patrons and the newspaper critics who reviewed it. As if we didn't have enough to do, Ginger and I, along with Dorothy's competent assistant and close friend, Hildegarde Bennett, opened a summer camp in Flat Rock, N.C. The Mt. Pinnacle Dance Camp was held at a camp owned by a Jewish family. The enrollment totaled about fifty students. We kept the camp going for several years.

In 1962, four major events happened. At the top of the list was the birth of our son David Michael Barnett, who was born on March 11. Soon after the birth, Ginger was back at work full time. During the pregnancy, Dorothy had asked Ginger and me to join her in watching a modern dancer audition for a job. Carl Ratcliff and his wife, Peggy—who was a visual artist, mainly working with enameled copper—had moved to Atlanta from California because Peggy had family here. Carl probably knew of Dorothy's reputation for integrating classical ballet and modern dance technique and it is no surprise that he sought her out. Carl got the job. He began teaching one or two classes a week at the school. He had been trained by the modern dancer Lester Horton in California. Horton was responsible for training a number of important people in America's rapidly growing modern dance community, such as Alvin Ailey. In addition to dancing in Horton's company, Carl had also danced in several Hollywood movies. After leaving Horton, Carl and a former Horton dancer, Bella Lewitzky, had teamed up for several years. She would visit Atlanta on more than one occasion to work with Carl. Once Carl was hired by Dorothy, he began choreographing works for ACB, and he danced in the company. After David was born, Ginger started working with Carl. It was the beginning of her transition from bunhead to barefoot dancer. A third major happening was the official announcement of my position as artistic director of ACB (I had actually been fulfilling most of the day-to-day responsibilities of the position since my arrival in 1958). My four-year mental debate on whether to choose a career at Rich's or a career with ACB ended. I quit my job at Rich's. Dorothy had effectively retired as artistic director in 1961, however, because I was still working at Rich's, Merrilee had become interim artistic director. Another change in 1962 was that I became administrative director of the Atlanta School of Ballet, with Merrilee as the director.

It would have been a fantastic year, had it not been for the tragic Orly Field catastrophe on June 3, 1962. Several of the one hundred and six Atlantans who died in the crash of the Boeing 707 upon takeoff at the airport outside of Paris, France, were major supporters of the Atlanta Art Association. They were on an organized museum cultural tour. Although I knew a lot of them, none was actively involved with ACB. Atlanta arts community leaders decided to build a complex dedicated to the arts as a memorial to those that died. It was Dick Rich who led the fundraising campaign to design and build what would become the Atlanta Memorial Arts Center on Peachtree Street. ACB did our part when we gave the proceeds from the 1964 *Nutcracker* to the Memorial Arts Center building fund.

Ginger and I were so busy dancing, teaching and raising the two kids, that getting to Washington to visit my parents was difficult to do. Fortunately, Dad and Mom visited us in Atlanta a few times, although Mom more often. She adored Ginger and the boys. There were instances when Ginger took the boys to Washington in the summer and left them with Mom and Dad. I would fly there a few weeks later and pick them up. There were even a few trips in January. Surprisingly for two young kids used to Atlanta's more temperate climate, the boys liked the frigid-cold winters in Washington. (After graduating from high school, Rob lived in Washington for about two years.) When they were older, Ginger, and strong-arm peer pressure from friends, got our sons interested in playing ice hockey in Atlanta, and they were good. On mornings when the boys had to be on the ice at 4:00 a.m. or 5:00 a.m. (it was the only time the team could reserve the rink), Ginger devotedly took them. Needing a caffeine charge while waiting to pick them up, she would drive to the nearby Dunkin' Donuts. She got to know the regulars really well, including a few local policemen. There was an ice-skating rink in Buckhead, near Roswell Road, and another out in Marietta. It was in Marietta that the Flames, the professional ice hockey team, played. We had season tickets and Ginger and I would take the boys to the games. Thus, the winter sports in Washington were a real thrill for our boys. Unlike in Atlanta with its artificial ice rinks, they could ice skate out in the wild on a frozen pond and play in the heavy snow. One winter in Washington David disappeared in a snowbank. Luckily for David, Dad dug him out, and fast.

When Mom visited us in Atlanta she had to make biscuits every time she came. Dick, especially, loved Mom's biscuits. Even though her life in Wenatchee was so much different from mine in Atlanta, she never showed any envy because of our lifestyle. She was proud of my achievements, and she was proud of Ginger's, too. And she and Dick got along extremely well. Mom truly enjoyed Sunday mornings (the one day Ginger and I had off) eating brunch with family and friends inside the pool house. After playing bridge, Dick's second passion was playing tennis. Routinely, his tennis group gathered on Sunday and played before joining our family for brunch. Our son Rob got to play some, too, until he was fourteen and began to beat Dick's tennis friends; then they wouldn't let him play much anymore. The adults drank mint juleps, real mint juleps. There was another significant difference between Washington and Georgia, although a difference that was not pleasant for any of us—the anti–Semitism and anti-integration practices in the South. It is not that Mom and Dad didn't know about these discriminatory laws and practices in the 1960s, it was that in Washington people did not have the same experiences as those residing in other parts of the country, especially in the North and the South. I grew up playing and working with people from lots of different religious and ethnic groups. In fact, the valedictorian of my high school graduating class in 1943 was black.

The Rich family showed their disagreement with Atlanta's discriminatory laws and practices in many ways. For instance, when Dick was encouraged to join a prominent, distinguished private club, he said no, because many of his Jewish friends were not allowed to join. When Ginger turned eighteen she was invited to be a debutante at this same club and said no because her Jewish friends were not invited. The New York City Metropolitan Opera used to tour. In Atlanta the performances were at the Fox Theatre and every year Dick bought center orchestra section tickets. On more than one occasion he gave his tickets to Martin Luther King, Jr., and his wife, Coretta. She was a singer and loved the opera. Because Rich's department store had to follow the local, state and federal laws that were discriminatory, however, there were a few troubling happenings that affected the family anyway. We even had to have police protection at the house for a brief period when the sit-ins were going on in small towns and big cities throughout America. Government laws barred blacks from eating in the same restaurants as whites, and Rich's department stores had restaurants. When some black students from the local black universities staged a sit-in in the Magnolia Room at Rich's, there was a lot of publicity because police arrested the respectful and well-behaved young men and women for violating the law. Dick thwarted the Jim Crow era laws and rules whenever he could unless his actions would cause Rich's a huge fine—or worse. Peer pressure he shrugged off, though, even if it meant alienating friends. I know that it was because of Rich's importance in the community and Dick's actions supporting the Civil Rights Movement that our family was targeted. For example, the boys got some anonymous and threatening telephone calls, which had us all frightened. For a while we had to keep the interior lights in the house turned off at night, and police patrolled our property. We surmised that the threats were coming from members of the Ku Klux Klan. The Atlanta Civic Ballet and the school were not affected, however. And during this troubling era I tried to stay focused on running the company and earning money to support the family.

Even though the economy had suffered a mild recession beginning in 1958, extending through 1961, ACB was not greatly affected. And by the mid–

1960s we were on a fantastic onward-and-upward rollercoaster ride. Morale could not have been higher. Touring with the Colonel's Original Ballet Russe company throughout Europe was a real learning phase—the ballets, and the people I danced with, were my introduction to this wonderful world of dance. Next, being a first-generation dancer at NYCB was truly extraordinary for me, because I was at the start of something that was so new and important in the evolution of ballet in America. I was fortunate to be with this genius Balanchine: Just being in his space made you learn stuff. Joining ACB, however, as associate artistic director, was like starting my professional ballet career all over again: I had to learn a new set of skills. It was not easy at first, but after seven years of hard work and lots of learning I was having so much fun. Life was busy, sometimes too busy, but great nevertheless. My vision on how to grow ACB, to move it upward to the next level, to make it a professional company, was always on my mind. And it was going to get even better … so I thought.

Chapter Nine

The Atlanta Ballet

My vision to take Atlanta Civic Ballet to professional status was sorely thwarted beginning in the 1960s because of a couple of serious missteps that tested my patience. In addition to the scholarship program that provided financial support to individual dancers to study at Balanchine's SAB or the San Francisco School of Ballet, the Ford Foundation also provided support to companies that wanted to advance from non-professional to professional status, and ACB was on the foundation's list of candidates. Dorothy, however, decided that if ACB accepted the foundation's support (and consequently its oversight), it would strengthen Balanchine's aim to centralize ballet in America, which was the opposite of what she was doing with the regional ballet movement. And she was very vocal about it. Interviewed for an article in *Dance Magazine* in 1964, she said, "The acute need to keep a balance between our centralized professional activities and our decentralized regional semi-professional activities cannot be ignored."[1] I was with Dorothy and representatives from the Ford Foundation at a meeting to discuss which regional ballet companies should be supported and therefore can confirm what Helen Smith would write in a *Dance Magazine* article: that "Ballet Society of the New York City Ballet was offering to take many regional companies under its wing by offering such lures as access to Balanchine choreography, costumes, and potential large grants from Ford. Alexander perceived this as a threat to regional ballet, a gobbling up by a big New York company of the little companies in the hinterlands… 'I knew I was sacrificing the Atlanta Ballet for regional ballet,' said Alexander."[2] Consequently, ACB was kicked off the Ford Foundation list. Two regional ballet companies that did take advantage of, and benefit from, the Ford Foundation grants were Boston Ballet and Pennsylvania Ballet. Dorothy came to regret her decision. Later, she said it was a mistake. Balanchine was not happy with her decision, either. While Dorothy's decision not to get involved with the Ford Foundation made it harder for me to move ACB up to professional status, I was determined that it would not stop me. Then in 1965 an Atlantan, Chris Manos, presented

an opportunity that seemed even better than that of the Ford Foundation—
a union with his Municipal Theatre.

Theater Under the Stars (TUT) was started about the early 1950s to present summer musicals in Atlanta's Chastain Park, an outdoor theater with a seating capacity of about 6,000. It is like the Muny in St. Louis, although on a much smaller scale. Ginger and I had danced in two summer TUT musicals, *Carousel* and *Wizard of Oz*. Musicals are popular entertainment in cities because they usually make money (paying big-name Broadway stars to perform is often worth it); whereas, theater arts productions are a bit iffy when it comes to ending the year with a profit. Chris, however, believed he had the magic touch: that he could offer the Atlanta community both musicals and theater arts (what was sometimes referred to as highbrow arts) productions and make a profit on both. Around 1964, Chris decided to augment the TUT summer entertainment at Chastain Park with an Atlanta opera company and a theater company—his "Grand Opera Season"—he called it. The companies were not under TUT, though, but under the umbrella of his Municipal Theatre enterprise.[3] When Chris decided to add a ballet company to this Municipal Theatre consortium he chose ACB, and Dorothy and I did not hesitate to say yes. Each company was to perform for one week at Chastain Park. The fundraising campaign to build the Atlanta Memorial Arts Center (lead by Dick Rich), had progressed to the stage where the opening date had been set—1968. We were told that the complex would have at least two state-of-the-art theaters for ballet and opera productions. Once the center was opened, Manos intended for the opera, theater and ballet companies to perform their fall and winter seasons there. To make certain no other arts organization in the Atlanta area got first scheduling rights to the theaters, Chris submitted a proposal to the Arts Alliance board of directors to lease theater space in the Memorial Arts Center for three years. At ACB we were feeling really good about this union with Municipal Theatre. At last ACB would have a home theater. Because Dorothy, the Board and I were so certain that merging with Municipal Theatre was the best business decision ever for taking the company to professional status, we gave Chris practically everything he wanted to manage ACB, including most of our money. We kept our own board, though.

The ballet's first production under the auspices of Municipal Theatre was in summer 1965—an ambitious (some would say you-must-be-out-of-your-mind) full-length *Swan Lake*. Chris Manos was the managing director of the production. I was the ballet master, along with a lot of other responsibilities, including dancing in the performance. I contacted David Blair, a principal dancer with London's Royal Ballet, to stage the Royal's Petipa-Ivanov version. ACB would make history as the first U.S. company to perform this version in its entirety. There were about sixteen dancers plus nine apprentices in ACB. I figured I could add another ten from the school for a total of maybe thirty-five dancers. David and I wanted a cast of at least fifty, though, and the search for more dancers began. (There was no cast B, and I kept my fingers crossed that there would be no serious injuries or illnesses requiring last-minute substitutes.) The contract included rented costumes from Royal Ballet and salaries and expenses for a few leads and soloists, including David Blair and his wife, Royal Ballet dancer Maryon Lane; Lupe Serrano from ABT; and four soloists from Ruth Page's Chicago Opera Ballet. Also hired was Lupe's husband, Kenneth Schermerhorn, a conductor with ABT. The remaining dancers recruited were not paid; and neither was Ginger nor I. Because I had been an adjudicator at regional ballet festivals, I already knew of some prospects to invite who were not only technically proficient but willing to pay their own expenses for the rehearsals and performances. Auditions were held to find the additional soloists and corps de ballet required, and dancers auditioned from all over: Texas, Boston, Pennsylvania, Tennessee, South Carolina, Florida and California. From Georgia there were dancers picked from civic ballet companies such as Ruth Mitchell Dance Company and Pittman Corry's Southern Ballet.

The plan was to perform the ballet nightly for one week. Opening night was August 24. David Blair was Siegfried and Lupe Serrano was Odette and Odile. Ginger and I danced the Neapolitan pas de deux. Pittman Corry was Von Rothbart. Dorothy was the queen mother. Chris Manos had a set department, and they built the sets. The pick-up orchestra was filled with musicians from The Atlanta Symphony Orchestra.

It was David Blair's first time to stage the full-length ballet. It was my first time to organize such an ambitious production or to be a ballet master for a full-length *Swan Lake*. There were only about four hectic weeks to rehearse all the dancers, most of whom were learning their roles for the first time. Tech and dress rehearsals are always stressful when you're putting music, sets and props, lighting and dancing together for the first time. Add in the unpredictable summer weather dancing in an open-air venue—especially on days of high humidity and temperatures of 92-degree heat—and emotional and physical stresses can cause a person's blood pressure to soar. The logistics involved in mounting such a major production were almost as overwhelming as a migraine headache. Every detail was examined, from what I would do in the event of an electrical failure to costume worries. And the latter became real when the borrowed costumes from Royal Ballet did not arrive on schedule: they were sitting in the bowels of a ship stuck in the Jacksonville harbor because of a maritime strike. We had to plead for a shipment to be air-expressed from London and some of the Royal Ballet costumes sent were from ballets other than *Swan Lake*. Not surprisingly, there were lots of high-adrenaline-pumping days before the launch of this mammoth production that kept us all in a furious-frenzy-state of nervous excitability. *Patience and tolerance* was the mantra of each day. Still, there were some emotional outbursts, some unkind words spoken because of a flare-up of tempers, that required Dorothy, Ginger or me to have to soothe more than a few hurt feelings. While I did my best to appear calm, to act as if I had no worries, I definitely felt like Atlas—the world was weighing heavy on my shoulders. Opening night is always fraught with lots of questions, and worries. For instance, would there be enough patrons to occupy enough seats in the 6,000-plus theater to avoid embarrassment? How would the patrons respond to our performance?

Opening night, holding my breath, I practically hyperventilated counting the cars slowly entering the parking lot. Even though advanced ticket sales were great, I was pleased to observe more and more well-heeled and well-dressed people standing by their cars, enjoying the ritual pre-show tailgating party. As the crowd grew larger the sounds of happy people grew louder. Then, one by one the musicians showed up, adding their welcome discordant warm-up notes to the festive atmosphere. Satisfied when all seemed as it should be, I rushed back stage to put on my makeup and to get into my costume. A stage manager announced that the gates were open; and I could hear the sounds of people laughing and joking while strolling into the open-air theater to take their seats. The musicians silenced their instruments. There was a loud burst of applause from the audience when, right on time, Schermerhorn took his place on the podium in the orchestra pit. He raised his baton. Then, with his commanding and decisive downbeat, the first notes of the beautiful Tchaikovsky melody floated up into the heavenly summer air. At the end, the Atlanta audience could not have been more expressive in their enthusiastic response. Opening night was a tremendous success. And so was the entire week of performances. "The unthinkable becomes inevitable when the daring take command," wrote the *Dance Magazine* reviewer George Beiswanger in his article "Swan Lake in Atlanta."[4] He said, "Suffice it to say that four weeks of intensive training served to bring to flower that which forty years of regional soil-building and seed-nurturing had made ready."[5] It was high praise indeed to Queen Dorothy and to all of us disciples in the regional ballet movement.

Another big happening was ACB's first full-length production of Balanchine's *The Nutcracker*. I had only set parts of the ballet before; thus, I got in touch with the former NYCB dancer Victoria "Vicky" Simon, who is experienced at staging the entire ballet. Vicky was one of the original candy canes who danced with me in the "Candy Cane" divertissement in NYCB's 1954 premiere. She is a good friend, and she stayed with Ginger and me. I recall that *The Atlanta Constitution* newspaper (as a gift to the city) sponsored the ballet by purchasing every seat in the theater. Any person wanting to attend had to request a ticket by mail, however. Consequently, every seat in the Municipal Auditorium on Courtland Street was taken; and there was a waiting list for tickets. AB's first full-length *The Nutcracker* closed the year with great fanfare and lots of cheers.

In 1966, I received a telephone call that no son or daughter wants to get. James "Jim" Garfield Barnett had died. I was shocked by the devastating news. The last time I spoke on the telephone to my seventy-seven-year-old Dad he was in good health. He was maintaining a physically active lifestyle; he was still hunting. In fact, he had been hunting when he died. It was not unusual

A photograph of Virginia Barnett performing with the Atlanta Ballet in *The Nutcracker*. Virginia is the principal dancer in the center (by Marion D. Ware, from author's collection, *George Balanchine's The Nutcracker*®, choreography by George Balanchine © the George Balanchine Trust)

for him to be gone from home overnight or not to tell Mom where in the woods he might go to hunt. But after he had not returned home for a couple of days, Mom had called a relative to ask about Dad's whereabouts, who in turn called another relative, until finally a cousin was found who just happened to have talked to Dad about where in the woods he planned to hunt. The cousin and the coroner drove up into the mountains and found Dad's truck. They soon found his body, the rifle by his side. He had had a massive heart attack or a stroke. If there is one thing I will remember most about Dad it was his fondness for bear cubs. While he might have gotten criticized from some people for taking visitors up the mountain to shoot brown and grizzly bears, his treatment of orphan bear cubs was beyond reproach. Whenever he found two cubs (and there were usually two, not one) hiding up in a tree, he would coax them down. He would carry them by horseback to our house and secure them in a stall in the barn if it was cold, or in the yard. Never inside our house, though—Mom would have killed him. I can remember a time when Dad took a nap in the front yard, two cubs curled up by his side. After a few days, he would call the forest rangers, and they would take the cubs to a zoo or release them in the reserve. If while riding in the forest Dad found a half-eaten horse, it was a sure bet that a renegade old bear had killed it. Most bears lived on berries but, occasionally, there would be an old bear that had gotten a taste of fresh meat. Once that happened wild and domestic animals were at risk for their lives, and ranchers had little choice but to protect the horses and cattle that roamed the mountain ranges freely—the bear had to be found and killed. And if it was a female bear with cubs, Dad would take the orphaned cubs home. One day Dad witnessed a 300-pound female bear drop down out of a tree—landing on a grazing, unsuspecting horse's back, crushing the spine and killing the horse instantly. On this occasion, Dad decided to hunt and to trap the bear; he didn't want to kill her. He and a few friends succeeded in trapping her but then she ran, and the heavy log she dragged got caught between two trees. Not having a tranquilizer gun, they had to manhandle her to try and secure a metal coffee can (holes were punched to allow air to circulate) on her jerking face while avoiding her sharp teeth. After she was muzzled Dad spotted two cubs up in the tree. Deciding that momma was really old, and that she was not going to live much longer, one of the men shot her. After coaxing the cubs out of the tree, they put them in gunny sacks. The sacks were slung across a horse's back, one cub on each side, and they were carried down the mountain. It was an incredibly hot day, and it took a couple of hours to get down to the house. Dad then put the cubs on leashes and took them to the creek to cool off and get a drink. Unfortunately, one cub drank too much water. He got sick and died.

Dad kept the surviving cub a little longer than usual but eventually gave him to the rangers to let loose in the reserve. Balanchine and Dick Rich were impressed with my dad—a real American wild-west cowboy. Dad was adventurous, a brave man but not a daredevil. He was tough, yet tender. I miss him very much.

Dad with an orphan bear cub that he rescued and brought home.

The Municipal Theatre's 1966 Chastain Park summer ballet production was the full-length *Sleeping Beauty*. Again, David Blair came to Atlanta to stage the Royal Ballet's version, which was based on Petipa's choreography. Again, Dorothy danced, or rather pantomimed, the role of the queen mother. David and his wife danced the two leads. Anne Burton and I danced the "Bluebird" divertissement. Ginger danced Lilac Fairy, and Carl Ratcliff was Carabosse. I held auditions to fill the soloist and corps de ballet positions. Once again the weather cooperated and the production was a success for ACB.

After years of wishing and planning, the company officially became professional in 1967. I dropped the word *Civic,* and the Atlanta Ballet (AB) was born. One of the first things I had done in 1966 when establishing AB was to telephone Anne Burton to offer her a job—a paying job in our new professional company. She agreed. I recruited Anne for many reasons, including

Here I am performing "Bluebird" in the Atlanta Ballet's *Sleeping Beauty*. To the right is Anne Burton Avery.

as my regular partner. Having partnered with her before she moved to New York City on the Ford Foundation scholarship, I knew that the two of us were perfect in height and temperament. It is a dancer's dream to find the perfect partner; sometimes it happens, but many times not, even after years of tries. Anne and I were a perfect match in every way, including technical proficiency and artistry. There was our mental telepathy, too, the ultimate non-verbal communication between partners. In August the officially professional Atlanta Ballet performed *Giselle* at Chastain Park. The nine AB company members were paid. David Blair staged the ballet and he and his wife danced the leads. Reluctantly, Virginia was Myrtha, Queen of the Willies. She hated the role. Although she was good, it just wasn't her thing. Anne Burton and I danced the Act I peasant pas de deux. Had this been a typical year, performing our first full-length *Giselle* would have been considered another fantastic milestone in the company's 39-year history; and, despite two nights cancelled because of rain, I believe it was good for AB. I do not know if this unusually rainy summer affected Chris's TUT musical productions, but it did hurt Municipal Theatre's bottom line. Rainouts at Chastain Park were not my biggest concern, however. What had many of us at AB biting our nails with nerve-racking worry was Municipal Theatre's forthcoming inaugural performance in the Memorial Arts Center scheduled for October 1968. Chris had decided to produce *King Arthur*. It was a huge collaboration among the theater, opera and ballet companies to show off our importance as a prominent arts organization in Atlanta. Although twelve months away, already the collaboration, and our announced tenancy in the Memorial Arts Center, were creating a buzz of curiosity in the local and national press. Chris Manos was taking a high-stakes gamble with such an over-the-top production, though. If he failed, AB failed. Overly confidant, he was not minding the expenses on the *King Arthur* production, which had lots of us at AB on edge, our emotions fueled by apprehension that Municipal Theatre might be a leaking boat.

The official grand opening of the Memorial Arts Center complex was Tuesday October 5, 1968. The art school and museum were the first to have their inaugural openings, followed by the Atlanta Symphony Orchestra's inaugural performance in Symphony Hall. Municipal Theatre inaugurated the Alliance Theater on October 29. *King Arthur* was the first, and only, collaboration among Municipal Theatre's opera-theater-ballet consortium in the new Memorial Arts Center, because it was the beginning of the end. The big idea to use *King Arthur* to showcase the Municipal Theatre consortium, to proclaim our permanent tenancy in the new Memorial Arts Center complex, was a big bust, although it would be months before most people realized it. Days and even a few weeks after the production, if one listened to the Memorial Arts Center's powers-that-be and the local and national newspaper journalists, the production was a huge success. But only because a lot of us worked

Anne Burton Avery and I were regular partners (courtesy Anne Burton Avery).

hard behind the scenes to make it seem so. (Despite the obvious fact that the stage was too small, the orchestra pit too small and the number of seats too few for such a huge production.)

On opening night, as I watched the black tie-dressed patrons fill the 860 or so seats in the Alliance Theatre, my feelings were more disappointment than elation. As I was sitting next to Ginger in the audience, my thoughts pivoted between wishing the best for the AB dancers to wishing I was at home with the family. There were too many friends and celebrities to entertain to slip quietly away, however. In the audience that night were the widow Mrs. Martin Luther King; actresses Patricia Neal and Joan Fontaine; opera diva Marian Anderson; and dancers Ted Shawn and Dame Alicia Markova. *King Arthur,* by John Dryden and Henry Purcell, is what could be called an operetta. It is mostly singing and talking—and a little bit, a very little bit, of dancing. The choreographer was the New York City–based Joyce Trisler, and because of the sets, actors and singers (the cast was about 200), she could not do much more than have the dancers weaving and strolling around the stage, trying their best not to knock elbows or run into anyone or anything. The most dynamic dance was performed by an accommodating brave dancer who juggled three balls in the air. The opera is the story of the conflict between the Saxon King Oswald and the British King Arthur, both of whom are in love with the beautiful young Emmeline. I was not impressed with the story or the performance. Anne Burton and Joey Carman were two of the AB dancers who did their best with the uninspiring and unimpressive choreography. A review of *King Arthur* in *The New York Times* did not even mention the dancing or dancers.[6] The only good thing to happen because of *King Arthur* was that Anne Burton met her future husband, Eddie Avery. He was an actor in the production. At a rehearsal, when he saw Anne, he was instantly smitten.

Why was *King Arthur* not performed in Symphony Hall? I am asked. Chris had gone way over Municipal Theatre's budget on the production and the cost to rent Symphony Hall was too high for him to pay may have been one reason. And even if we did rent the Hall, the costs to equip the stage with the lighting and sound equipment required to mount the production (as we soon learned) were too expensive. Years before, during the early planning stage of the construction of the Memorial Arts Center, I had been given a copy of the blueprints, which I sent to the well-known theater designer in New York City, Jean Rosenthal. We were friends, and she graciously designed a plan for the main two theaters—Symphony Hall and the Alliance Theatre—at no charge. Proudly, I had passed along her design plan to the powers-that-be. I do not know what happened to her plan, but it was not used. Consequently, the theaters that were built proved to be inadequate for at least two organizations under the control of Municipal Theatre—the opera and AB. The auditorium in Symphony Hall had 1,800 seats, and we had been told three years before that this state-of-the-art hall would have a stage wide and deep enough to accommodate our needs for the much-needed income-generating full-length *The Nutcracker* we planned to put on every December. For AB's fall and winter rep seasons, we most likely would use the Alliance Theatre. In December 1969, *The Nutcracker* was performed in Symphony Hall. While the seating capacity in the Hall was adequate, the stage was terrible for ballet. It was a stage constructed for symphony orchestra concerts—a concert hall—and it certainly was not state-of-the-art for opera and ballet. It seems that someone with a lot of authority had hired a young kid from an Ivy League university to create the architectural design for the theaters instead of using Rosenthal's design. The kid was too inexperienced for a project of this size, and I have no clue as to why he was hired to design what we were led to believe would be a state-of-the-art theater for music, opera, theater and dance. AB did hold a few, but very few, programs in Symphony Hall. First, the cost to rent the hall was too high for AB's budget. Second, because there was no lighting for productions, such as *The Nutcracker*, we had to rent and install lighting equipment and then pay to uninstall the lighting equipment. In addition, there were the costs to remove boosters and sound boxes before a performance, then to put them back. The Alliance Theatre was not a practicable option either. Although the cost to rent the theater was much less than Symphony Hall, there were too few seats in the auditorium to make much money, if any. Ballets performed in the Memorial Arts Center theaters were not going to earn the cash needed to keep AB going and growing, much less to ever have an endowment.

Soon after the *King Arthur* debacle, Chris informed me that Municipal Theatre was so deeply in debt that he might have to declare bankruptcy. Chris had gambled and lost.[7] Dorothy and I were devastated by the bad news. "We were so excited that we lost all business sense. That season makes me want to say to every ballet director everywhere: be sure to get good business advice!"[8] said Dorothy. There were many emergency board meetings convened to look at our options for surviving. We discussed whether to join the Memorial Arts Center (now the Woodruff Arts Center), but when we were told of the costs involved we could not afford to; our assets were gone. Municipal Theatre had spent every penny we had. Despite our serious financial crisis, we managed to perform the scheduled rep program at the Memorial Arts Center in November. On the program was Balanchine's *Symphony in C.* Mr. B came to Atlanta for the performance. He was wined and dined at a gala organized by the Atlanta Ballet Guild in his honor.

"*Spring, 1969*: The Municipal Theatre [*sic*] has gone under. The Atlanta Ballet takes a big breath, rattles its tin cup urgently, and finishes the season on its own,"[9] wrote Doris Hering in *Dance Magazine*. The official folding of Municipal Theatre was definitely not what I had envisioned for the company's 40th anniversary. And AB came so close to folding, too. This second serious misstep in the history of Atlanta Ballet was a humbling experience for both Dorothy and me. Because we had done the right thing by not abolishing the Board when we merged with Municipal Theatre, there were about thirty dedicated supporters to help raise the money to keep the company limping along. I reorganized the company back to non-professional status. Not surprisingly, most of the dancers left. Only about eight remained, mostly females. The Board did its part fundraising and the artistic and administrative staff did its part slicing expenses, and although it was an enormous struggle, after a few months we were able to return AB to professional status. Those subsequent years with only eight full-time dancers were exceptionally hard, however. The first year of the reorganization, I picked as many capable high school students from the school as possible to dance in the company's spring season program. Yet having so few dancers, and mostly females, affected choreography and programming. Joseph "Joey" Carman grew up in the school. He was an exceptionally talented dancer, and to highlight his ability to please a crowd I choreographed a ballet for him, *Joey and Friends*. It was light, fun, humorous, and with a lot of color to brighten the company's mood. I contacted Boston Pops conductor Arthur Fiedler, requesting permission to use his composition of some Beatles songs, and he graciously gave his consent. The ensemble of lady friends each wore a different colored mini-dress in the brightest lollipop-colored fabric we could find and afford. The tights and pointe shoes were dyed to match the color of the costume. As Doris Hering wrote in her *Dance Magazine* review, the women "flirted and strutted and basked in the sunshine of Joey's ingenuous grin."[10] And I have to agree with her that out of the four pieces on the rep program that spring season, *Joey and Friends* was the most enthusiastically received by the patrons. Doris concluded her article applauding AB's grit in surviving the Municipal Theatre consortium collapse. She wrote that AB "deserves the support of the Atlanta Arts Alliance, the fundraising structure behind the Art Museum, the Atlanta Symphony Orchestra and the Alliance Theatre Company. What other arts organization came through the Municipal Theatre debacle with its head so high, its continuity so undisturbed?"[11] At AB we were truly grateful to Doris Hering for her public acknowledgment of our refusal to give up and die. But joining the Atlanta Arts Alliance was not going to happen. Joey went on to have an impressive ballet career. He danced with Joffrey and was a soloist with Dutch National Ballet. He danced with AB again for one year, partnering Maniya Barredo, then joined ABT. Today he is an author and writer for esteemed publications such as *The New York Times* and *Los Angeles Times* and *Dance Magazine*. In addition to dance, he publishes articles on classical music, opera, theater, and films.

It was a relief to us all when a great opportunity occurred: AB was thrilled to say yes to an invitation to perform at the Delacorte Theatre in New York City for the 105th annual New York Dance Festival sponsored by the New York Shakespeare Festival. We rattled the tin cup for donations and raised enough money to make the trip. AB performed several works. Anne Burton and I danced a piece. Carl Ratcliff and Ginger performed their collaboration "The Bix Piece." One published review was exceptionally positive for both the company and Anne: "The Atlanta Ballet scored with another full-scale project, *Schubert—Fifth Symphony,* in which a young lady named Anne Burton was breathtakingly good. She also sparkled in the first night's *Valse* with Robert Barnett..."[12] Dayton Civic Ballet and Sacramento Ballet performed, also. Several of us watched the company of Twyla Tharp perform, a choreographer and dancer I had never heard of before. "She'll be very important, one day," said Carl. Because I needed more male dancers in the company, it was my lucky day when I met the dancer Tom Pazik in New York City. We met in a costume shop and started talking. This chance encounter led to Tom joining AB as a dancer.

Besides becoming one of my best friends, he would be a major player at AB for the next twenty-two years, including associate artistic director and resident choreographer. In addition, he would become a much-loved teacher at the Atlanta School of Ballet. Tom was a master at organizing children's ballets and lecture demonstrations. And he would prove to be a darn good costume builder, too.

Believing that AB had turned the corner, just when I was feeling really optimistic about AB's future, another financial misstep occurred. It was caused by over-spending on a gala to honor Dorothy for fifty years of outstanding achievement, not just

This photograph was taken in the 1970s in Atlanta.

for the regional dance movement but for her outstanding contributions to the progression of dance in America. The decision to hold such an extravagant celebration was made with good intentions, but bad business practices almost did us in, again. The consequence was a deficit that shoved AB back into a financial crisis state. The big event started with Mayor Sam Massell proclaiming March 16, 1973, "Dorothy Alexander Day." At the "Night of Stars" evening ceremony, actress Joanne Woodward introduced Nancy Hanks, Chairman of the National Council of the Arts (National Endowment for the Arts). Hanks' tribute was so apropos to capturing Dorothy's accomplishments. She said (and it was written in the gala program, which is in the Dorothy Alexander collection at Emory University),

> For Dorothy Alexander who epitomizes the artist as visionary. Just as great architects have foreseen cities which then came to be, she danced and made dances. She built a company, The Atlanta Ballet. She built a national dream, regional ballet. Behind it all was the faith that someday the people of Atlanta—and Americans everywhere—would cherish dance as a meaningful part of their lives. Because of her, that day beckons.[13]

Atlanta Ballet performed *Serenade.* Guest dancers were Arthur Mitchell and Lydia Abarca, Dance Theatre of Harlem; Judith Jameson, Alvin Ailey; Ivan Nagy and Natalia Makarova, American Ballet Theatre; Edward Villella and Violette Verdy, Allegra Kent and Peter Martins, New York City Ballet. The guest conductor was Robert Irving from NYCB, who led the Atlanta Symphony Orchestra. Following the performance at the Atlanta Civic Center patrons and guests were feted at Phipps Plaza. The dinner was in the solarium and the organizers had gone all out to make the place look like an elegant ballroom. Round tables and chairs had been rented for the elaborate dinner and ceremony. As ladies in small groups of two and three got up from their chairs to go powder their noses, whispers and chuckles could be heard throughout the room. Dresses, especially those that were black, had white stripes down the back. Someone had decided to paint the wooden chairs white and the paint had not dried. The dry cleaners in Atlanta were very happy. The celebration to honor Dorothy was a critical success nationally and locally. But it was a financial fiasco for AB. The night of the gala Joanne Woodward announced that Georgia Governor Jimmy Carter had signed a proclamation naming Atlanta Ballet "The State Ballet Company of Georgia." As proud as everyone felt, the title came with no monetary compensation. And if we did not start making better business decisions, Georgia's official State Ballet Company would cease to exist.

One of our worst business practices was not recruiting board members who understood their roles and responsibilities as trustees. In those years when the company had grown from a regional non-professional civic ballet company to a professional ballet company, trustees had not been recruited who could provide the business experience and expertise required. Furthermore, there were too many on the board who expected to do nothing more for AB than attend VIP events, such as the Atlanta Ballet annual ball. Weaknesses were evident on the administrative side of AB, also. There was a general manager position, but no CEO position on the HR organization chart. Because of the frequent turnover in the leadership position—and because most of the new hires lacked the experience and competency needed to do the job right—more than one general manager got AB committed to projects that pushed the company into financial trouble. Probably most importantly, there was a serious disconnect among the trustees and the administrative and artistic sides of the company. Usually the Board consisted of about thirty-five members, although there were a few years that it numbered fifty. Lack of continuity was a big problem: The board was a revolving door of trustees entering and leaving. Three or four stayed for years, but too many trustees appeared and then disappeared quickly. There were no real obligations to be a board member, such as a minimum monetary donation or a requirement to attend a specific number of meetings every year, for instance. Out of forty to fifty board members, AB was lucky if nine made any effort to provide the guidance and assistance needed during those years of financial crises. I used to go to the meetings, and if it was at the end of the company's fiscal year, and if there was a deficit, then the artistic staff was told to cut expenses to make up the difference, even if it meant letting people go, including dancers. AB was so fortunate when Carole Brockey Goldberg joined the Board. She was the company's only real development officer, even though it was a volunteer position. Her husband, Joel Goldberg, was president of Rich's department store (and later chairman and chief executive officer), and therefore she knew a lot of prominent business leaders in the Atlanta community. She and Ginger had known each other for years, which is how I became friends with her. Carole had no reluctance to telephone or visit people and ask for money. Although she knew that fundraising was not something I liked to do, nevertheless she would take me by the hand to go visit businessmen (and a few women) in the community. She raised a lot of money for the ballet.

In addition to the aggressive fundraising campaign Carole was leading to get us out of the financial mess, we applied for and received a National Endowment for the Arts (NEA) grant to tour the U.S. No town was too small. In fact, that was NEA's purpose for supporting this touring program—to bring the arts to Americans who would otherwise not be exposed. Usually, a dance company stayed in a small town for a couple of nights. In addition to one or two performances—in a real theater, if we were lucky, or a high school auditorium, if not—company dancers visited a high school or two and presented lecture demonstrations in the auditorium or gym. When on tour we were called the Atlanta Ballet Touring Ensemble. This was done to satisfy the paperwork required. I remember a tour to Flint, Michigan. We stayed for several days, and it was freezing. We were rehearsing in the basketball gym and some basketball players stopped to watch us. And they snickered. Still, we must have done something to impress them, because on the night of the performance they were all there. Atlanta Ballet Touring Ensemble traveled from one town to the next in two small buses: one with the dancers and stage crew and one with the costumes, props, and audio equipment. Included on

the trips were an accompanist, and some-times a conductor, who arranged for pick-up musicians so that AB could perform with a live orchestra. I insisted that every person in the troupe dress up when we were out in public, because on tour we all represented the Atlanta Ballet, and as rep-resentatives we had to look our best. If we went to a party and I didn't believe some dancer was appropriately dressed, she or he stayed on the bus. We traveled in good weather and bad. Even driving our buses through snow and ice. To this day Anne and I still laugh about the time we per-formed in a small university town in North Dakota during a blizzard. The pick-up musicians in the orchestra pit were awful, and when we got to the second act *Nut-cracker* pas de deux they quit playing. Despite the horrific weather, the audito-rium was packed. Anne and I continued dancing as if nothing was wrong. Unknown to the audience, we were softly humming the music throughout the entire pas de deux.

My final performance as a principal AB dancer was in 1974. I was forty-nine years old. I was the artistic director and a principal dancer and directing the com-pany that was touring constantly. Artistic

My years of classical ballet train-ing and performing were worth it (by Marion D. Ware, from author's collection).

and administrative responsibilities were taking up so many hours of the day that it was just too difficult teaching, choreographing, trying to stay in shape and dancing. While I tried to get home every night to eat dinner with the family, it was getting harder and harder to do. Something had to go; I had to make a choice. I was still in good physical condition, but it was time to stop. My final dance was in Atlanta. Anne Burton and I danced the second act *Nutcracker* pas de deux. I had told no one at the office, not even Anne, about my retirement. I knew that she, especially, would get too emotional to dance our final dance. After the performance, when I told her I was stopping, she broke down. There was no big announcement, no retirement party. I left quietly.

In 1975, our family suffered a very sad loss. Dick suffered a massive stroke while in a hospital in Houston, Texas, and died. He had had a few strokes previously, and he was in Texas being treated by the famous heart surgeon Michael Debakey. The house was put on the market. Once it sold, Ginger, the two boys and I moved into a small condo.

My beautiful Ginger and her father, Dick "Gramps" Rich, at home on 27 West Andrews Drive in Atlanta's Buckhead area.

That same year AB was a guest company at the Alaska Festival of Music in Anchorage. The costumes were shipped, and all arrived except the tutu for Black Swan. Tom Pazik, our costume guru, found a fabric store and purchased the materials to make a tutu. He had a portable Singer sewing machine with him. Four hours later the ballerina was on stage wearing her beautiful new costume, even more exquisite than the one that never arrived.

In the 1970s through the 1980s AB was performing *The Nutcracker* either at the Atlanta Civic Center or at the Fox Theatre. The Civic Center, which is not open anymore, had an adequate-sized stage, but sitting in the auditorium felt like, and sounded like, watching a show in an aircraft hangar. If there was a choice of watching a performance at the Civic Center or the Fox Theatre, most patrons would have voted for the Fox. Patrons love to watch live performances at the Fox. A lot of performers aren't so excited about it, though. As wide as the stage is, it is so shallow, it's like a Kabuki theater. Usually, it is not possible to make any money performing ballets at either the Civic Center or Fox. With one exception: thank goodness for *The Nutcracker*. Except for the traditional Christmas *The Nutcracker*, making a profit from performances in Atlanta was like pulling teeth. That's true for a lot of ballet companies, which is why almost every major (and a lot of mid-sized) classical ballet companies perform *The Nutcracker* in December. The one December I experimented and offered *Sleeping Beauty*, we almost lost our shirts. The Atlanta community was not supportive of our annual spring program no matter what was performed or where. And we tried just about everything. Another downside of performing at the Fox or Civic Center, even *The Nutcracker*, is that dancing for an audience of less than about 1,000 patrons, with more than 3,500 empty seats staring you in the face, can be a de-motivator and demoralizing. One way we did fill the seats at the Civic Center, and I do mean every seat, was with the Kids in Step program. Sarah duBignon, a Guild member, had daughters in the school, and she conceived the project and ran it. Eventually, it became so successful that it was a full-time job. I believe in the early days of the program the price for a ticket was 25 cents. The school districts in the Atlanta area bused the kids to the performance, and still do so today. As of 2018, AB performs *Nutcracker* at the Fox. There's nothing more electrifying than dancing in front of 4,500 wildly applauding, laughing, eyes-wide-with-excitement kids, many of whom are watching a ballet performance for the first time.

In 1978, about the same time America was in an economic recession—something to do with an energy crisis—AB suffered another critical financial downturn. The company had about "thirty-seven dollars in the bank, owed $150,000 in back debts, was operating on a $200,000 current deficit, and was committed to a tour the coming season...,"[14] a tour of *Peter Pan*. It was to be a new version choreographed by Tom Pazik. It was a great idea, a crowd pleaser that would have made a lot of money. Unfortunately, we learned midway into the project that we could not get the rights. The debt of $150,000 included the losses incurred from the closing of the Municipal Theatre in 1969 and the over-budget expenditures from the 1973 gala. To make matters worse, subscriptions for the 1978/79 season declined sharply, from about 1,400 to less than 900, because of the Board's error in deciding to put off the annual spring subscription campaign to the fall. "Lack of funds" was their reason for the postponement. Once again Carole Goldberg, now Chairman of the Board, was the ballet's savior. She always looked like a million bucks and was such a hard worker for the company. AB was fortunate that she stayed for ages. The Board, thanks to an NEA matching grant, hired a consultant to help us learn what we were doing right, what we were doing wrong, and give recommendations for improvements. I recall that the recommendations were to "Get the company known in Atlanta as well as on tour, set up standing committees on the board, embark on a five-year plan, and hire appropriate administrative staff."[15] During the seven years of touring we logged about 30,000 miles annually. We did it because we made more money touring than performing at home. In 1977, we were on the road for twenty-six weeks. As a result, AB was better known nationally than at home. The company was better known in other Georgian cities, such as Columbus and Valdosta, than at home.

What the consultant's report showed was that while my vision to grow AB into a first-rate, nationally-ranked company had happened, the number of administrative staff on the payroll to support a company of this size had not kept up with the growth on the artistic side. Carole replaced the current general manager with a man who was more experienced working at an arts organization. In addition to managing AB, he was the business manager and development director as well. The consultant's report was a wake-up call for the Board and the Guild. The Board of thirty-three members learned it needed to be more business-oriented. The Guild learned that it needed to help in ways other than organizing so many small fundraising programs, such as becoming more involved in subscription sales.

With the administrative duties and responsibilities in the competent hands of Carole and the trustees on the board, and the new general manager, I could now return my attention to running the company and the school. I had bought Dorothy's half ownership in the school, and Merrilee Smith and I were co-directors. Most important, I had more time to spend with the family. Mom was eighty-three and although in excellent health, mentally and physically, she wasn't visiting us in Atlanta any longer. It was up to Ginger and me to take the boys to see her in the summers. The 50th anniversary celebration of AB's founding was somewhat low-key because of the financial situation. But we were still alive. We had survived. We were still the oldest continuously operating ballet company in America. What had looked so bleak a few months earlier for AB's next fifty years, if it would even exist for another fifty years, was now looking golden again.

AB was now up in size to about nineteen professionals and nine apprentices, and the recent addition of talented, highly-skilled females and males had made the company stronger than ever. Regrettably, Anne Burton, now

Anne Burton Avery because she married Eddie, resigned. Eddie had a job transfer that took him to Dallas, Texas. Counting the days when she was a student in the school and the years in AB as a principal dancer, together we had experienced a lot of great highs and weathered a few critical lows. She was close friends with Ginger and the boys. Not only was I going to miss Atlanta's favorite ballerina, I would miss my good friend, too. Yet, even with the loss of Anne, and although small in number, AB had some exceptionally talented dancers in the company. There was the principal ballerina Maniya "Honey" Barredo and her husband, dancer Mannie Rowe; Kathy McBeth (now Kathy McBeth Hutcheson); and two males who had been trained at the school, Joey Carman and eighteen-year-old Gil Boggs. Tom Pazik was not only a strong character dancer, but he was becoming a choreographer of national renown. The dancers were on a thirty-six-week contract and although not members of a union, they were paid union scale while on tour. I had refused to be paid a salary until the dancers were paid. Now, for the first time since joining the Atlanta Ballet, after twenty-one years, I was about to receive my first paycheck.

Chapter Ten

Families and Friends

Dorothy Moses Alexander: She was family. And not just for Virginia, who thought of Dorothy as a second mother, but for me, too. I learned so much from her, such as how to teach. Dorothy had studied kinesiology in college, and she knew about ligaments and tendons and muscles and how to use them, especially the muscles in the back. Ports de bras were her specialty. I lost count of the times that Virginia was praised for her gorgeous ports de bras—the carriage of the arms, back and head—that she had learned from Dorothy. Whenever Virginia complained that she was not born with classical ballet feet—that she didn't have banana feet—I tactfully reminded her that people weren't interested in her feet; it was her ports de bras they liked to see. Mr. B loved Virginia's ports de bras. He used to say in company class: "Do like Ginny. Do like Ginny." Because of Dorothy I learned a lot about teaching ports de bras. There were many other teaching tips I learned, also. After teaching kids at her dance school and in the public schools for fifty-plus years, she was a distinguished veteran. I remember a day that she watched me teach. I must have gotten excited, jumped out of my chair to demonstrate a step, and raised my voice a little too loudly. Later, she said, "Bobby, dear, if you whisper they will listen." Starting with the day she met us at the airport she took care of me, making sure that I had all the tips-of-the trade, and some tricks hidden in the cuffs of my sleeves, including how to run a ballet company and how to work with a board, which sometimes was a real patience tester. She would say, "Bobby, it makes no difference who gets the credit, it just makes a difference of how it all turns out."

From Dorothy I learned that it was not who you know that gets you where you want to be in life, but hard work, stick-with-it-grit and talent. It was a lesson we passed along to the dancers in the Atlanta School of Ballet and AB: If you have the talent, and you work hard enough, you will get a starring role. That did not mean a student or company member got every role he or she wanted, though. And there were lots of times when kids were disappointed that they did not get picked to dance the roles they wanted. But they knew we were fair. Neither Dorothy nor I had much use for auditions. I knew who could do what from watching them in class. Only if assigning dancers for a character part did we sometimes schedule an audition—to find out who was the best actor; who was the most secure in that area of performing. Dorothy and I taught our dancers to watch rehearsals, to learn a part even if they might never dance it, just as I had done in the Original Ballet Russe and at NYCB. When someone got hurt and Mr. B asked, "Who knows this?" I would raise my hand, which is why I got to dance so many different roles. It was by watching Herbert Bliss at rehearsals that I got to dance *Symphony in C*. Herbert was rehearsing one day and got a spasm in his back. A substitute was needed quickly. I knew the part and got picked. Maiqui Manosa—it happened to her at AB. She knew Maniya Barredo, they were both Filipina, and Maniya got Maiqui to move to Atlanta and enroll in the Atlanta School of Ballet. That first year she watched a lot of rehearsals. Then, on her own, she would slip into a vacant studio and practice. One day, in a rehearsal, I needed a replacement and asked, "Who knows this?" Maiqui, sitting in a corner of the room, raised her hand. She got the part, even though she was a student. She danced in the performance and danced the part really well. As a result, I gave her a contract to dance in AB.

Dorothy and I loved our students; we loved our company dancers. We gave hard classes; we demanded a lot. But we treated them all with respect. We made the necessary corrections without shouting, without insulting. Dorothy stayed involved in company affairs until she died. Upon my arrival in 1958, however, she became less and less active in running the artistic side of the company. Yet, even after her retirement as artistic director in 1961, she still let me know after every performance whether she liked it, or didn't like it—in her soft, southern-lady way of speaking. I have yet to meet another woman like Miss Dorothy. Although I was disappointed with the financial debts resulting from the "Night of Stars" black-tie celebration to honor Dorothy for fifty years of outstanding achievement in dance, it was worth it. That night was a recognition of this beautiful lady's many achievements, bestowed on her by dignitaries and celebrities locally and nationally that was well deserved and that the citizens of Atlanta can be proud of. It was a tribute to her "indefatigable devotion," as Ted Shawn had said so well in 1960, to growing ballet, not just in her beloved Atlanta community, but in America. And she did this by educating people living in small towns and cities on the importance of ballet as an art form. Balanchine wanted to bring the most talented, well-trained dancers from the regional ballet companies to SAB where he could polish them, and then pick the best to join NYCB. Dorothy believed differently. She wanted ballet and ballet dancers—well-trained classical ballet dancers—to be in lots of towns and cities throughout America, not just San Francisco or Chicago or New York City. Following the youth symphony orchestra model, which was common in the early to mid–1900s—Dorothy proved that kids could be trained in classical ballet to a level where they could be accepted into a youth regional ballet company, and that, eventually, the ballet company would have a sufficient number of well-trained, artistically talented youth to become professional. Dorothy disagreed with Balanchine that regional ballet teachers could not polish a dancer, that a talented student had to go to Balanchine's SAB. Balanchine tried to woo her to get her to agree with him, but it didn't happen. Even though disappointed, Mr. B had a lot of respect for this stubborn southern lady. And his visits to Atlanta to work with AB, for many different purposes, was evidence. "The great visionary of these American regional pioneers is Dorothy Alexander,"[1] said authors Mary Clarke and David Vaughan in *The Encyclopedia of Dance & Ballet*. Dorothy was a regional pioneer. And because of her, I became one of these pioneers, too.

Dorothy was always the lady in physical appearance and attitude. There was no doubt about her southern roots, yet she did not use the word *ya'll*. In the most stressful times she stayed calm. I never heard her curse. Her practicality, her subtle strength in getting people to agree with her on some really hard decisions, was inspiring. She worked tirelessly networking locally, nationally and internationally—cultivating influencers and supporters who could promote the Atlanta Ballet. She never let a person's first "no" stop her from asking again or from trying a different approach to getting what she believed to be important. And her efforts paid off big time. AB always got a lot of press coverage in newspapers such as *The New York Times* as well as the *Atlanta Constitution,* and in good magazines, such as *Dance Magazine.* Dance critics from New York City frequently flew to Atlanta to review AB performances. She was friends with key persons at the National Endowment for the Arts in Washington, D.C. Dorothy listened to others' viewpoints closely. She was not judgmental. Yet she was a woman who was open in telling you what she thought and convincing you why she was right. Only on a couple of emotionally-charged topics did she keep her views private. Subjects having to do with politics and religion, for example, were not subjects she talked about publicly. She choreographed more than eighty ballets. Not one was created to express her political views or to denote her thoughts on society's flaws. Rather, her themes were about dance as a celebration of life. Dance had helped her through serious illnesses as a child and as an adult, through the premature deaths of both her mother and father, and through a failed marriage. She had suffered. And this is what moved her to teach thousands of others about the importance of dance to manage those hardships that every person is going to encounter in life; to use dance to restore balance and to offer fulfillment. In an article in *Ballet News* on the company's fiftieth birthday celebration and how "the trail-blazing Atlanta Ballet and its founder are still looking forward," Dorothy explained her purpose, her raison d'etre:

> people were amazed that one family would produce an Episcopalian bishop, my brother, and a dancer, me. But I couldn't see anything odd about it. We both had something to say and each of us said it in a different medium. I had a great desire to elevate people and lead them to the mountain tops. I never had any thought of influencing or converting people. I simply wanted to lead them to that mountain where they would find, in their own terms, fulfillment.[2]

It is a purpose I learned from Miss Dorothy and which I pass along today.

In the early 1980s, even though federal arts funding had begun to shrink and the company had a $360,000 deficit,[3] on the artistic side AB was doing very well. In addition to Maniya Barredo, there was the talented young man, Gil Boggs, who had begun studying at the Atlanta School of Ballet in 1973 when he was twelve. His professional debut was the next year in *The Nutcracker*. At the age of twenty, Gil, now a soloist in AB, was picked at a regional U.S. competition to be one of seven to represent America at the International Ballet Competition in Varna, Bulgaria, in July 1980. I was the official U.S. coach at the competition. Mannie Rowe was an assistant coach. The competition in this "Olympics of Dance"[4] was stiff. Gil did not win a medal; no American did. Still, we were satisfied when he received a diploma as one of the top twenty dancers in the senior division. This was especially noteworthy given that he was the youngest in the senior division. The competition in Varna was a great learning experience for all of us—professionally and politically. As a communist country, Bulgaria was behind the Iron Curtain. Our every move was monitored and controlled, and because we were Americans, we were not always liked. As Gil said in an interview, "What you had to go through to keep sane was very difficult ... we didn't hear a thing—not in newspapers or on radio or television—about what was going on in the rest of the world. We were totally isolated."[5] The three of us were relieved to get back home. I would do it again, though, because it put AB on the international grid of outstanding ballet companies. Another positive thing to happen was that I met a young man in Varna—and he did win a gold medal—who would become a good friend of mine. Stanislav "Stas" Issaev would eventually move to the U.S. Not only would he have an affiliation with AB, but he and I would serve on the dance faculty at South Carolina Governor's School for the Arts. My return to a Communist country occurred sooner than I had expected. I was back behind the Iron Curtain the next year when I was head coach of the U.S. delegation to the International Ballet Competition in Moscow. It was my first time to see the famous Bolshoi Theatre, and it was sad to see what once had been a grand theater in such a bad state of decay. It needed a serious restoration. A highlight was coaching a young American dancer who won the gold medal, Amanda McKerrow.

I was a coach at the International Ballet Competition in Moscow in 1981. The young girl is the American dancer Amanda McKerrow, who won a gold medal.

The year 1980 marked an exceptionally important time in AB's thirteen-year history as a professional company: the decision was made to discontinue the Atlanta Ballet Touring Ensemble. It wasn't a difficult decision to make as we had just about ceased touring, reducing our trips to six weeks from the sixteen weeks the year before. In each city we often gave at least three performances, and then there were the master classes and lecture-demonstrations to do, also. For example, in 1980 the company performed Tom Pazik's *Cinderella* in Akron, Ohio; Lansing, Michigan; and Greenville, South Carolina. There was a rep program in Nashville, Tennessee, in December, which featured the second act *Nutcracker* pas de deux with Gil and Maniya. In Flagstaff, Arizona, we danced on the same program as an Indian Pow Wow. We danced in the big cities (big for Alaska, that is) of Anchorage, Fairbanks and Juneau.

There was a small town in Alaska where the oil company paid for the visit. That experience was not memorably pleasant, and not only because of the freezing-cold temperature, but because we slept on the floor in sleeping bags at a local church, instead of in private homes, which was the norm and much more comfortable. Thank goodness in the other Alaskan towns we stayed in private homes. Tom Pazik did the lecture demonstrations, which were about one hour. The dancers sat on the edge of the stage and answered questions from the kids in the audience. The kids were so fascinated about pointe shoes, and how girls stood on pointe, and partnering. At the end of the session, the kids were invited to come on stage and dance with the dancers, and some always did, entertaining us all. Regularly, the city leaders went all out to show us off, and we were treated very well. AB was accompanied by the Nashville Symphony Orchestra, for example, which the city officials paid for. Because live music had become too costly at home, we had cut expenses by using tapes for most performances. Thus, we performed to more live music on the tours than in Atlanta. Still, touring eventually lost its appeal for me, even though it was great for the company's reputation, ego and the bottom line. By 1980 the 30,000 miles of travel over sixteen weeks—plus two seasons in Atlanta every year—had us exhausted. AB was well known nationally but we needed to get better acquainted with the Atlanta community, chiefly the business community if we wanted more corporate sponsors. At last there was more money coming in from local businesses than in the company's history; some supporters were major international corporations. But we still needed more. Another reason to perform more at home was to raise awareness and get more people in the Atlanta community to attend performances. As Balanchine had done, and Dorothy as well, I wanted to educate people—to get them excited to watch us dance; to get them in the theater, not just once a year but twice, even three to four times a year. Season subscription sales are very important to a company's viability. Increasing performances at home to twenty-two from what the year before had been only ten, as well as reducing on-the-road performances, was an easy decision to make. What wasn't easy was my decision to restructure the company, which involved letting half of the fourteen professional dancers go and then to add seven new ones.

Restructuring is one of the most difficult decisions every artistic director at any dance company in the world must make. There is no way to avoid the fact that some people will be happy, while others will be unhappy, their feelings hurt. Nor is it easy to quickly get back to a peaceful work-dance place, because conflicting feelings make it difficult to hold meetings to talk about it calmly. Once the restructuring was done, once the emotional dust had settled, AB was fortunate that Maniya Barredo and Gil Boggs stayed, even though both could have made a lot more money somewhere else. Kathy McBeth Hutcheson, who had been on maternity leave, returned. Jill Murphy and Robert Rogers were two of the dancers recruited. The first black dancer in AB's history was hired. Susan Lovelle had been in Arthur Mitchell's Dance Theatre of Harlem. In addition to her technical skills and artistic talents, because Arthur Mitchell was a former dancer with NYCB, Lovelle already knew the Balanchine repertory performed in AB. She brought experience and was gracious and helpful in sharing her knowledge with the other AB dancers.

I got my good friend Melissa Hayden involved as a consultant, and she was a coach for some of the Atlanta Ballet dancers, also. As often as possible I sent Maniya to New York City for private coaching with Melissa on solos in Balanchine ballets that she would be dancing at AB. Melissa also came to Atlanta on several occasions to teach and coach the dancers. In an interview she was asked why she was a consultant at AB. She said, "I am doing this because of what is in the Atlanta Ballet.... I wouldn't be an artistic consultant if I didn't think highly of them. That Robert Barnett is a good friend just makes it better."[6] Melissa was right: the quality of the dancers and the programs offered was outstanding. What was needed was more dancers and live music and money to grow the company, if we wanted to be on the same level as major ballet companies in cities such as Boston, Philadelphia, Houston, and New York. Our performances were mostly at the cavernous Atlanta Civic Center. We hoped that our ambitious, newly created strategic plan to move AB up to the next level would fill a lot more of those empty seats. Restructuring the company caused me to lose a lot of sleep. And while these big changes were hard for me personally and incredibly painful, especially when I had to say goodbye to so many dancers in the AB family, I kept reminding myself to look at the overall picture: the picture of my vision for growing the company.

In addition to the restructuring on the artistic side of the company, there were changes on the administrative side, too, which affected morale in the building (some positive, some negative, depending on your point of view). Mainly, it involved a big turnover in staff. The changes allowed President and General Manager Ken Hertz to hire a full-time public relations employee. He also increased the Board to forty-five trustees—forty-five volunteers with the knowledge and experience to provide advice and direction on best practices; volunteers who were willing to work hard to grow the company.

In 1981, the restructuring of the company was completed although financial solvency was still a serious concern. At least ticket sales were looking good, though: in 1982 the budget showed that subscriptions had grown to

3,500 from 700 in just a few years. We were delighted to report that ticket sales were 62 percent of the budget this year.[7] Despite the financial concerns, when the company was invited to dance in New York, it was too good to pass up. AB held a fundraising party to raise money to pay the expenses. We gave three performances at Brooklyn College's Brooklyn Center as part of the Tribute to American Dance series. Most of the national reviews were of high praise. But what was really great about the performances in New York was that it got AB into negotiations with Brooklyn College for its newly created residency program.

In 1982, the company lost Gil Boggs, one of Atlanta's favorite male dancers. He auditioned for ABT. I wasn't surprised when Mikhail Baryshnikov, the artistic director, offered him a job. Gil and Maniya were regular partners, and there was no other male in the company that could replace him. It was fortunate that I found Nicolas Pacaña, principal dancer with Boston Ballet. He joined AB and became Maniya's regular partner. A good thing to happen that affected the company's bottom line was that thanks to the beneficence of Simon Selig, of Selig Enterprises, we could move into a huge building on Pine Street and Peachtree Street (a mid-rise building close

Virginia and I talking with George Balanchine after an Atlanta Ballet performance at the Alliance Theatre in Atlanta.

to the Fox and not far from the Civic Center) for such a nominal monthly rental fee that it seemed too good to be true. In this case, though, it truly was good, at least for the bottom line. Initially, AB occupied only the second floor of the building. An optical business occupied the first floor. Later, AB would have the whole building for offices, studios, a place to store sets, and an in-house costume room. If the Board fulfilled its agreement to make the fundraising goals and wipe out the deficit, AB could get back on track to establishing an endowment fund, as well as accelerating my vision for growing.

Balanchine died in 1983 at age seventy-nine. From then on AB paid the Balanchine Trust royalties for staging his ballets. It was money I was glad to pay, however. Tanny inherited many of his ballets, and royalty payments helped to support her. And AB could afford to pay. The deficit was paid off; in part, because of a $500,000 gift from an anonymous donor.[8] In part because so many of us on the artistic side—dedicated dancers and choreographers and artistic staff—stayed with the company through those difficult years, even though we were paid a pittance of what we could have earned at other companies. We did it out of love—for Dorothy and for AB. It was a humbling experience that so many of the dancers and artistic staff stayed during those hard years because of AB's purpose and mission and its historical importance in American dance. When I arrived in 1958 the budget was $16,000. The budget did creep upward, but only to about $65,000 by 1979, as I recall. It took twenty-six years, but by 1984 the budget had reached $2.5 million. My vision to grow the company was really happening. We were officially, both artistically and financially, on the list of the major ballet companies in America. In the 1978–79 season there were about 750 subscribers. In 1983–84 it was close to 6,500. In 1980 we were mostly a touring company; we gave less than twenty performances in Atlanta. In 1984, while there was at least one out-of-town gig—in Clearwater, Florida—we gave forty-five performances in Atlanta. Then there was more good news: the negotiations with Brooklyn College were finalized. We signed a one-week residency contract that would continue for five years. The reason given by Brooklyn College for extending this prestigious offer to AB was "after an exhaustive search of companies with fine dance proficiency, we chose The Atlanta Ballet because it offered all that and one more component: the potential of becoming one of the major companies in the country."[9] If the New York City dance elitists weren't aware of AB's stature in the nation before, they were now. Also, in Georgia, it helped increase the awareness of our reputation and importance nationally, which would help with fundraising and ticket sales. The spotlight was shining bright on the State of Georgia's official ballet company, and morale in our Pine Street building soared.

It is not easy for a ballet company to make the front page of the local newspaper, but in 1984 we were successful. "Atlanta Ballet on Its Toes,"[10] was the title of the *Atlanta Journal–Constitution* article on AB's residency at Brooklyn College. The performances were held at the Brooklyn Center for the Performing Arts. It was a big deal for them and for us. At the opening night performance there were critics from all over the U.S. to see why AB had been chosen for this residency program. Because of a combination of "high artistic standards, vision and strong administration,"[11] said the Brooklyn Center's general manager. The critics were in the audience opening night to decide if he was right. We were extremely nervous. It helped ease some of the butterflies in the stomach to think about the forty patrons in the audience from Atlanta, including a few University of Georgia alumni, who were members of the University of Georgia Alumni Association. During the performance there were lots of applause and whoops and bravos yelled out. When the curtain closed for the final time, we were all emotionally exhausted but pleased, and relieved. Dorothy and I couldn't have been prouder to witness what AB had achieved since its founding in 1929.

Throughout the 1980s Dorothy had continued to accumulate more and more awards. She was honored at the December 1980 National Association for Regional Ballet kick-off luncheon, in recognition of the regional ballet movement's upcoming 25th Anniversary year in 1981. The ceremony was at Lincoln Center in New York City. She received the Capezio Dance Award in 1981, an annual award given by the Capezio Foundation to visionaries of dance. It is one of the most important awards in dance, and along with the certificate she received a $5,000 check, which was a lot of money in 1981. This 30th anniversary Capezio award ceremony was held at The Julliard School on May 11. Violette Verdy presented the award to Dorothy. The award selection committee picked Dorothy because of her "steadfast belief that dance can flourish at the grass roots level and for her idealism and concern for high standards."[12] There was her 80th birthday celebration in April 1984. On opening night at the Fox, before the start of *Sleeping Beauty*, the audience sang "Happy Birthday" as she was handed an enormous bouquet of gorgeous purple iris flowers. The post-show reception, also at the Fox, had at least one hundred friends singing again while she sliced her chocolate birthday cake. Someone decided that a documentary on Dorothy's life was warranted. Fulton County Arts Council provided a grant, and the communications department at the University of Georgia was involved. (The DVD of the documentary can be purchased from the University of Georgia.) AB was filmed performing Balanchine's *Scotch Symphony*. Featured dancers included Anne Burton Avery, Virginia and Maniya. A very young Julianne Spratlin danced for a group of

Atlanta women enjoying afternoon tea; it was filmed at Rhodes Hall on Peachtree Street. "A Dance Memoir: Dorothy Alexander, A Great Georgian" had its premiere in September 1985 at the Atlanta Historical Society (now the Atlanta History Center) on Andrews Drive in Buckhead. The cost to attend was $40, which included a champagne reception, a showing of the film, followed by a dessert reception. The proceeds benefited the Atlanta Ballet Endowment Fund.

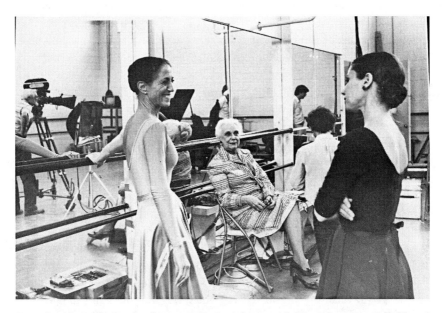

Dorothy Alexander in the dance studio in Atlanta with Virginia Barnett (left) and Anne Burton Avery (right) at a rehearsal for the documentary being filmed on Dorothy Alexander's contribution to dance in America (by Ellen Goldman, courtesy Anne Burton Avery).

Everyone of importance to Dorothy attended with two exceptions, Prissy, her eleven-year-old, spoiled French poodle, who was at home, and Merrilee Smith. After a brief illness, sixty-three-year-old Merrilee had died of cancer back in January. The graveside service was in Americus, Georgia. Merrilee's passing touched so many of us, and tears flowed down cheeks for many weeks. Merrilee taught the students in the lower division; therefore, when Anne Burton Avery was six years old, Merrilee was her first teacher. She praises Merrilee not only for the excellent classical ballet training but also for implanting a passion for teaching. Dorothy was truly saddened by the death of her colleague and close friend. Merrilee had been a dancer in Atlanta Civic Ballet before becoming a co-owner of the Atlanta School of Ballet. She had organized and run the school's non-professional Youth Ensemble company, which would become Atlanta Ballet II (ABII). They had known each other for at least forty years, and their relationship was like that of a mother and daughter.

In 1986, at the age of eighty-two, Dorothy had survived tuberculosis, eight major operations, and several bouts of cancer. Her eyesight was so bad that she could not drive her antique Chrysler. But she was still with it—still coming to performances and letting me know what she liked or did not like. She still dressed to the nines every time she was in the public eye. Her blue eyes still sparkled. In my eyes she was still the gorgeous southern lady who had met Virginia and me at the airport in 1958. As always, there was no complaining about her ill health or how much pain she was in, even though, once again, Dorothy had cancer. She received an honorary Doctor of Humane Letters from Emory University at the May 1986 commencement ceremony. Six months later, though, she was in the midtown hospital located within walking distance of AB's facility. On November 17, I stopped by to see her before going down the street to teach company class. She was in a lot of pain, clearly showing her distress. On my way out of the hospital, I bluntly asked a nurse to get her some relief. It was while I was teaching that the call came in to tell us that Dorothy had died. A graveside service was held on November 19. She was survived by three nieces and three nephews. Only one, Charlotte, lived in Atlanta, however. A memorial service was held December 3, 1986, at the Atlanta Civic Center. Remarks were given by colleagues, friends and a former student, Lane Bradbury. Dancers from ABII, Atlanta Ballet, Carl Ratcliff Dance Theatre, Gainesville Ballet Company, Charleston Ballet Company and Ruth Mitchell Dance Company performed. Maniya and Nicolas danced the second act *Nutcracker* pas de deux. Ginger danced *Avé Maria*. The next night was opening night for *The Nutcracker* at the Civic Center, and

Thanks to our founder, Dorothy Alexander, the Atlanta Ballet celebrates ninety golden years in 2019 (Atlanta Ballet archives).

the performance was dedicated to Miss Dorothy. Being part of the Miss Dorothy family for twenty-eight years was a motivation to not let the petty trifles in life get me down. Grace Noll Crowell, Poet Laureate of Texas in 1935, wrote "The Day." It is a poem that Dorothy loved and cited often. The last two lines of "The Day" are particularly reflective of Dorothy's philosophy of life: "Each night I paus [sic], remembering; Some day, adventurous, lovely thing." That was Miss Dorothy's way.

Highly-trained elite dancers, quality programs (with a live orchestra for *The Nutcracker*), a competent administrative and artistic staff, a board that was supportive and comprised of knowledgeable business men and women from the Atlanta community … everything seemed to mesh in the mid–1980s for growing AB. Except for one thing: We badly needed a permanent home theater. No developer had stepped forward to build a theater like the Tower. The Atlanta city government was not open to building a new theater either, much less a complex like New York City's Lincoln Center. Historically, arts organizations in every city and town in America always need more money; they are always rattling their cups for spare change. And since becoming professional AB was no exception. But we were doing okay. Our real need was a home theater if we wanted to be a major player equal to that of comparable dance companies in cities such as Houston and San Francisco.

The Atlanta School of Ballet was doing pretty well. I was the sole owner now that Merrilee had died, and there were four hundred students. I appointed Tom Pazik as the new director. He and I made some changes, such as extending the school year to eleven months from nine months and changing the name of the junior company from Youth Ensemble to Atlanta Ballet II (ABII). I asked Tom to strengthen the classical ballet training, mainly in the upper-level division in the school. We made changes to raise the quality of dancing in ABII. The junior company had an excellent reputation that was well-deserved because of the outstanding teachers. Even so, I thought we could do better. There were eight to ten dancers in ABII. Naomi-Jane Dixon Clark (who is married to dancer Christian Clark), danced in ABII, along with her good friend Julianne Spratlin. Both would become principals with AB. The level of talent among the students was good, and some were extraordinary. I have always considered all of my students special. But occasionally there would be one or two boys or girls so exceptionally gifted that it was impossible even for a person who knew nothing about ballet not to notice. I cannot name them all, but one who helped me with this book is Caroline Cavallo.

Caroline started dance training at one of the school's small branches when she was nine, probably the one on Johnson's Ferry Road. The next year she was encouraged by a teacher to take classes at the Buckhead school on Cains Hill Place where Merrilee taught. Caroline became one of Merrilee's babies. Merrilee taught Cecchetti technique up to level four. The Vaganova syllabus was taught in the upper levels. Vera Volkova, a former Vaganova student, came regularly to Atlanta to teach in the summer, and Caroline learned a lot from Volkova. Caroline recalls that she learned a lot from my classes, too. She liked the fast footwork and fast tempi, and the complicated steps with a lot of quick changes in weight from one foot to the other, in the variations I taught. It was a technique class similar to what Balanchine had taught me. I am gratified to say that Caroline and a lot of my students called me "Mr. B." For instance, I did not show the variations over and over again. "There was no show-the-step-five-times-until-you-got-it," she said.[13] Caroline was one of those students who almost always got it, and she executed the steps in the variations brilliantly. My teaching style is to keep the barre and center work simple—no mind-bending tricks. I correct the flaws but do not do so by insulting a student. I do not yell. I try to speak at a volume that is almost a "whisper," as Dorothy advised me to do. Technique without artistry is not good dance. Therefore, in addition to teaching students how to master technique, I also teach them the skills of artistry—passing along the tips of the trade that were taught to me. Over the years, many professional dancers have told me how much they learned from my technique classes and my style of teaching, and how much it was appreciated. Caroline is one of those. She got hired at Royal Danish Ballet not only because she was gifted with the perfect ballet body, but also because she worked incredibly hard to master the classical ballet technique training, beginning at an early age. As important, she showed a talent for artistry.

In December 1985, as a tribute to Merrilee, I had no worries asking fifteen-year-old Caroline Cavallo to dance the Sugar Plum Fairy role in *Nutcracker*. She tells me that to dance this classic ballet in memory of Merrilee "was mind-bogglingly HUGE!"[14] And that she was "proud that I could dance for her one last time. All thanks to Mr. B," she said. This performance, a tribute to Merrilee, a very special lady in my life, and watching Caroline dance so expressively, is one of those memories that I will never forget. Merrilee's baby became my baby. And I was the "proud ballet father," that Caroline called me. Caroline was a student at The Galloway School when she studied with me, and the school administrators allowed her to leave campus to take classes at the Atlanta School of Ballet during the day. She graduated high school early, and immediately became a full-time company member of AB. I didn't even move her from pre-professional to apprentice status, and then to full-time professional status in AB; she was that good. In her will, Merrilee had left her baby ballerina money to fly to Moscow to watch the International Ballet Competition. Anne Burton Avery accompanied her. In 1989, when Caroline was prepared, she competed. AB was generous in assisting. We helped with fundraising and sponsors. A costume was built for her in our costume shop. I arranged for a Russian interpreter/agent to be with Caroline. While Caroline was not a medal winner, she was a finalist.

Frank Anderson, artistic director of Royal Danish Ballet, had come to Atlanta to teach in the Summer Intensive program, and he had seen Caroline dance. Frank was so impressed that he asked my permission to invite her to Royal Danish Ballet to take classes. Of course I said yes. I was not surprised when she was offered a contract to join the Royal Danish Ballet, a world-renowned company that was not known for hiring non–Danes. Caroline fell in love with Denmark, and she felt that Royal Danish Ballet and the Bournonville technique were a good fit for her. Even so, the stress on whether to go or to stay with AB was a "guilt-ridden"[15] time for her, she said. We talked about it. I told her that if it didn't work out she could always come back to the AB family. "I walked out of his office as if I had won the lottery ... and I vowed to myself that I wouldn't let him down,"[16] she said. She did not. In 1992, she was promoted to soloist. She was promoted to principal in 1997. She was knighted by Queen Margrethe II in 2000. She won the Reumert Award for dancer of the year.

I never stopped following her career. Peter Martins from NYCB had set *Swan Lake* on Royal Danish Ballet, and Caroline knew the roles of Odette and Odile. When Peter called her two days before a NYCB performance of *Swan Lake* (he needed her to dance the roles of Odette and Odile to save the show, he told her), Virginia and I were in the audience. Because Royal Danish Ballet has a mandatory retirement age of forty, Caroline retired in December 2010. She is married to Eugene Hye-Knudsen, who is the leading cellist with the Aarhus Symphony Orchestra. They have two sons. Today, she is a guest teacher for the Royal Danish Ballet as well as the Royal Danish Ballet School. Back in 1989 I had hoped that Caroline would dance one year with Royal Danish Ballet and then decide that AB was the better fit, that she would come back home. In hindsight, it probably was a good thing that Caroline did not return. Once again, AB was teetering precariously on the edge of a financial cliff.

"The Atlanta Ballet is in crisis,"[17] wrote Helen Smith in the July 23, 1989, *The Atlanta Constitution.* "On the eve of its 60th anniversary, the oldest ballet in the nation is besieged with financial and leadership problems." In ten years the company had grown from an annual budget of $600,000 with about 850 subscribers to $3.2 million with nearly 7,000 subscribers. However, growth pains were hurting the company. There was a $1.4 million deficit, and the Board demanded changes, and AB's president and General Manager was ousted. The times were tough in general, for all the arts. Arts funding at the national, state and local levels had fallen. Symphonies, museums and operas were affected. Too many ballet companies in the U.S. had died or were in the process of reorganizing. Small companies, such as Virginia and Carl Ratcliff's modern dance company, were particularly vulnerable and in jeopardy of folding. While AB could take some comfort in knowing that we were not alone in our financial struggles, it didn't help the bottom line or our prospects for survival. We had to come up with a workable plan to stay alive. In addition to the president and general manager leaving there were layoffs and turnover in the administrative staff that he had supervised. I was traveling when a lot of board meetings were held, extending late into the evenings, devoted to the crisis. Once back in Atlanta I walked into the Pine Street building that was in a state of upheaval and unrest. Along with my leadership team we looked for ways to cut costs, without losing dancers or asking them to dance at reduced salaries or changing the programming for the season, as thousands of tickets had already been sold. Board members and volunteers got on the phones to ask for monetary gifts to save the ballet—$25, $50, $100. No amount was too small. Corporate friends were called upon to help us out of this financial emergency. Of the consultants brought in to evaluate the situation and make recommendations, one after the other commended the company for maintaining its high-quality performance standards and for its low turnover in artistic staff and dancers. Also commended were the volunteers. The weaknesses cited the most in the reports were on the administrative side of the company, including the lack of leadership and the high turnover in staff. There was more dismal news: business men and women on the Board told us that the U.S. had been in a state of robust growth since 1982; now, though, we were in the early days of entering an economic recession, and we had to get prepared for the worst.

Raising money from corporations and individuals during good times is not easy, and in bad economic times it is especially hard. So, while such news about an economic recession was not good to hear, it did tell us that we had to take some extreme measures to cut costs. Of course, an increase in income was also pursued, such as raising the price of tickets. In addition, fundraising efforts had to be ramped up, even though we were handicapped with a limited staff and a small budget for marketing and advertising. We had to not only work harder to increase income, but to work smarter. That sounds easier than it is when there is a deficit of money to support operating expenses, hire staff, or to pay for advertisements. Because of the limited number of staff employed, just getting thank you notes mailed to those donors who did give was a big deal, and often not done. Some givers were understanding; some so frustrated they refused to give again. Thankfully, there were a lot of volunteers who pitched in to help in the office. Women, many of them members of the Guild, were constantly in and out of the building doing all sorts of tasks, such as stuffing envelopes to get invitations to the big fundraising events in the mail—the annual ballet ball invitations, for instance. A website and other social media methods of communication that we rely on today did not exist; nor did we have the computers and software—or staff to use the computers—even if they did. Of the many cost-saving changes that occurred, one in particular caused a firestorm of complaints—the ballet's orchestra was dissolved. We were scheduled to perform in Athens at the University of Georgia. In a newspaper article we learned that some students had organized a boycott to protest the suspending of the orchestra. We drove the seventy miles anyway and danced a pretty good show. When live music was not used for *The Nutcracker,* some musicians in the ballet orchestra picketed. The musicians, wearing tuxedos, playing excerpts from *The Nutcracker* on the sidewalk in front of the Fox, caused the patrons to have to walk through a music-gauntlet to get inside the theater. Carole Goldberg's golden touch was badly needed. But she was no longer a constant presence at AB.

Even though the school I owned was not affected seriously by the financial and leadership problems at AB, nevertheless changes were occurring there, also. We had been in the Cains Hill Place facility since the 50s, and the lease was affordable until the real estate in the area became so pricey that the landlord jumped the rent from $1,700 a month to $3,400, and then notice was given that it was increasing to $4,000. The director, Tom Pazik, and I decided to close the location. We had opened a smaller branch at Johnson Ferry Road the year before. Students in the lower levels studied there. Those in the upper levels moved to the Pine Street location. The ABII nonprofessional company was housed there as well, which was a good move because it gave these dancers more contact with AB dancers.

While the Pine Street building was a good facility as far as size to accommodate our needs, and for its location near the theaters, the building badly needed repairs and a major renovation. It was shabby in appearance, inside and out. There were a lot of complaints from parents and volunteers about driving to Midtown where parking was not easy to find and which had to be paid for. My attention during this dramatic phase when we were on the downhill-roller-coaster track was on protecting the dancers, however, and not the inadequate facility. I wanted to protect their jobs. I wanted to provide our loyal patrons with a season that showed we were still dancing at the same high standard as in the years before—a level of excellence that we had worked so hard to achieve. And we did. The 60th birthday gala opening was on September 21 at the Civic Center. Twenty-one professionals and fourteen apprentices performed, for the first time in Atlanta, Balanchine's *Stars and Stripes*. I choreographed two new works: *Fascinating Rhythms* and *Reflections For*, which were tributes to Merrilee Smith and to Dorothy Alexander. And there was a live orchestra in the pit.

By the end of 1989, I was grateful that the financial crisis had not affected the dancers or artistic staff to the point of instability. We cut expenses, but never lowered our standards. This occurred because of the great leadership team in place—dancers, choreographers, and artistic assistants, such as principal dancer (and senior advisor to the younger dancers) Maniya Barredo. There was Maniya's now former husband, Mannie Rowe. Mannie was my right-hand man, although his official position was ballet master. We were so fortunate to have such a fantastic protect-the-ballet team. And when not touring, Carl Ratcliff and Virginia were always ready to jump in and assist with whatever was needed, also. If the Board did their part, I knew that AB would be okay. What was missing in this crisis compared to the others we had survived in my thirty-one-year history with the company was Dorothy's calmness, her practicality, and her optimism that always helped to keep our spirits high and to keep our focus forward.

Chapter Eleven

A New Direction

I am an optimist by choice. But I must admit that the first four years of the 1990s do not hold as many pleasant, fun memories as the previous four decades of my professional ballet career. I was sixty-five years old, in good health, and not even thinking about ending my professional dance career yet. But there were the occasional fleeting thoughts flickering around my brain from time to time of what it would be like to pursue a new direction and what that direction would be. Virginia was having similar thoughts about her career. Because of reductions in federal, state and local funding, and the skimpy support for the arts in general among the Atlanta community, the Carl Ratcliff Dance Theatre was struggling to survive. In four years she would be sixty—did she still want to be dancing? The early 1990s was an era when the arts programs in the U.S. were struggling. Reductions in the NEA touring program, for example, was seriously limiting the opportunities for educating kids on the importance of the arts in society. Budget cuts at the federal, state and local levels were affecting kids in grades K-12 as the arts curricula were watered down or eliminated in school districts. Dance, which had once been a noticeable, if not an integral, part of the physical education curriculum, was on the chopping block waiting for the sharp blade to strike. Dorothy, who had been one of the first to add dance and movement to the physical education curriculum in the Atlanta public school system that served as a model for school districts throughout the U.S., would have been fighting mad. I was really thankful for our Kids In Step program, and kept my fingers crossed that the Atlanta and area public school systems would not stop supporting the program.

As Ginger and I looked at the world around us and discussed the major changes occurring, we knew that the year 1990 was the beginning of a decade that was going to be of great importance to our future career plans. What new direction did we want? There were more questions than answers. Whatever the direction, however, it had to give us more time together and with less backstage-dance drama. There had been too many years when finding time to relax, enjoy long, leisurely visits with our grown sons, and to take vacations to the West Coast to visit relatives seemed almost impossible to schedule. There were gigs where both of us were paid to stage a ballet, such as *Serenade,* which was great. Still, there were lots of days when Ginger got on a plane at the Atlanta airport headed in one direction, and I got on a different plane headed in another. Adjudicating and teaching master classes at SERBA and being involved with the other regional ballet associations required lots of travel. Living the good life is not supposed to always be easy. But the roller-coaster ride of good years-bad years, because of AB's spells of financial difficulties and the consequential all too frequent turnover in administrative staff, was getting harder and harder to stomach. Furthermore, I had yet to reach the goal of increasing the number of AB dancers to thirty-two. The 1990–1991 season started with twenty-one dancers and fourteen apprentices on a thirty-four-week contract. There were maybe forty-six members on the Board. The chairman was Lynda Courts. She had been a student in Dorothy and Merrilee's school, and she had danced with Atlanta Civic Ballet. Tom Stark was the new Executive Director, a former vice president of an international corporation. He was hired to fix AB's problems, a temporary replacement for the former president and general manager. A lot of new people, a lot of abrupt, big changes, and yet I was determined to stay optimistic. It's not that my spirits were dragging the ground. It's just that they weren't bouncing as high as I would have liked in the bright-blue-ballet sky. The word "fun" was not a word I uttered often.

I have always told my students and company members to "leave your troubles at the door" whenever they walked into the studio. During AB's financial recessions and depressions, the students and company dancers did. And I did the same. Thus, as we entered the 1990s, I could not have been prouder of our dance family's dedication to their art and to AB. Also propping up our spirits was that the five-year residency at Brooklyn College had been more successful than imagined. Occurring at the same time as the residency were cultural arts trips that we undertook, which resulted in an unexpected bonus: a group of die-hard AB fans from the New York area who joined AB patrons on some fun foreign excursions. Traveling in small groups to see some of the finest ballet companies in Russia, Europe and Asia got AB lots of new, very supportive friends that made us known in the New York City area. And there were other good signs that we were on a slow climb up the roller-coaster track. Tom Stark was replaced by Charles Johnston, the former headmaster of Trinity School, a private school in northwest Atlanta. The Board had raised maybe about $600,000 in pledges. Drastic changes to cut expenses had significantly reduced the deficit. While the lack of a live orchestra had affected ticket sales, particularly *The Nutcracker* in 1989, AB was now crawling out of the financial pit. It was a great relief when there was even more good news to announce to our patrons who had remained loyal: "Live Music is Back!" proclaimed an ad published in *The Atlanta Constitution*. The ad was for *The Red Shoes,* with a live orchestra in the pit at the Atlanta Civic Center. This thankfully good newsworthy happening came about because of a collaboration (we shared costs) with Ballet South of Birmingham, Alabama. The choreographer was Ballet South's Thor Sutowski, who had been a resident guest choreographer at AB in 1987. Also on the program were the pas de deux from *Le Corsair* and my neoclassical piece *Arensky Dances.* Now, if we could only find a decent-sized home theater. By budget size AB was the third-largest arts organization in the Atlanta area, behind the Atlanta Symphony Orchestra and Alliance Theatre. We were the only arts organization of the three not to have our own home theater, however. I consoled myself that while the pace of financial recovery at AB was much slower than ideal, at least the train was inching upward and no longer plummeting downward.

Because of AB's annual performances on the campus of the University of Georgia in Athens, which is about seventy miles northeast of Atlanta, an instructor in the university's dance department and I had become friends. Because of her connections in Taipei, I had made two trips there to teach and coach. As a result, AB was invited to visit the country in November 1990 and perform four shows. I recall that the Taiwanese government paid most of the expenses for the trip; we could not have done it otherwise. The rep program was *Serenade, Four Temperaments,* and *Prodigal Son.* There was a total of thirty-four dancers. Corps members included a few of the Taiwanese dancers I had taught. Also in the corps de ballet was fifteen-year-old Julianne Spratlin, who was in ABII. At age ten she had danced Mary in *Nutcracker.* Julianne was a talented young student who was working hard to master her craft, and I had no hesitation in assigning her increasingly difficult parts in the classic full-length story ballets, such as *Coppelia* and *Romeo and Juliet.* We talked about her pursuing a professional ballet career once she graduated from high school. I knew that she would go far. Flying to Taipei was AB's first international trip since the 1950s. The flight to Taipei and the performances went well. The flight home was not so good. Our plane was delayed in Seoul, Korea. We slept on benches, on the floor, anywhere we could find a comfortable place to lie down and sleep in the airport overnight. I believe there was only one store open that offered food, and we cleaned them out. Still, when the minister of culture in Taipei asked me to return to teach ballet for six weeks in the summer, and asked Virginia to teach modern dance, we did not hesitate to say yes.

AB was in need of a male dancer, a tall male dancer to partner the taller girls. Usually, Maiqui Manosa returned to the Philippines in the summers to dance. One summer a company she was dancing with was involved in a cultural exchange program with the National Ballet of China. One dancer and one choreographer representing the Philippines were to go to China. One dancer and one choreographer from China were to go to the Philippines. Filipina Maiqui Manosa was the dancer chosen. Wei Dongsheng was the dancer for China. Maiqui called me to talk about this exceptional male dancer she was dancing with. She sent me a videotape. Not only was Wei a principal dancer with an internationally famous company, he had to be six feet tall. I began recruiting him to join AB. The first time the offer was made Wei said no. He did not want to leave the National Ballet of China or give up the perks, including a comfortable apartment paid for by the government. I was determined, though, and months later I made the offer again. This time Wei said yes—but for one season only. And on one condition: he was married; his wife, also a dancer in the National Ballet of China, had to come dance in AB, too. Luckily, the political iceberg between the U.S. and Communist countries, such as China, had begun to thaw. Also, travel restrictions in China had eased. It wasn't simple, but we did get all the official documents approved so that Wei and Jenny could leave China and live in the U.S. for one year. Wei remembers that he and Jenny Jue Chen were the first married couple to be allowed to leave Communist China together; the year before it would not have been permitted. Knowing that the leave of absence was for one season only, the Chinese government held Wei and Jenny's apartment for them. Maiqui helped the couple to find an apartment near the Lindbergh Marta station. Once the couple had settled in, I picked up the twenty-four-year-old Wei in my jeep and drove him to a dealership to help him buy his first American car. Twenty-plus years later, Wei and Jenny still live in the Atlanta area.

Not long after the couple's arrival in the fall of 1991, I lost my best friend: Ralph Emanuel "Mannie" Rowe, Jr. He died at age forty-four. Mannie was not only my right-hand man, he was my right arm. For so many of my works, Mannie Rowe was the ballet master, putting the polish not only on my ballets but on the ballets of many a guest choreographer. And he choreographed, too. He had been an excellent dancer in his youth, until a knee injury caused an early retirement. He was an outstanding teacher and loved by his students in the school and the company dancers. He had mentored Gil Boggs, who was now a principal with ABT. He was close friends with our boys. Mannie had stayed at our home on more than one occasion to take care of David and the dogs when Ginger and I were traveling. He was active in the regional ballet movement and was a frequent teacher or speaker at seminars and workshops across the U.S. For the past four years he had been married to a New York free-lance costumer, Judanna Lynn, and they had commuted between their homes in New York and Georgia. Judanna designed some costumes for AB. Just before his death he was promoted to associate artistic director. Mannie died in November 1991. Only three days earlier there had been another sad loss. Ginger's younger brother, Michael Peter Rich, died at age fifty-three. Because Michael and Mannie were in the same hospital, although on different floors, son David remembers visiting them both before their deaths. Another death a few weeks later was equally sad. Vera Idella Barnett died at age ninety-nine. She was living in a senior-living facility, but still mentally with it and physically mobile. On December 15, she and Winnie had spent a pleasant day eating lunch at a restaurant in Wenatchee, enjoying each other's company. Mom had her hair done, too. They returned to Mom's home and continued talking until Mom said she wanted to take a nap. Winnie stopped at Lois's house for a quick visit; Lois was going to spend time with Mom tomorrow. Once Winnie was home, she got the telephone call: Mom had passed peacefully, in her sleep. There were so many deaths those last few months of 1991 that our family cried a lot of tears during the holiday season.

Virginia and my mom, Vera Barnett, and our sons Rob and David, at Mom's home in Wenatchee, Washington.

The year 1992 marked the beginning of the biggest collaboration project in AB's history, far exceeding the full-length *Swan Lake* production at Chastain Park. It was a full-length *Swan Lake* with Cleveland San Jose Ballet, and it was performed in three different cities. Artistic Director Dennis Nahat, who had gained fame from his role in the popular 1977 ballet film *The Turning Point*, and I were good friends. Nahat and I wanted to raise local and national attention on the importance of our two outstanding companies, and to make some money at the same time, and we believed it possible by sharing the costs, the resources (such as sets and costumes), and dancers and

With Kailo at my mom's house in Wenatchee, Washington.

artistic staff. After months of preparation, this enormous collaborative production launched on March 3, 1993, at the Cleveland State Theatre and concluded on March 14. The next performance was in San Jose, California. From March 26 through April 4 the ballet was performed at the Center for Performing Arts. We finished in Atlanta. The ballet was at the Civic Center from April 15 through April 25. Dennis and I began talking about a second collaboration—*Sleeping Beauty,* probably in 1995.

A second, although much smaller, collaboration project was in May 1992 with son David and the rock band "Tom Grose & The Varsity." David and Rob were, and still are, into sports—Rob is the family golfer and David the ice hockey player. Growing up, Rob had little interest in dance. He was around it most of his young life because Ginger and I took the boys to the school when we taught classes and to the theater when we were rehearsing. The boys were expected to do their homework and to stay out of trouble, but I think they actually spent more time running around and playing games in the dark auditorium or backstage or, if at the school on Cains Hill Place, walking down the street to buy snacks at the city's famous bakery-deli. Following after his

Gramps (Dick Rich), Rob never showed much enthusiasm for the arts. David on the other hand may not have wanted to dance—he certainly did not want to take ballet or modern dance lessons—but he got a kick out of the theatrics that surrounded it, including dressing in the feetless modern dance tights he saw Ginger and Carl Ratcliff wear all the time. He liked to get into the makeup

My family: Virginia and our sons Rob and David, circa 1963, in Atlanta.

kits Ginger and I had at home and paint his face. If guests were in the house (Yogi Berra, for instance, or Dick's good friend *Wizard of Oz* strawman Ray Bolger), David provided some fun entertainment that had us all laughing. In the early 1990s, my grown-up son had a career in the music production business, and he is the one who probably came up with the idea of AB collaborating with the local band. The piece was part of the "1992 Dedication Series" at the Georgia Tech Theatre for the Arts. We hired a black choreographer based in New York City, my friend Louis Johnson, to create "Rockin' to the Pointe." It definitely met the goal of being a high-voltage rock ballet. Some of the AB diehard patrons had problems with it. I thought they needed the education, though.

This same year AB started a one-week summer residency in Asheville, North Carolina. It was sponsored by the Haywood County Arts Council. If funding was secured, the residency would expand to six weeks every summer. There were several reasons for wanting to be in Asheville during the summer, and not just because it was a lot cooler in the mountains than in the humid, hot Atlanta's low-rise hills. It kept the dancers working; that is, working with AB and not free-lancing with other companies where they might be hired away. From Balanchine I had learned the importance of keeping dancers together as many months of the year as possible. That is why he began the England tour in 1950, and I wanted to do something similar at AB.

There were many other significant events in the early 1990s. Tom Pazik had been ill for some time. While he had had chemotherapy treatment that left him weak and sick and using a wheelchair, in October 1993 we were pleased that he was able to attend a tribute in his honor at a local theater. The proceeds were used to assist with AIDS research. In November Ginger and I held our annual Thanksgiving dinner gala for friends and family. It was not unusual for us to share dinner with twenty to thirty guests in our small condo. Wei and Jenny, and other AB dancers from other countries who had no family nearby, came to the Barnett Thanksgiving feast. Wei loved my cooking. I am really top-notch with the baked goods (daughter-in-law Jackie loves my light-as-air pumpkin chiffon pie) thanks to the lessons learned from my mother. Thanksgiving Day started out well, until we got the telephone call: Tom Pazik had died in a local hospital. Julianne Spratlin and Tom were very close. He was her teacher, her mentor. Julianne and Kathy McBeth Hutcheson were with him when he passed. Soon, Ginger and I were at the hospital, too. We invited Julianne and Kathy to our home. The guests had left, and the four of us shared Tom Pazik stories. We laughed, and we cried.

In the spring of 1994 I was in Florida setting a ballet and got a call that was completely unexpected. The Executive Board of the Atlanta Ballet had met and decided that I had to cut about two million dollars out of the 1994–1995 season budget. I resigned. I left because there had been just too many times when a budget would be set, and then, in the spring, the Board would say that we could not do the last season as planned. Sometimes, they voted to cut it. I would explain that we had to do it; that season tickets had been purchased and the company, having spent the cash, did not have the money to give it back. Dumpy facilities in the Pine Street location and a *Nutcracker* production held together with spit and glue were one thing, but the Board's decision to eliminate a program with season tickets already sold, and to dock the dancers' salaries, was too much. It was no secret that I was thinking about retiring. In fact, the need to devise a succession plan had been discussed. That telephone call in the spring of 1994, however, shoved me over the cliff.

Upon my return to Atlanta from Florida I walked into the studio to teach company class. The dancers had not a clue. After telling them I was retiring, in July, every one of them was stunned into silence, and then we all cried. We struggled on. But at the end of the session there was not a dry shirt or leotard in the room: our clothes, especially mine, were soaked with sweat and tears. My last official day on the job was July 1, 1994. My title was now artistic director emeritus. Today, looking back, I believe that in some ways my leaving was meant to happen. And that AB eventually benefited. My leaving abruptly woke people up, and the company has prospered. I'm not the kind of person who dwells on things. I just move on. Ginger, however, not so much. If Atlanta wants to be a city comparable to New York City, San Francisco, Boston and Houston, for example, it has got to do more to support the arts. Sports are all well and good. But a major-player city must have the arts, too. And then there is the international reputation to consider as well. Ginger, especially, was disappointed in the Atlanta community's lack of support for the arts.

Suddenly, both Ginger and I were headed in a new direction. The Carl Ratcliff Dance Theatre had folded, and America's first professional modern dance company in the Southeast was never resurrected. I still had my Atlanta School of Ballet to run, however, although ABII was dissolved. The Johnson Ferry Road branch was closed and the school moved to Chastain Square on Roswell Road. Chic Murphy was the Executive Director. Andrea Pell was director of the pre-professional division, and Joanne Lee was director of the lower-level division. Dodi Olson, mother of Christian Clark, a student at the school and then an AB dancer, was the receptionist. David, who was still in the music production business, moved his office to the school to help out with the accounting and finances. Now that the school was in good management hands, I could pay more attention to my work with the regional ballet associations, especially SERBA. Since 1958 I had attended every SERBA festival, and many other regional festivals, working either as a master teacher and/or adjudicator, and also serving on boards. I am still involved today. Not being artistic director at AB gave me more time to travel to set ballets and to teach master classes at companies all over the world. Most important, I had more time to spend with Ginger and the family and with friends. Ginger and I began to plan the next phase of our life together. After so many years of living in a small condo because of our hectic schedules, we wanted a more peaceful way of living, in a bigger house to entertain, and with lots of land so that Ginger could nurture her gardens. The first question was where did we want to live? It had to be a city, preferably a small city, where the government and the residents were passionate about the arts. Ginger and I bought property in Waynesville, North Carolina, and began to build our new home in the Smoky Mountains. It would take two years to complete the house. In the meantime, most months were spent in Atlanta.

Upon my departure from AB, Tim Cronin, the associate artistic director, was appointed interim artistic director. The man hired as the AB artistic director was John McFall. I knew John, having brought him in to premiere his ballet *The Watchers* on the AB company in 1985. Soon after he arrived at AB he established a dance education school, and for a year or two there were two schools closely associated with AB. After some consideration, the AB Board offered to buy my school, and the negotiations began.

In 1996, the Waynesville house was finished, and we moved in. The negotiations to sell my school to AB were finalized and the deal was closed in 1997. From then on there was no need for us to make the four-to-five-hour drive from our house to Atlanta except for important occasions.

Two such important occasions occurred almost immediately after our move. Carl Ratcliff, who had cancer, died. A memorial service was held at his home in Lilburn, Georgia, at his Red Arrow Ranch. The second occasion for our drive back to Atlanta was in October. The Atlanta Chamber of Commerce Arts and Business Council awarded me the Coca-Cola Lifetime Achievement Award for Outstanding Arts Leadership. It was a recognition of my professional dance career with Colonel d 'Basil's Original Ballet Russe, New York City Ballet, and Atlanta Ballet. A lot of high praise was heard that Monday night on October 21, 1996. I gave an acceptance speech but kept it short. I wasn't going to make my audience suffer. (I don't want to hear a long-winded speaker; it upsets me.) While I was humbled and delighted by this unexpected award, in my speech I did give a poke-in-the-face scolding to the business leaders and community movers-and-shakers present for failing to provide the financial backing for the arts that most cities of the same size do.

Then, in November, Ginger and I were back in Atlanta. A Carl Ratcliff memorial dance performance was held at the small but appropriate 14th Street Playhouse where they company had often performed. Ginger danced one of Carl's pieces. Maniya Barredo and Kathryn McBeth Hutcheson danced, also.

Except for the death of Jerome Robbins in 1998, the rest of the decade was filled with terrific happenings for Ginger and me. Most notably, our first

Here I am with dancers Anne Burton Avery (left) and Maniya "Honey" Barredo in Atlanta.

grandson arrived. David was now married to Jackie, and they had a son, Aaron, in 1998. The next decade was filled with lots of family fun and thrills, also. Robert married Elizabeth. They had a son, Ryan, in 2004. In celebration of our 50th wedding anniversary, Ginger and I took the six members of our family to Jamaica in 2007. While the family spent hours on the beautiful beach, I spent hours shopping. Buying clothes for Ginger was what I loved to do, as it was of no interest to her. Of course, I had to visit the jewelry stores, too. Elizabeth was pregnant on the trip. Thank goodness she suffered no major discomforts or illness. Grandson Austin was born in 2008. Life in Waynesville was good. But the arts community is so exceptional in Asheville that Ginger and I sold our house and moved.

My professional ballet career has been extraordinary, and the accolades given to me for my years of service have been many. I have served as a juror, such as the Competitor Selection Committee juror for the 6th annual USA International Ballet Competition in Jackson, Mississippi. I was a master teacher, also. I have traveled extensively setting ballets, teaching, lecturing. It is hard to believe, but I was actually persuaded out of retirement to dance again in 2010. John McFall proposed the idea. It was James Kudelka's *Four Seasons*. When I was asked, I refused to do it unless Anne Burton Avery could be persuaded to come out of retirement and dance in the piece as well. She agreed. To prepare, I did weeks of barre work every morning. After all, my last dance had been in 1974, and I wasn't sure how my balky knee would hold up. Ginger said that I was out of my mind. After the ordeal was finally finished I was satisfied with my performance. It felt great to be eighty-four and to be able to get up there on that stage and move around, although I did have to be treated by a naturopath for a pinched meniscus during the final rehearsals. Still, I did it. I did the dance. But that's it for me. My professional ballet career is going to only involve coaching, teaching and setting ballets. And I am still sticking to that plan at the mature age of ninety-four.

Chapter Twelve

Passing It Along

Writing this autobiography has been a literary pas de deux: my partner, Cynthia Crain. I have led, and she has followed, and together we have danced on the stage of what has been a most memorable journey. It is a journey of reflection on those valuable lessons I learned that benefited me not only professionally, but personally. In 2017, I set Balanchine divertissements—"Sugar Plum Fairy," and "Spanish" and "Candy Cane"—on some Atlanta Ballet 2 dancers. Afterwards, a few of the boys came up to me and asked: what was it like to dance for Mr. Balanchine? It is a question I have been asked a lot in my seventy-years-plus of dancing, teaching, coaching and setting ballets. As always, it is a question I am delighted to answer.

It was from Mr. B that I learned that dance could exist on its own without a narrative; that a choreographer could use only steps and movement to express the feeling of the musical composition, such as his ballet *Symphony in C*. Dedicated to learning as much as I could, I studied Mr. B's style and methods when he taught company class. I attended as many of his rehearsals as possible, even when I wasn't cast, to learn how to choreograph, how to select dancers, and to learn more about technique and artistry. In Mr. B's neoclassical ballets the steps and movements could be very fast. I remember him telling the women to spring up—to attack. Don't roll up on pointe. With a spring up you have to bring your toes under your pointe shoes to do it correctly; the woman must be right up on her metatarsals. If the ballerina rolls up onto her pointes, she is too late to stay in time with the music. I can remember dancing some of his petit allégro combinations without once placing my heels on the floor between steps in order to keep in time with the music. And to be cast in a Balanchine ballet a dancer had to keep time with the music. Mr. B wanted the traditional classical ballet technique methods taught in the school and in company classes, and he didn't care whether it was Vaganova, Cecchetti, Bournonville or a combination of the three. What was different about his classes (and he regularly taught company class) was that he added his own unique style. For example, while Nijinska wanted the hips square (the Cecchetti technique), Balanchine wanted the downstage hip open, because he said it was more aesthetically pleasing to the audience. Also, I learned a lot from Jerry Robbins and from the many guest choreographers, such as Freddie Ashton. Still, there was no one like Mr. B. "One of the most significant things Bobby did was to bring the Balanchine ballets to Atlanta Ballet,"[1] Dawn Mullins, a former dancer, told Cynthia Crain. Yes, I was a disciple. A disciple who did my part to grow ballet in America. By living down South in Atlanta (which a reputable New York City dance writer called the boondocks), for so many years, I was able to spread the word, to educate a lot of people who could not get to New York City, on Mr. B's style of technique and his neoclassical ballets—his American-style neoclassical ballets. And for that to have happened, I must thank Dorothy Alexander.

It was such an honor when she offered me the positions of associate artistic director and principal dancer in her ballet company, and she taught me a lot. She pushed me in directions I might never have considered, such as choreography, for example. When I first arrived in 1958 Dorothy was not doing much choreography anymore, although we kept many of her eighty-plus works in the Atlanta Ballet (AB) repertoire for years. And while I did not create as many ballets as Dorothy, her pushing got me to do my fair share, because it had to be done. That's what most artistic directors do I soon learned upon my arrival in Atlanta; it is part of the job. I was a utility choreographer. My way of creating a new work was to start with movement, with combinations, to create patterns, and then to find the music to fit my choreography. Because of the hours spent watching Mr. B, I knew that he often chose music first, then he added movement, combinations and patterns. I took a slightly different approach. I liked to first think about a style and tempo, a 6/8 tempo, for instance. I liked fast movement and quick changes in direction, and this I did learn from Mr. B. Also, I was influenced by the way he constructed a ballet. Often, he had two or three movements, sometimes four movements, using different-sized casts, whereas I usually choreographed a thirty-minute ballet with two or three movements, with different-sized casts. I choreographed at least two or three new ballets a season, and there are a couple that I am especially proud of. The one I would like to see performed again one day is a harp concerto created for eight boys and seventeen girls. Although I choreographed a lot of works as artistic director at AB, choreographing was not my favorite thing to do. My bag was to entertain and to educate. Teaching and coaching and setting Balanchine ballets is what got me up and about every day, and still does. Whether walking into a studio in Taipei or Atlanta, I love the smells and familiar sights and sounds. Like the sound of resin cracking as a dancer grinds her pointe shoe inside the resin box; hearing the excited voices of dancers sitting on the floor warming up, stretching their rubbery bodies; watching the kids at the barre and in the center, pushing their bodies to the outer limits. Then, at the end of a really demanding and exhausting two hours, smelling the sweet sweat of a job well done.

From both Balanchine and Dorothy, I learned a lot about teaching. Classical ballet technique-training is hard. It takes years to master. Placement is everything. Many of my students know me for my prickly comments when I spot a ballerina who is off her leg. It doesn't happen as much with the boys, but then they don't dance on pointe. Whenever I catch a female not standing properly on her leg, that's when I call for a pause in the action and take the time to teach her (and the other girls and guys in the class who should be watching and learning) how to stand correctly; how to pull up the muscles in the front of the hip. Also, I am known for my attention to artistry. Artistry is so important, especially in the lead roles in the traditional story classic ballets, such as Odette or Aurora or Giselle. Artistry is not a series of drills that can be mastered after hours and hours of practice, like technique training. Nor can a dancer be taught how to feel. Dorothy once told Anne Burton that she could not dance the principal role in *Giselle* until she had suffered a real tragedy, because only then would she know how to express what the peasant girl felt upon learning that her lover, Prince Albrecht, had betrayed her. Eventually, a mature Anne, once she had experienced tragedy in her life, did dance *Giselle*. And she was *Giselle*—the young and naïve, head-over-heels-in-love peasant girl, who goes mad. While I can give tips or coach young dancers on how to express themselves in certain roles—a turn of the head, the placement of the arms, a splaying of the fingers, whether to smile or frown, for instance—artistry is a gift that a dancer is born with. What I can do, however, is to nurture and to hone that gift. Artistry and self-expression have to work together, and it is completely a personal thing: Hate, adore, or sad—those are examples of self-expression. And a dancer must be real; otherwise the audience will see through the phoniness in a minute. Anne Burton was real, no matter what role she performed. So was I. That is why Balanchine, Robbins and Ashton gave me all those dramatic roles. When I walked onto the stage to dance I became another person; no longer was I Robert Barnett. When coaching a dancer in a role I ask them what they see, what is it that they feel in a movement? I ask: if you hug or shake someone's hand in a ballet, what do you feel when you do it? Are you doing the motion because I tell you to, or because you feel it? That is self-expression. On that stage, a dancer has to show the audience that he has something important to say. You must become the character, and not just through the steps and combinations, but with the gestures: the head, the arms and even down to the tips of the fingers. And, equally important, do not get sloppy with your ankles, feet or the toes.

That does not mean that technique is laid by the wayside to concentrate on artistry, that once mastered there is no need to further one's training other than to take company class. A dancer has to continue honing technique until retirement. And no dancer is too senior to not need constant teaching and coaching. For example, Margot Fonteyn worked privately with coaches until the day she quit dancing. How is classical ballet technique-training different from when I started in the 1940s compared to today? I am frequently asked.

Anne Burton Avery in *Giselle* (courtesy Anne Burton Avery).

One big difference is that today classes are more technically athletic. And while dancers are performing incredible feats that wow patrons and judges at competitions (the woman's leg repeatedly knocking against her earlobe, for example), I do think this trend to make ballet look more athletic has gone too far. There is a trade-off between athletic feats and aesthetics. Athletic style dancing may be fine for dance-reality shows on television. But it has no place in the theater if ballet wants serious respect as an art form. As I said in an interview, the "art and classicism of ballet is lost. Epaulement and refined port de bras are being brushed aside for super technique.... What is missing from training today is a variety of styles and understanding of time periods. This is killing the artistic aspects of classical ballet today."[2]

Another change I do not like seeing is the artistic director's absence from teaching company class. I remember being asked in an interview whether the artistic director of a ballet company should teach: Definitely, was—and still is—my answer. Nijinska, when she was artistic director of Rubenstein's company in the 1930s, taught company class—a really demanding company class in the morning, followed by hours of rehearsing that might extend late into the night. While no professional ballet company operating today can require dancers to dance as many hours as they did in the 1930s, it still is important for the artistic director to teach company class. Mr. B was always in the studio teaching because he was deciding who to cast in his ballets. By teaching, he knew what every dancer was good at and what was not his or her thing. And that is why I did the same as artistic director at AB, no matter how busy my schedule.

Students often ask me: what does it take to become a professional dancer? "First of all, take care of your body! Second, come to class to work hard. Leave your problems outside. Third, attitude is everything. See in the mirror what's really there, and not what you want to see."[3] Fourth, follow your passion. To work in a profession that requires hours and hours, and many years, of training, a dancer must love what she or he is doing. Also, be willing to accept the possibility that even if you do work hard and have the ambition, you may not succeed. Not everyone who has a passion for classical ballet performing has the talent, the physical requirements (the agility, the flexibility, or the mental facility to memorize parts quickly, for example), the tolerance for physical and emotional pain, or the innate ability required for musicality. I have friends who cannot carry a tune, and they will never be professional singers. If a dancer cannot keep time with the music, then classical ballet is not the career for her or for him. Fifth, you have to be able to accept criticism well, too, and constant criticism requires developing a thick skin. And last, after years of training, if you do continue to develop and to progress, make sure you are prepared before you start auditioning to get accepted into a professional ballet company. Most dancers audition too soon, before they are ready to be seen. Wait until you are well-trained, beautifully polished, and that when you are in an audition you complete everything asked of you. And do it well with a good attitude. It is not only a matter of auditioning and getting into just any company; consider whether that company is right for you. Don't take two hours to audition one day and then run out and leave. Find a company that seems to be a good fit and take class every day. See how the teachers teach, observe rehearsals, know the company's repertoire. Make sure a company is the place you really want to be if offered a job.

With the merging of classical ballet and modern dance, have we gone too far and has there been a watering down of classical ballet? I am asked. No. Although dancers do have to be more versatile in the kinds of dance classes required today than when I started my training with Nijinska. Because contemporary ballet works (works that rely on a dancer having both a classical ballet technique foundation and modern dance technique fundamentals) are part of the repertoire in almost any mid-sized to large ballet company in the world, a dancer must be able to perform both classical (Marius Petipa and Lev Ivanov's famous thirty-two fouettes in *Swan Lake*, for example) and contemporary (rolling on the floor, a friend calls it) choreography. Wei Dongsheng says that he had a difficult time the first few years he danced with AB in the early 1990s because he had had no training or experience dancing contemporary ballets with the National Ballet of China.[4] The grand pas de deux in *Swan Lake* he could dance effortlessly. Balanchine's neoclassical *Square Dance* was a real struggle—at first. Mr. B is responsible for launching a demand for more versatile dancers. He was an experimenter who changed the look of classical ballet. *Stars and Stripes,* for example: He said that he choreographed the ballet because he liked the music; that it did not need a narrative. Yet the ballet still requires the dancers to have a classical ballet foundation; it is not a ballet for a Broadway hip-hop-hoofer-trained dancer.

To reiterate, because it cannot be stressed enough, mastering and continually honing technique is important to be a professional classical ballet dancer, but so is artistry. A student may have the right attributes: long arms, long neck and long legs, for instance; but if she performs on stage like an empty taxi cab, the audience will not want to watch. I would much rather see someone on the stage that excites me rather than see someone who has the perfect classical ballet body. Pretty feet, precise pirouettes—or triple tours and a series of sharp, crisp brisé volé for the boys—will not cut it without artistry. I've watched dancers perform technically difficult roles, such as the

Bluebird male solo in *Sleeping Beauty*, and perform flawlessly—technically. Yet the audience's applause was not enthusiastic because the dancer did not dance. I mean the steps were all there correctly, but the piece wasn't danced. You have to show that you are enjoying being on that stage. And there is a difference between artistry and personality. I don't always like a performance when a dancer mugs for the audience. Most important, ballet is not about tricks, it's about aesthetics. It's an art form. Athleticism for the sake of it, the way it is often being done now, is not art. Virginia was beautifully proportioned, and she knew how to move. She was outstanding both technically and artistically when she danced the role of the Dewdrop Fairy.

My views on programming? It did not take me long working with Dorothy to understand the importance of good programming. Often, I brought in guest choreographers for a program, in addition to the one piece on the program that was mine, because variety is key. Usually, a program included three, or maybe four short works if one was a pas de deux. Also, I learned to never make an audience watch a program that is more than two hours. I don't recommend two intermissions either; too many patrons will leave at the second one. After the first one or two pieces on the program I often used a five-, maybe ten-, minute pause, followed by a pas de deux, then a fifteen-to-twenty-minute intermission, followed by the last ballet—a grand finale. Because AB was not that big, everyone danced in the last piece. On a typical program I tried to do something traditional; followed by a war horse pas de deux from iconic ballets, such as *Le Corsair* or *Swan Lake*. I ended the program with a real dance piece. For example, Balanchine's electrifying *Stars & Stripes* ballet, the music by John Philip Sousa, was a real crowd-rousing finale.

In recognition of my experience and dedication to passing along what I learned, I have been pleased to be asked to teach a lot since leaving AB in 1994. For a while, back in the early 2000s, I was on the dance faculty at South Carolina Governor's School for the Arts, also known as the Governor's School. The director of the ballet program was Stanislav "Stas" Issaev. I had met Stas in Varna, Bulgaria, at the 1980 competition when I was the U.S. coach and my student, Gil Boggs, was a contestant. Gil did well but did not medal. Stas did win a gold medal, however, and we became good friends. In 2017 I was asked by a former student, Jeffrey Rockland, to teach master classes and give lectures at Kent State University in Ohio. Just this past summer I taught classes at Maniya Barredo's Metropolitan Ballet Theatre. In addition to teaching and coaching, I have continued to set a lot of ballets. After leaving Atlanta, there were many summers when Virginia and I spent several weeks in Hawaii with Ballet Hawaii or in the Philippines with Philippine Ballet Theatre. There were other international gigs, but these two places we visited the most.

In 2017, Nancy Reynolds, the Director of Research at the Balanchine Foundation, invited me to New York City for a project she oversees. I was filmed coaching dancers in "Candy Cane" and *Stars and Stripes* for the foundation's archives. Other good friends involved were Patricia Wilde, Allegra Kent and Gloria Govrin. And Patricia Wilde and I were back in 2018 for a second videotaping of Balanchine works. It was such a privilege to be asked to participate in the recording of Balanchine ballets for the video archives so that they will not be forgotten and lost. I wish this was being done for the excellent neoclassical ballets premiered by the different Ballets Russes companies, especially those works of Fokine's, Massine's, Nijinsky's and Nijinska's.

I feel so privileged to be allowed to set Balanchine works for companies throughout the U.S. A lot of dancers inherited Balanchine's ballets when he died, and many of them have been given to the Balanchine Trust to manage. The George Balanchine Trust was established in 1987. The Founding Trustees were Balanchine's former assistant, Barbara Horgan, and the late NYCB dancer Karin von Aroldingen. The office of the Trust has many responsibilities, including the business of licensing Balanchine's ballets. His works are copyrighted; thus, the trustees are responsible for protecting the Trust's copyrights and trademarks. Both owner and the Trust get a percentage of the royalties. When a company wants to license a Balanchine ballet it must get permission from the Trust, and the officers are particular about who will set the ballet. Over the years, the trustees have never given me a bad time when I have asked for permission to set a Balanchine ballet. In summer 2018, for example, I set Balanchine's *Tschaikovsky Pas De Deux* on the Atlanta Ballet. It was such a pleasure not only working with the energetic and enthusiastic young couples, but to work in the studio along with Atlanta Ballet's fourth artistic director, Gennadi Nedvigin.

Regrettably, Dorothy's choreography was not copyrighted. She did not want it to be. In fact, she destroyed her notes. She believed that eventually her ballets would be out of date, and she did not want them seen. Dorothy did, however, collect and keep a lot of paper chronicling her career—meeting minutes, playbills, newspaper and magazine articles, for example. She kept some in the garage at her Ansley Park house but, thank goodness, not all. A fire in the garage destroyed what was there. She called me one day and said she wanted to give what remained of her collection away, and she asked me where to place it. I suggested that she give the collection to Emory University in Atlanta. I could not recommend that she keep these valuable historical documents at the AB facility because there was no archivist on staff to inventory and to maintain this important collection. The collection is at Emory. This was Dorothy's way of passing it along.

In an interview with Kristi Casey Sanders for her article "The Man Who Brought 'The Nutcracker' to Atlanta,"[5] she wanted to know what I wanted my legacy to be. I want to be remembered for the growth of the Atlanta Ballet, I quickly replied. And I want to be remembered for entertaining audiences and for educating them about the ballet, including its importance as an art form. Hopefully, I've been able to do that, especially through the education program Kids In Step. Sharon Story danced in AB's *The Nutcracker* for a couple of years before she left, or I should say returned, to Boston Ballet. The Atlanta community is lucky that when she retired from dancing she chose to live in Georgia. Since 1996, she has been the dean of the Centre for Dance Education at AB, skillfully and superbly supervising an enrollment of about 1,200 students at schools in three locations. Thanks to her, the Kids In Step program that Sarah duBignon and I began continues today, educating kids— many of whom are from disadvantaged neighborhoods—on what this wonderful world of ballet is all about. The program brings close to 20,000 kids annually from city, county, and private schools, and even homeschoolers, to see AB programs, such as a one-hour abbreviated *Nutcracker* performance at the Fox Theatre every December. The purpose of the program is to educate children about ballet and its importance as an art form; to provide an opportunity for kids to enjoy an enchanting one hour of beautiful music, spectacular sets, a lot of wow-rousing dancing, and the magic that only a real, live ballet production can offer. In addition, it is an opportunity for kids to watch highly-trained, experienced professional dancers; and to learn what an important role AB plays in the Atlanta community. It is a very important program as far as cultivating a future audience for AB. Watching as more than 4,000 kids fill the Fox Theatre and hearing their loud hoots and yells and wild clapping of excitement is a hair-tingling-thrill experience. In the middle of the program there is a pause. While the dancers take a much-needed break to towel off the sweat, a stage manager talks to the kids on what is happening behind the scenes when the dancers are on the stage performing—the lighting, the sets, and the wondrous special effects that make *Nutcracker* such a magical, special Christmas tradition. It is through the launching of Kids In Step that I continued Miss Dorothy's mission, one of her resolute rules, of giving back to the community. I am so gratified that today, thirty-plus years later, the current AB administrative and artistic staff keeps the program, and thus Dorothy's mission, and my mission, still going.

I have been humbled over the years by the praise, and by the many official tributes I've received, to thank me for doing my part, for passing it along. For example, in 2000, Ginger and I flew to New Orleans to participate in a ceremony to honor the living legends—dancers who had performed in the

Ballets Russes companies. The 65 of us standing on stage that night beamed with pride as we were applauded by the many students, dance fans and scholars from all over the world. I am so fortunate to be one of the few dancers still around to tell the exciting tales of what it was like to tour and dance in the Colonel's Original Ballet Russe. When NYCB had a 50th anniversary celebration in 1998, we old-timers were invited to attend. David and Rob went with Virginia and me. At the end of the performance a ceremony was held and about one hundred former and present NYCB dancers came up on the stage to be recognized by an appreciative audience. Virginia and I felt so proud to be among the small group of first-generation dancers standing on the stage. NYCB was only fourteen months old when I joined

the company, and the few tickets sold in the 1950 winter season did not foretell a long-term future for Balanchine and Kirstein's company. Seventy years later the New York City Ballet is thriving. It is one of the most, if not the most, well-endowed ballet companies in America. We first-generation NYCB dancers and staff must have done something right.

While work has been a fabulous journey and continues to be a fun ride, my friends and family are a source of great joy. Sadly, my sister Lois M. Butler died at age ninety-one in 2008. My sister Winifred "Winnie" Barnett Lewis, at age ninety-seven, died the same year a few months later. Still, there are lots of family in Washington to get me back there, or my nieces visit me in Asheville. A yearning to visit the old home place (or one of them anyway) took a niece and me to Conconully one year. We looked for the land my parents had homesteaded. Along the narrow highway there was an overlook, where we parked

I was honored at the 2014 Atlanta Ballet Ball (by Charlie McCullers, courtesy Atlanta Ballet).

the car and got out to breathe the fresh mountain air and to take in the gorgeous view. She pointed to a huge sign. The Okanogan County Historical Society had hung a sign that recognized the Barnett Bluff, a tribute to the settlers, including my parents, who had homesteaded the Scotch Creek Basin. Subsequently, while in Washington for a family reunion, I took my two sons and their wives and children to see it. My life continues to be filled with family gatherings in Asheville and Atlanta. Grandson Aaron Michael Barnett is David and Jackie's son. He is in college, and a good ice hockey player who also loves the arts. He is one of the only males in the family who enjoys going to see ballets, on his own, without being bribed to do so. Rob and Elizabeth's sons are Austin and Ryan. I will join anyone, but it is mostly the grandsons, at an arcade in Asheville for fun and games. I assist in cooking some meals, too, including the traditional Thanksgiving turkey-and-all-the-trimmings meal. Grandson Austin loves my pancakes. Not only is he an excellent golfer, but he shows an interest in cooking, and he may one day become the next generation master chef in the Barnett family. My mother would be really pleased.

Our fiftieth wedding anniversary celebration in Jamaica with the family in 2007. From left are grandson Aaron; Virginia; grandson Ryan; Rob and his wife, Elizabeth; me; and David and his wife, Jackie. Elizabeth was pregnant with grandson Austin.

Virginia and me at our home in Asheville, North Carolina.

At my home in Asheville, Cynthia and I take a break from writing to look at the YouTube video of Royal Danish Ballet dancers demonstrating the Bournonville technique. Among the dancers is Caroline Cavallo, and I am the proud "Papa," that Maiqui Manosa calls me. I insert a disc in the DVD player and we watch *Serenade,* the ballet that I set on Ballet Hawaii dancers in summer 2017. The dancers dance Balanchine's iconic ballet beautifully. Again, I feel so very proud. And yet also sad. Virginia and I had a history of setting the ballet together in Hawaii. This time I was alone. At a rehearsal, I presented each dancer with a single red rose so that Virginia could be with us in spirit. Pamela Taylor Tongg, director of Ballet Hawaii and once a ballet mistress at AB, and I hugged, and we brushed off our cheeks some tears.

I drive Ginger's car. The boxy, bold-red Mini Cooper is a testament to her practical personality: its black and white checkerboard-patterned side mirrors and roof top a show of her proficiency in strategic planning and attention to details. And her concern for safety: "I want every truck driver to be able to see my car," she told me. When driving seventy miles per hour on the interstate between Asheville and Atlanta, I truly appreciate how much she was right. The home we lived in with Dick Rich and our two boys on West Andrews Drive in Buckhead was torn down and replaced with a more modern home. Thank goodness the great memories still stand, however. There are Ginger's albums to look at, the fascinating story of her professional dance career. "She danced like an angel,"[6] says Wei Dongsheng. Approachable, humble, and wise—these are only a few of the words friends use to describe Virginia. On October 16, 2016, the Atlanta Ballet had a special event at the Atlanta Ballet's Michael C. Carlos Dance Centre, in the "Virginia Rich Barnett Studio." The room was filled with friends and family from throughout the United States who came to Atlanta to attend this much deserved tribute—a memorial celebration of her life. Arturo Jacobus, President and CEO of Atlanta Ballet, made some very kind introductory remarks. Dean Sharon Story and David spoke also. Now that she

Above: In 2016 Atlanta Ballet hosted a very special memorial event at the Michael C. Carlos Dance Centre, in the "Virginia Rich Barnett Studio," to recognize Virginia's dedication and contributions. This photograph was on the cover of the event program (by Lucinda Bunnen, from author's collection).

Right: Sharon Story is the dean of Atlanta Ballet's Centre for Dance Education and a former Atlanta Ballet dancer (by Kim Kenney, courtesy Atlanta Ballet).

I gave this photograph to Atlanta Ballet to be hung on the wall at the Michael C. Carlos Dance Centre.

is gone, David calls me every morning to check in. Ginger's sister, Sally, her husband Dick and I go to the movies, and we like to critique the good books we have read. I am lucky to enjoy such good health, my energy still high. With my work, my travels, my friends and family, there are no spare hours to be bored. Ginger used to ask, "Bobby, when are you going to retire? … when are you really going to retire?" My answer was, and still is, a smile.

In 1943, my aim was to be a fashion designer. Thanks to Igor Youskevitch, I changed my mind. Thanks to Michio Ito, Nijinska, David Lichine, and many others, I received the high-quality training required to be successful in realizing my dream to become a classical ballet dancer. It has been a most rewarding career. It has offered the fulfillment that Dorothy Alexander believed ballet, whether a vocation or avocation, could help a person to achieve. Most importantly, I have been fortunate not only to do what I want in life, but to have had the loving support of my family to do it my way. Teaching, coaching and setting ballets: that is what keeps the game of life interesting. It keeps my feet dancing—the waltz on the path still onward and upward—on what has been a beautiful, memorable journey.

Chapter Notes

Chapter Two

1. Clarke and Vaughan, *The Encyclopedia of Dance & Ballet*, 45.

Chapter Three

1. Taper, *Balanchine: A Biography*, 136.
2. *Ibid.*, 140.
3. Homans, *Apollo's Angels: A History of Ballet*, 398.

Chapter Four

1. Reynolds and McCormick, *No Fixed Pointes: Dance in the Twentieth Century*, 269.
2. Taper, *Balanchine: A Biography*, 201.
3. Brown, Dennis. "The Muny Saga: 1940–1949 'This Grim Business of War,'" 37.

Chapter Five

1. Vaill, *Somewhere: The Life of Jerome Robbins*, 311.
2. *Ibid.*, 154.
3. *Ibid.*, 117.
4. d'Amboise, *I Was A Dancer*, 89.
5. Steichen, "Balanchine's 'Bach Ballet' and the Dances of Rodgers and Hart's *On Your Toes,*" 293.
6. Garafola, *Legacies of Twentieth-Century Dance*, 243.
7. Milberg, *In Balanchine's Company: A Dancer's Memoir*, 133.
8. Martin, "Ballet of Ashton Danced at Center," 21.
9. Reynolds, *Repertory in Review: 40 Years of The New York City Ballet*, 101.
10. Taper, *Balanchine*, 151.
11. Balanchine and Mason, *101 Stories of the Great Ballets*, 388.
12. Walczak and Kai, *Balanchine the Teacher*, 7.

Chapter Six

1. Taper, *Balanchine*, 261.
2. Milberg, *In Balanchine's Company*, 15 and 16.
3. Taper, *Balanchine*, 249.
4. d' Amboise, *I Was a Dancer*, 95.
5. Milberg, *In Balanchine's Company*, 114.

Chapter Seven

1. Milberg, *In Balanchine's Company*, xv.
2. Barnett interview, Lobenthal, 16 June 2011, 49.
3. "Dancers to Be Wed," *The New York Times*, 19 April 1957, 15.
4. "Two Dancers Married," *The New York Times*, 28 July 1957, 51.

Chapter Eight

1. Dorothy Alexander and the Atlanta Ballet Collections, Box 1, Folder 6, Stuart A. Rose Manuscript, Archives, and Rare Book Library, Emory University.
2. "Eleanor Howard, Publisher, and Lucile Marsh, Educational Editor, Travel Cross Country to Meet Teachers," *The American Dancer* (May 1944). Also "South's Interest in the Arts Fully Expressed in Famed Atlanta Civic Ballet," Box 1, Folder 12, Dorothy Alexander and the Atlanta Ballet Collections, Stuart A. Rose Manuscript, Archives, and Rare Book Library, Emory University.
3. Kamarck, *Arts in Society*, 11.
4. Joseph Carman, email, 26 July 2018.
5. Manchester, "Dance: Regional, Nonprofessional Ballet Companies Hold Lively Springs Festivals," 8.
6. "Dance Magazine's Annual Awards Presentation," *Dance Magazine*, 30.

Chapter Nine

1. "The Ford Foundation Controversy," *Dance Magazine*, 34.

2. Smith, "The Atlanta Ballet: Fifty Golden Years," 93.

3. Herbert, "Will Success Spoil Manos' Municipal Theater Project?" 9.

4. Beiswanger, "Swan Lake in Atlanta," 37.

5. *Ibid.*, 39.

6. Schonberg, "Music: 'King Arthur' Opens Alliance Theater in Atlanta Center," 43.

7. Kay, "'King Arthur' Faces Challenge," 7-F.

8. Anderson, "Turnabout for Atlanta Ballet," D22.

9. Hering, "Atlanta Ballet in Dance Repertoire—1970," 93.

10. *Ibid.*, 94.

11. *Ibid.*

12. Baker, "Dance at the Delacorte: Terpsichore throws a picnic in the park," 59.

13. Hanks, "An Historic Evening of Dance: Night of the Stars," Gala Program (March 16, 1973), Box 2, Folder 9, Dorothy Alexander and the Atlanta Ballet Collections, Stuart A. Rose Manuscript, Archives, and Rare Book Library, Emory University.

14. Smith, "The Atlanta Ballet: Fifty Golden Years," 88.

15. *Ibid.*, 89.

Chapter Ten

1. Clarke and Vaughan, *The Encyclopedia of Dance & Ballet*, 288.

2. Terry, "Miss Dorothy's Way," 15.

3. Horosko, "How to Parlay a Six-Figure Deficit into a $2.5 Million Budget," 66.

4. Smith, "Gil Boggs Carries U.S. Hopes to The Olympics of Dance," 3.

5. Smith, "Atlanta's Gil Boggs Both Winner, Loser at Varna," 2.

6. Yearley, "NYC Dancer Joins Atlanta Ballet as Advisor," 9-E.

7. Williams, "It's Feeding Time for the 'Arts Monster,'" 2-B.

8. Horosko, "How to Parlay a Six-Figure Deficit into a $2.5 Million Budget: Atlanta's Brooklyn Connection," 68.

9. *Ibid.*

10. Smith, "Atlanta Ballet on Its Toes," 46A.

11. *Ibid.*

12. Pikula, "Capezio Honors Dorothy Alexander: America's Pioneer in Regional Dance," 90.

13. Caroline Cavallo, former principal with Royal Danish Ballet and former student of Robert Barnett in Atlanta, GA, letter emailed and dated January 31, 2018.

14. *Ibid.*

15. *Ibid.*

16. *Ibid.*

17. Smith, "Atlanta Ballet's Future Requires a Leap of Faith," N-1.

Chapter Twelve

1. Dawn Mullins, former Atlanta Civic Ballet dancer, Atlanta, GA, May 2, 2018.

2. "Robert Barnett: Teacher's Wisdom," *Dance Magazine*, 81.

3. *Ibid.*

4. Wei Dongsheng, former Atlanta Ballet dancer, Atlanta, GA, May 31, 2018.

5. Sanders, "The Man Who Brought 'The Nutcracker' to Atlanta," e-newsletter.

6. Wei Dongsheng, former Atlanta Ballet dancer, Atlanta, GA, May 31, 2018.

Bibliography

Books, Journals, Newspapers and Special Collections

Alexander, Dorothy. "Blueprint for a Civic Ballet." *Dance Magazine* (February 1954): 49.

Alexander, Dorothy. Personal documents collection (1904–1986). Dorothy Alexander and the Atlanta Ballet Collections, Stuart A. Rose Manuscript, Archives, and Rare Book Library, Emory University.

Amberg, George. *Ballet in America: The Emergence of An American Art.* New York: Duell, Sloan and Pearce, 1949.

Anderson, Jack. "Ballet Is Booming Across the Country." *New York Times* (October 19, 1980): 308–309. Accessed September 17, 2017. https://query.nytimes.com/search/sitesearch/#/archives.

Anderson, Jack. "Ballet Russe." *Dance Heritage Coalition* (2012): 1–3. Accessed February 20, 2018. http://www.danceheritage.org/treasures/russe_essay_anderson.pdf.

Anderson, Jack. "A Happy Gathering of the Ballets Russes." *New York Times* (June 25, 2000): 23–24. Accessed July 20, 2018. https://www.nytimes.com/2000/06/25/arts/dance-a-happy-gathering-of-the-ballets-russes.html.

Anderson, Jack. "Turnabout for Atlanta Ballet." *New York Times* (March 22, 1981): D22. ProQuest Historical Newspapers, The New York Times (1851–2007). Accessed October 1, 2017. http://www.proquest.com.proxy.libraries.smu.edu.

Baker, Robb. "Dance at the Delacorte: Terpsichore Throws a Picnic in the Park." *Dance Magazine* (November 1972): 57–60.

Balanchine, George. *Choreography by George Balanchine: A Catalogue of Works.* New York: The Eakins Press Foundation, 1983.

Balanchine, George, and Francis Mason. *101 Stories of the Great Ballets.* New York: Doubleday, 1989.

Barzel, Ann. Ann Barzel Rare Book Collections, the Newberry Library, 60 West Walton Street, Chicago, Illinois.

Beaumont, Cyril W. *Complete Book of Ballets: A Guide to the Principal Ballets of the Nineteenth and Twentieth Centuries.* New York: Grosset & Dunlap, 1938.

Beaumont, Cyril W. *The Diaghilev Ballet in London: A Personal Record.* London: University of Oxford Press, 1940.

Beiswanger, George. "First Repertory Program Reviewed." *Dance Magazine* (January 1969): 49–50.

Beiswanger, George. "The Sleeping Beauty in Atlanta." *Dance Magazine* (October 1966): 46–48.

Beiswanger, George. "Swan Lake in Atlanta." *Dance Magazine* (October 1965): 36–40.

Bond Perry, Cynthia. "'A Vision a Star': Dance as Art, Inspiration and Social Change in Atlanta." Master's Thesis, University of Georgia, 2017.

Bond Perry, Cynthia. "Where Dorothy Danced: How a Young Artist Made a Place for Dance in Atlanta." *ArtsATL* and Stuart A. Rose Manuscript, Archives and Rare Book Library, Emory University (April 4, 2017). Accessed August 17, 2018. https://artsatl.com/dorothy-danced-young-artist-place-dance-atlanta.

Brown, Dennis. "The Muny Saga: 1940–1949 'This Grim Business of War.'" Accessed August 17, 2018. https://muny.org/saga/.

Carroll, Mark. "Let's Stage a Fight! Massine's Symphonic Ballets in Australia." *Brolga* 6 (June 2007): 14–26.

Chazin-Bennahum, Judith. *René Blum & The Ballets Russes: In Search of a Lost Life.* New York: University of Oxford Press, 2011.

Chujoy, Anatole. "Atlanta Pioneers in Setting Regional Ballet Festival." *Dance News.* (January 1956): 5.

Chujoy, Anatole. *The New York City Ballet.* New York: Alfred A. Knopf, 1953.

Clarke, Mary, and David Vaughan, eds. *The Encyclopedia of Dance & Ballet*. New York: G.P. Putnam's Sons, 1977.

Collins, Nicole Dekle. "Interview—Robert Barnett, Former New York City Ballet Dancer and Longtime Artistic Director of Atlanta Ballet." *DanceTabs*, February 16, 2017. Accessed September 25, 2017. http://dancetabs.com/2017/02/interview-robert-barnett-new-york-city-ballet-and-longtime-director-atlanta-ballet.

D'Amboise, Jacques. *I Was a Dancer: A Memoir*. New York: Alfred A. Knopf, 2011.

"Dance Magazine's Annual Awards Presentation." *Dance Magazine* (June 1960): 29.

"Dancers to Be Wed." *New York Times* (April 19, 1957): 15. Accessed April 14, 2018. https://www.nytimes.com/1957/04/19/archives/dancers-to-be-wed-robert-barnett-and-virginia-rich-of-city-troupe.html.

Dolin, Anton. *Pas de Deux: The Art of Partnering*. New York: Dover, 1969.

English, Cordelia. "Ballet 'Who' in Atlanta." *Dance Magazine* XVIII, no. 5 (May 1944): 8.

Fokine, Vitale. *Fokine: Memoirs of a Ballet Master*. Boston: Little, Brown, 1961.

"The Ford Foundation Controversy." *Dance Magazine* 38, no. 2 (February 1964): 34.

Garafola, Lynn. *Legacies of Twentieth Century Dance*. Middletown: Wesleyan University Press, 2005.

Garafola, Lynn. "Lincoln Kirstein, Modern Dance, and the Left: The Genesis of an American Ballet." *The Journal of the Society for Dance Research* 23, no. 1 (Summer 2005): 18–35. Accessed September 19, 2017. http://www.jstor.org/stable/40004077.

Gintautiene, Kristina. "The Black Crook: Ballet in the Gilded Age (1866–1876)." New York University Dissertation. Ann Arbor: University Microfilms International, 1984.

Goodman, Saul. "Biography of Robert Barnett (1925-VVVV)." *Dance Magazine* (January 1955): 36–37.

Grant, Gail. *Technical Manual and Dictionary of Classical Ballet*. New York: Dover, 1967.

Greenhill, Janet. "Pas de deux: Atlanta Ballet and Cleveland San Jose Ballet Join Forces." *Dance Magazine* (April 1993): 50–53.

Greenhill, Janet. "Spotlight on Carl Ratcliff: Pretend You're an Actor." *Dance Teacher Now* 14, no. 7 (September 1992): 22–26, 28–30.

Grigoriev, S. L. *The Diaghilev Ballet: 1909–1929*. Baltimore: Penguin, 1960.

Gustaitis, Rasa. *Melissa Hayden: Ballerina*. London: T. Nelson, 1967.

Haney, Lynn. *Naked at the Feast: A Biography of Josephine Baker*. London: Robson Books, 2002.

Herbert, Dick. "Will Success Spoil Manos' Municipal Theater Project?" *Atlanta Constitution* (December 11, 1965): 9. Accessed August 6, 2018. https://www.newspapers.com/image/398566009/?terms=Municipal%2BTheater.

Hering, Doris. "America Dancing." *Dance Magazine* (July 1994): 54–57.

Hering, Doris. "Atlanta Ballet in Dance Repertoire—1970 Symphony Hall, Atlanta, March 12–14, 1970; a Review." *Dance Magazine* (May 1970): 93–98.

Hering, Doris. "Atlanta Civic Ballet … Company of Contrasts." *Dance Magazine* (March 1959): 53–55.

Hering, Doris. "The Beautiful Gesture." *Dance Magazine* (January 1969): 46–48.

Hering, Doris. "A Kind of Oneness: Regional Ballet and Its Festivals, What Do They Mean to American Dance?" *Dance Magazine* (May 1970): 72–78.

Hering, Doris. "My Glad Is Very Big: Dorothy Alexander." *Dance Magazine* (May 1973): 95.

Hering, Doris. "Regional Ballet-USA: Tickets for the Bug Man." *Dance Magazine* (February 1963): 52–53.

Hering, Doris. "Regional Ballet—USA." *Dance Magazine* (December 1963): 6–7.

Hering, Doris. "Regional Ballet: What's It All About?" *Dance Magazine* (September 1966): 49–59.

Hering, Doris. "Robert Barnett Resigns from Atlanta Ballet." *Dance Magazine* (July 1994): 18.

Homans, Jennifer. *Apollo's Angels: A History of Ballet*. New York: Random House, 2010.

Horosko, Marian. "Atlanta's Rejuvenated Ballet: How to Parlay a Six-Figure Deficit into a $2.5 Million Budget." *Dance Magazine* (April 1993): 66–69.

"The Howard." *Atlanta Constitution* (July 24, 1926): 12. ProQuest Historical Newspapers, Atlanta Constitution (1849–1986). Accessed January 2, 2011. http://www.proquest.com.

Howard, Ruth Eleanor. "Eleanor Howard, Publisher, and Lucile Marsh Educational Editor, Travel Cross Country to Meet Teachers." *The American Dancer*, Box 1, Folder 12, Dorothy Alexander and the Atlanta Ballet Collections, Stuart A. Rose Manuscript, Archives, and Rare Book Library, Emory University.

Hughes, Allen. "Dance: Atlanta Still Makes History." *New York Times* (September 5, 1965): 270. Accessed May 21, 2018. https://www.nytimes.com/1965/09/05/archives/dance-atlanta-still-makes-history.html.

Hughes, Allen. "First Complete U.S. Production of 'Swan Lake' Given in Atlanta." *New York Times* (August 25, 1965): 29. Accessed May 21, 2018. https://www.nytimes.com/1965/08/25/archives/first-complete-us-production-of-swan-lake-given-in-atlanta.html.

International Dictionary of Ballet: Vol I. Detroit: St. James Press, 1993.

International Dictionary of Ballet: Vol II. Detroit: St. James Press, 1993.

International Encyclopedia of Dance. Vol. 5. New York: Oxford University Press, 1998.

Kamarck, Edward L. "Symposium on the University and the Creative Arts." *Arts in Society* 2, no. 3 (1963): 11.

Kavanagh, Julie. *Secret Muses: The Life of Frederick Ashton.* New York: Pantheon Books, 1996.

Kay, Terry. "'King Arthur' Faces Challenge." *Atlanta Constitution* (October 27, 1968): 7-F. Accessed August 6, 2018. https://www.newspapers.com/image/398622988/?terms=Memorial%2BArts%2BCenter.

Kendall, Elizabeth. *Balanchine & the Lost Muse: Revolution & the Making of a Choreographer.* New York: Oxford University Press, 2013.

Kirstein, Lincoln. *Ballet: Bias and Belief.* New York: Dance Horizons, 1983.

Kirstein, Lincoln. *Movement & Metaphor: Four Centuries of Ballet.* New York: Praeger, 1970.

Kirstein, Lincoln. "The Policy of a Ballet Company." *Playbill.* Published in the January 1976 New York City Ballet performance *Playbill*, 1976.

Kriegsman, Sali Ann. *Modern Dance in America: The Bennington Years.* Boston: G.K. Hall, 1981.

Lester, Keith, and Clement Crisp. "Rubinstein Revisited." *Dance Research: The Journal of the Society of Dance Research* 1, no. 2 (Autumn 1983): 21–31.

Levy, Suzanne Carbonneau. "The Russians Are Coming: Russian Dancers in the United States, 1910–1933." New York University Dissertation. Ann Arbor: University Microfilms International, 1990.

Lihs, Harriet. *Appreciating Dance.* Highstown, NJ: Princeton Book Company, 2008.

Lobenthal, Joel. "A Conversation with Robert Barnett." *Ballet Review* 41, no. 4 (Winter 2013–2014): 36–52.

Lobenthal, Joel. *Wilde Times: Patricia Wilde, George Balanchine, and the Rise of New York City Ballet.* Lebanon, NH: ForeEdge, 2016.

Lowry, W. McNeil. *The Performing Arts and American Society.* Englewood Cliffs, NJ: Prentice-Hall, 1978.

Macaulay, Alastair. *Margot Fonteyn.* Guernsey: Sutton, 1998.

Madden, Ethan. *Anything Goes: A History of American Musical Theatre.* New York: Oxford University Press, 2013.

Manchester, P.W. "The Colonel's Ballets Russes." *Dance Chronicle* 6, no. 1 (1982): 84–89.

Manchester, P.W. "Dance: Regional, Nonprofessional Ballet Companies Hold Lively Spring Festivals." *New York Times* (May 28, 1961): 8.

Manchester, P.W. "Giselle Goes to Georgia; Blair Sets Work for the Atlanta Civic Ballet." *Dancing Times* (October 1967): 24.

Martin, John. "Ballet of Ashton Danced at Center: 'Illuminations,' Based on the Poems of Rimbaud, Receives Impressive Production." *New York Times* (March 3, 1950): 21. Accessed April 14, 2018. https://www.nytimes.com/1950/03/03/archives/ballet-of-ashton-danced-at-center-illuminations-based-on-the-poems.html.

Mayer, Charles S. "Ida Rubinstein: A Twentieth-Century Cleopatra." *Dance Research: The Journal of the Society for Dance Research* 21, no. 2 (Winter 1988): 33–51.

Maynard, Olga. *The American Ballet.* Philadelphia: Macrae Smith, 1959.

Maynard, Olga. *American Modern Dancers: The Pioneers.* Boston: Little, Brown,, 1965.

McLyman, Meghan Karleen. *Ballet Companies in the United States: Analysis of Partnerships, 1995–2000.* Master's Thesis, American University, 2000.

Milberg Fisher, Barbara. *In Balanchine's Company: A Dancer's Memoir.* Middletown: Wesleyan University Press, 2006.

Murphy, Anne. "Reports: Brooklyn." *Ballet News* 6, no. 7 (January 1985): 39.

Nijinska, Irina, and Jean Rawlinson, eds. *Bronislava Nijinska: Early Memoirs.* New York: Holt, Rinehart and Winston, 1981.

Noverre, Jean Georges. *Letters on Dancing and Ballets.* Translated by Cyril W. Beaumont. London: C.W. Beaumont, 1930.

Papich, Stephen. *Remembering Josephine.* New York: Bobbs-Merrill, 1976.

Pikula, Joan. "Capezio Honors Dorothy Alexander: America's Pioneer in Regional Dance." *Dance Magazine* 55 (June 1981): 90.

Pousner, Howard. "At 84, Barnett Dancing Back into Atlanta Ballet Fold." *Atlanta Journal-Constitution* (March 30, 2010). Accessed September 24, 2017. http://www.accessatlanta.com/entertainment/calendar/barnett-dancing-back-into-atlanta-ballet-fold/lIL7bFZ1UKS193YMfOBeqL/.

Prevots, Naima. *Dancing in the Sun: Hollywood Choreographers: 1915–1937.* Ann Arbor: UMI Research Press, 1987.

Reynolds, Nancy, and Malcolm McCormick. *No Fixed Points: Dance in the Twentieth Century*. New Haven: Yale University Press, 2003.

Reynolds: Nancy. *Repertory in Review: 40 Years of the New York City Ballet*. New York: The Dial Press, 1977.

"Robbins' Stint with NY Ballet Troupe Proof of Crafts Hole on Members." *Variety* 177, no. 1 (December 14, 1949): 56.

"Robert Barnett: Teacher's Wisdom." *Dance Magazine* 80, no. 9 (September 2006): 80–81.

Sanders, Kristi Casey. "The Man Who Brought the Nutcracker to Atlanta." *Encore Atlanta* (December 17, 2008). https://encoreatlanta. com/2008/12/17/the-man-who-brought-the-nutcracker-to-atlanta. Accessed July 20, 2018.

Sandomir, Larry. *Isadora Duncan: Revolutionary Dance*. Austin: Raintree Steck-Vaughn, 1995.

Scheijen, Sjeng. *Diaghilev: A Life*. New York: Oxford University Press, 2009.

Schonberg, Harold C. "Music: 'King Arthur' Opens Alliance Theater in Atlanta Center." *New York Times* (October 30, 1968): 43. Accessed June 30, 2018. https://timesmachine. nytimes.com/timesmachine/1968/10/30/issue. html?action=click&contentCollection= Archives&module=ArticleEndCTA&region= ArchiveBody&pgtype=article.

Severn, Margaret. "Dancing with Bronislava Nijinska and Ida Rubinstein." *Dance Chronicle* 11, no. 3 (1988): 333–364. JSTOR. Accessed February 18, 2011. http://www.jstor.org/stable/ 1567661.

Severn, Margaret. "Scenes from a Dancer's Life, Part One: 1910–1919." *Dance Chronicle* 15, no. 3 (1992): 253–290. JSTOR. Accessed February 18, 2011 http://222.jstor.org/stable/1567820.

Shehan, Patricia K. "The Riches of Ragtime." *Music Educators Journal* 73, no. 3 (November 1986): 22–25.

Siegel, Marcia B. "Modern Dance before Bennington: Sorting It All Out." *Dance Research Journal* 19, no. 1 (Summer 1987): 3–9. JSTOR. Accessed September 14, 2017. http://www. jstor.org/stable/147764.

Smith, Helen C. "Atlanta Ballet Celebrates Sixty." *Dance Magazine* (October 1989): 20.

Smith, Helen C. "The Atlanta Ballet: Fifty Golden Years." *Dance Magazine* (November 1979): 88–94.

Smith, Helen C. "Atlanta Ballet on Its Toes." *Atlanta Journal-Atlanta Constitution* (April 8, 1984): 46A. Accessed July 28, 2018. https:// www.newspapers.com/image/384690185/? terms=%22Atlanta%2BBallet%22.

Smith, Helen C. "Atlanta Ballet's Future Requires a Leap of Faith." *Atlanta Journal–Atlanta Constitution* (July 23, 1989): N-1, N-2. Accessed July 7, 2018. https://newspapers.com/image/ 400309536.

Smith, Helen C. "Atlanta's Gil Boggs Both Winner, Loser at Varna." *Atlanta Constitution* (July 24, 1980): 2, 5-B. Accessed July 2, 2018. https://www.newspapers.com/image/3993 63508.

Smith, Helen C. "Dancewatch: Atlanta." *Ballet News* 7, no. 9 (March 1986): 33–34.

Smith, Helen C. "Everything Comes Up Roses for Ballet." *Atlanta Constitution* (September 21, 1981): 1-B. Accessed July 3, 2018. https:// newspapers.com/image/399355032.

Smith, Helen C. "Gil Boggs Carries U.S. Hopes to the Olympics of Dance." *Atlanta Constitution* (June 26, 1980): 3. Accessed July 2, 2018. https://www.newspaperscom/image/3994 30369.

Soares, Janet Mansfield. *Martha Hill & the Making of American Dance*. Middletown: Wesleyan University Press, 2009.

Starr, Larry, and Christopher Waterman. *American Popular Music: From Minstrelsy to Mp3*. New York: Oxford University Press, 2014.

Steichen, James. "The American Ballet's Caravan." *Dance Research Journal* 47, no. 1 (April 2015): 69–94.

Steichen, James. "Balanchine's 'Bach Ballet' and the Dances of Rodgers and Hart's *On Your Toes*." *The Journal of Musicology* 35, no. 2 (Spring 2018): 267–293.

Strong, Leonard V. "National Association for Regional Ballet: What it offers and how it works." *Dance Teacher Now* 6, no. 3 (May–June 1984): 24–31.

Stuart, Otis. "U.S.A.: In the boondocks? Regional ballet in the U.S.A." *Ballet International* 8, no. 11 (November 1985): 32–33.

Sussmann, Leila. "Anatomy of the Dance Company Boom: 1958–1980." *Dance Research Journal* 16, no. 2 (August 1984): 23–28.

Taper, Bernard. *Balanchine: A Biography*. Los Angeles: University of California Press, 1996.

Terry, Walter. *The Dance in America*. New York: Harper & Row, 1971.

Terry, Walter. "Focus on Atlanta: Miss Dorothy's Way" *Ballet News* 1, no. 9 (March 1980): 14.

Topaz, Muriel. "America Dancing: Regional Dance Series, Part I." *Dance Magazine* 71, no. 7 (July 1997): 42–44.

Topaz, Muriel. "Regional Dance: Creating Dances for RDA." *Dance Magazine* LXXI, no. 12 (December 1997): 96.

Trudeau, Melanie. "Igor Youskevitch." *Performing Arts Magazine* (September 1979): 13.

"Two Dancers Married." *New York Times* (July

28, 1957): 51. Accessed April 14, 2018. https://www.nytimes.com/1957/07/28/archives/two-dancers-married-robert-barnett-weds-virginia-richboth-of-city.html.

Vaganova, Agrippina. *Basic Principles of Classical Ballet: Russian Ballet Technique.* New York: Dover, 1969.

Vaill, Amanda. *Somewhere: The Life of Jerome Robbins.* New York: Broadway Books, 2006.

Van Praagh, Peggy, and Peter Brinson. *The Choreographic Art.* New York: Alfred A Knopf, 1963.

Walczak, Barbara, and Una Kai. *Balanchine the Teacher: Fundamentals That Shaped the First Generation of New York City Ballet Dancers.* Gainesville: University Press of Florida, 2008.

Walker, Katherine Sorley. "Finding René Blum." *Dance Chronicle* 35 (2012): 114–118.

Williams, Dick. "It's Feeding Time for the 'Arts Monster.'" *Atlanta Journal–Atlanta Constitution* (February 20, 1982): 2-B. Accessed July 3, 2018. https://www.newspapers.com/image/399523992.

Windreich, Leland. "The Colonel's Company." *Dance Chronicle* 14, no. 1 (1991): 116–123.

Woolf, Vicki. *Dancing in the Vortex: The Story of Ida Rubinstein.* The Netherlands: Harwood Academic, 2000.

Yearley, Midge. "NYC Dancer Joins Atlanta Ballet as Advisor." *Atlanta Journal and Constitution* (May 11, 1980): 9-E. Accessed July 3, 2018. https://www.newspapers.com/image/399331971.

Young, Henry. "The National Endowment: Preparing for the Future." *Dance Magazine* (January 1980): 50–52.

Zeller, Jessica. *Shapes of American Ballet: Teachers and Training Before Balanchine.* New York: Oxford University Press, 2016.

Video and Film and Audio

Balanchine: Dance in America. Documentary film produced by Kultur. West Long Branch, NJ, date unknown.

Balanchine: Orpheus and Serenade. "New York City Ballet in Montreal." Vol. 1. Video Artists International, Pleasantville, NY. Date unknown.

Barnett, Robert. "Review of University of Alabama Ballet." Interviewed by Walter Terry, 1979, audio: *MGZTCO 3–989. Jerome Robbins Dance Division, New York Public Library for the Performing Arts.

Cavallo, Caroline. "The Bournonville School." October 7, 2012. https://www.youtube.com/watch?v=lGmh14Qn6EQ

Cohen, Janice. "Interview with Janice Cohen Adelson." Interviewed by Meg Stillman, November 23, 1998, audio: *MGZTCO 3–2142. Jerome Robbins Dance Division, New York Public Library for the Performing Arts.

Jerome Robbins: Something to Dance About. Documentary film directed by Judy Kinberg. Written by Amanda Vaill. www.pbs.org or Netflix DVD.

Martha Graham. Documentary film produced by Nathan Kroll. The Criterion, Janus Films, 1957.

Rich, Virginia, and Carl Ratcliff. "Interview with Virginia Rich and Carl Ratcliff." Interviewed by Marian Horosko, radio station WBAI, 1969, audio: *MGZTC 3–1913. Jerome Robbins Dance Division, New York Public Library for the Performing Arts.

Symphony in C. Video: *MGZID-1710. Jerome Robbins Dance Division, Victor Jessen Video Archive, New York Public Library for the Performing Arts.

Western Symphony. Robert Barnett and Allegra Kent dancing in the 3rd Movement. https://www.youtube.com/watch?v=umTeitzn6o8

Interviews and Written Correspondence Contributions

Carman, Joseph. Former Atlanta Ballet dancer. Letter e-mailed and dated July 26, 2018.

Cavallo, Caroline. Former principal with Royal Danish Ballet and former student of Robert Barnett in Atlanta, GA. Letter emailed and dated January 31, 2018.

Dongsheng, Wei. Interviewed by Cynthia Crain. Former Atlanta Ballet dancer. Atlanta, GA, May 31, 2018.

Mullins, Dawn. Interviewed by Cynthia Crain. Former Atlanta Civic Ballet dancer. Atlanta, GA, May 2, 2018

Story, Sharon. Interviewed by Cynthia Crain. Former Atlanta Ballet dancer. Current Dean, Centre for Dance Education. Atlanta, GA, July 14, 2018.

Websites

American Ballet Theatre. www.abt.org/education/archive/index.

Atlanta History Center. Atlanta Ballet records 1955–2002. Kenan Research Center at the Atlanta History Center, 130 West Paces Ferry Road, Atlanta, GA.

Atlanta Journal and Constitution. http://www.ajc.com/.

Dorothy Alexander and the Atlanta Ballet Collection, Stuart A. Rose Manuscript, Archives, and Rare Book Library, Emory University.

Fabulous Fox, Atlanta. https://www.foxtheatre.org/about/fox-historystory.

Fabulous Fox, St. Louis. https://www.fabulousfox.com/theatre-info/about-us.

Ford Foundation. https://www.fordfoundation.org/about/about-ford/our-origins/.

The George Balanchine Foundation. http://www.balanchine.org/balanchine/chrontitlelist.jsp

Global Performing Arts Database. www.glopad.org.

http://ahc.galileo.usg.edu/ahc/view?docId=ead/ahc.MSS963-ead.xml.

https://findingaids.library.emory.edu/documents/Atlantaballet634/?keywords=Dorothy+Alexander.

Internet Broadway Database. www.ibdb.com.

Internet Movie Database. www.imdb.com.

The Jerome Robbins Foundation. http://jeromerobbins.org/catalog-of-work.

The MUNY Archives. http://muny.org/archives/.

The MUNY Saga. https://muny.org/saga/.

National Endowment for the Arts. https://www.arts.gov/50th.

New York City Ballet. www.nycballet.com/researchers/archive.html.

New York Public Library for the Performing Arts. www.nypl.org.

New York Times. https://query.nytimes.com/search/sitesearch/#/archives.

Newberry Library. www.newberry.org.

Regional Dance America. http://www.regionaldanceamerica.org/history.html.

San Francisco Ballet. www.sfballet.org/interact.

Social, Folk Dance. http://www.socalfolkdance.com/master_teachers/joukowsky_a.htm.

Southeastern Regional Ballet Association. www.serbaballet.org.

YouTube. http://youtube.com.

Index

Numbers in **bold italics** indicate pages with illustrations

203

Scotch Symphony (ballet) 159

Sears & Roebuck Catalog 17, 26, 39

Selig, Simon (also Selig Enterprises) 157

Serenade (ballet) 2–3, 82, 85, 103, 125, 143, 169–170, 191

Serrano, Lupe 132; *see also* Blair, David

Servicemen's Readjustment Act of 1944 (also GI Bill) 37, 41

Shawn, Ted 116–117, 124, 139, 151; Jacob's Pillow 110

Shearer, Moira (also *The Red Shoes* film) 62

Simon, Victoria "Vicky" 80, 110, 133, *134*

Slavenska, Mia 110

The Sleeping Beauty (ballet) 81, 112, 136, *137*, 147, 159, 173, 186

Smith, Merrilee 2, 104, 110–111, *118*, 119–121, 126, 148, 160, 162–164, 167, 169; *see also* Atlanta School of Ballet

Sobotka, Ruth *107*

Sokolow, Anna 103

Sommers, Ben 119, 196; *see also* Capezio Ballet Makers; Capezio Foundation

Song of Norway (musical) 66–67

Sorrin, Ellen viii

South Carolina Governor's School for the Arts (also Governor's School) 153, 186

Southeastern Regional Ballet Association (SERBA) 116, 120, 125, 169, 177; *see also* regional ballet movement

Southern Ballet 65, 132; *see also* Corry, Pittman "Pit"

"Spanish" (divertissement, *The Nutcracker* ballet) 2, 180

Spirit of St. Louis (airplane) 67; *see also* Lindbergh, Charles

Spratlin, Julianne viii, 159–160, 162, 170, 175

Square Dance (ballet, Balanchine) 185; *see also* ballet, neoclassical

Stars and Stripes (ballet, Balanchine) 96, 167, 185–187

Stern, Teena 112; *see also* Carl Ratcliff Dance Theatre

Story, Sharon vii–viii,188, *192*; *see also* Centre for Dance Education

"Sugar Plum Fairy" (divertissement, *The Nutcracker* ballet) 2, 163, 180

Sullivan, Ed 70; *see also Toast of the Town*

Swan Lake (ballet) 81, 91–92, 107, 131–133, 164, 173, 185–186, 196

Swayze, John Cameron 70; *see also Camel News Caravan*

Les Sylphides (ballet) 34

Symphony Hall, Atlanta 138–140

Symphony in C (ballet, Balanchine) 73, 75–77, 96, 103, 140, 151, 180

Taglioni, Marie 56

Tallchief, Maria 38, 67, 80, 83–84, 87, 92

Tallchief, Marjorie 38

tap dance (also tap-dancing) 1, 26–27, 30, 36, 66

Taper, Bernard 48, 67, 195; *see also* Balanchine, George

Taylor, June (also June Taylor Dancers) 70

Tchaikovsky, Pyotr Ilyich 2, 57, 82, 133, 187

Tchernicheva, Lubov 45

television, the Golden Era 69–70

Terry, Walter 196

The Texaco Star Theater (musical) 70; *see also* Berle, Milton

Tharp, Twyla 142

Theater Under the Stars (also TUT) 131, 137; *see also* Manos, Chris

Toast of the Town (television) 70; *see also* Sullivan, Ed

Tobias, Roy 80

Todd, Caroline "Carol" 124

Tom Grose & The Varsity (band) 173

Tongg, Pamela Taylor viii, 82, 186, 191; *see also* Ballet Hawaii

Tower Theater 125, 162

Trisler, Joyce 139; *see also King Arthur*

Tschaikovsky Pas de Deux (ballet) 2, 187

The Turning Point (film) 173; *see also* Nahat, Dennis

University of Georgia 159, 166, 170

University of Georgia Alumni Association 159

Up in Central Park (film) 41

USA International Ballet Competition (Jackson, Mississippi) 179

The Vagabond King (musical) 66

Vaganova Ballet Academy 37, 163, 180; *see also* Imperial Ballet Theatre

Vaganova syllabus 50, 83, 163, 180

Variety (magazine) 61–62, 71–72

vaudeville halls 50

Verdy, Violette 143, 159

Vienna State Ballet (also Vienna State Opera Ballet) 58

Villella, Edward 143

Volkova, Vera 163

Walczak, Barbara viii, 74, *75*, 80, 84, 87, 96, 195

waltz (dance) 21

Warburg, Edward 82

Warm Springs, Georgia 93, 107–108; *see also* Balanchine, George and LeClercq, polio

Wassilieva, Yania 53; *see also* Joukowsky, Anatol

Wenatchee, Washington 24, 26, *27*, 107, 127, *172, 173*

West Side Story (musical) 74, 90

Western Symphony (ballet, Balanchine) *84*

Whiteman, Paul 70; *see also Paul Whiteman Presents*

Wilde, Patricia "Patty" *80*, 96, 100, 110, 187

Wizard of Oz (film) 175; *see also* Bolger, Ray

Wizard of Oz (musical) 131

Woizikowski, Léon 49; *see also* Les Ballets de Léon Woizikowski
Woodruff Arts Center (also Atlanta Memorial Arts Center) 140
Woodward, Joanne 143
Works Progress Administration (also WPA) 123
World War II 22–23, *29*, 32, 36–37, 50, 82, 88

Yokosuka Naval Base (also spelled Yokoska) *32*, 33–34
Youskevitch, Igor 31–32, 52, 60–61, 124, 193

Zimmerman, Jill (also Jillana) 80
Zoritch, George 124